Aesthetics, Ethics and Trauma in the Cinema of Pedro Almodóvar

Aesthetics, Ethics and Trauma in the Cinema of Pedro Almodóvar

Julián Daniel Gutiérrez-Albilla

EDINBURGH
University Press

In memory of my beloved mother, siempre

Edinburgh University Press is one of the leading university presses in the UK. We publish academic books and journals in our selected subject areas across the humanities and social sciences, combining cutting-edge scholarship with high editorial and production values to produce academic works of lasting importance. For more information visit our website: edinburghuniversitypress.com

Edinburgh University Press Ltd
The Tun – Holyrood Road
12 (2f) Jackson's Entry
Edinburgh EH8 8PJ

First published in hardback by Edinburgh University Press 2017

Typeset in Monotype Ehrhardt by
Servis Filmsetting Ltd, Stockport, Cheshire,
and printed and bound by CPI Group (UK) Ltd
Croydon, CR0 4YY

A CIP record for this book is available from the British Library

ISBN 978 1 4744 0010 7 (hardback)
ISBN 978 1 4744 3167 5 (paperback)
ISBN 978 1 4744 0011 4 (webready PDF)
ISBN 978 1 4744 2772 2 (epub)

Contents

Figures

Acknowledgements

I started working on this book while I was teaching at Newcastle University, back in 2008. I had the pleasure to work with Ann Davies, whose graduate course on Almodóvar I inherited, and which helped me shape in many ways my thinking here. I was also fortunate to work with Sarah Leahy, who enthusiastically welcomed me into the graduate programme in Film Studies from the outset. I would like to express my deepest thanks to my former colleagues and graduate students at Newcastle University, as this book will always remind me of my time there with them.

I had the opportunity to present earlier drafts of this book to colleagues and friends from Europe. I am grateful to Isabel Santaolalla, Jo Evans, Rob Stone, Alfredo Martínez-Expósito, Santiago Fouz-Hernández, Chris Perriam, Tom Whittaker, Sally Faulkner, Sarah Wright, Fran Zurian, Parvati Nair and Alberto Mira. In the United States, I had the honour to share parts of this book with several friends and colleagues. I remain deeply grateful to Jon Snyder, Isolina Ballesteros, Teresa Vilarós, Steven Marsh, Barbara Zecchi, Eva Woods, Alberto Medina, Isabel Estrada, Susan Martin-Márquez, Enrique Álvarez, Víctor Fuentes, Susan Larson, Robert Trumbull, Cristina Moreiras, Gema Pérez-Sánchez, Jill Robbins, Cristina Martínez-Carazo, Marvin D'Lugo, Kathleen Vernon, Tatjana Pavlovic, Dean Allbritton, Patricia Keller, Sarah Thomas, Camila Moreiras, Ana Moraña and especially my former colleague and dear friend Marsha Kinder for enthusiastically reading and discussing parts of this book with me. I could not have written this book without Marsha's wonderful personal and professional support and invaluable advice. Paul Julian Smith deserves my deepest thanks. He generously agreed to be a respondent to a special panel I organised at the Society for Cinema and Media Studies Conference in Montreal in 2015 to commemorate the twentieth anniversary of the publication of his pioneering book on Almodóvar. I am also deeply grateful to Jo Labanyi. She invited me to New York University as a Visiting Scholar on two occasions where I was able to work on this manuscript. I thank both Jo and Paul for their thoughtful advice and their inspiring conversation. I am also honoured to express my sincere and deepest thanks to Griselda Pollock and Bracha Ettinger. While I lived in

Britain, I attended several conferences organised by Griselda Pollock. Her lectures transformed me intellectually and personally. This book attests to the significant influence and impact of her inspiring research on my thinking through many years. I also had the distinct honour and pleasure of meeting Bracha Ettinger at a conference on maternal subjectivity in London, in which Griselda Pollock also participated. Bracha Ettinger's theoretical work is the 'heart' of this book. She is the most fascinating feminist thinker I have ever encountered. I hope that this book does justice to her complex psychoanalytic work. It has been a great privilege to have had conversations with Ettinger throughout this process.

Nor could I have written this book without the inspiring intellectual atmosphere that I have the privilege to enjoy at my current institution, the University of Southern California. I am honoured to express my deepest thanks to my colleagues and students, who are seriously committed to establishing a productive dialogue between critical theory and philosophy, and Latin American and Spanish cultural texts: Sherry Velasco, Roberto Díaz, Erin Graff-Zivin, Samuel Steinberg, Natalia Pérez, Gian Maria Annovi, Brenno Kaneyasu-Maranhao, Ronald Mendoza de Jesús, Panivong Norindr, Natania Meeker, César Pérez, Jackie Sheean, Veli N. Yashin and Akira Lippit. I am deeply grateful to Guillermo Rodríguez-Romaguera and Justin Evans whose help has been instrumental in preparing the final version of this book. I am especially grateful to Peggy Kamuf for her rigorous feedback on parts of this book. And I should also thank Bertha Delgado and Amelia Acosta for their administrative support, as well as the Vice Dean of Humanities at the Dornsife College of Letters, Arts and Sciences, Peter Mancall, for his leadership and enthusiastic support of my research.

Chapter 1 is a substantial revision of the article 'Returning to and from the Maternal Rural Space: Trauma, Late Modernity, and Nostalgic Utopia in Almodóvar's *Volver* (2006)', *Bulletin of Hispanic Studies*, 88:3 (2011b), 321–38. Parts of Chapter 2 appeared in 'Becoming a Queer Mother in and through Film: Trans-sexuality, Trans-subjectivity, and Maternal Relationality in Almodóvar's *All About my Mother*' in *A Companion to Spanish Cinema*, ed. Jo Labanyi and Tatjana Pavlovic, Malden and Oxford: Blackwell (2013a), pp. 563–80. Chapter 3 is a substantial revision of 'Inscribing/Scratching the Past on the "Surface" of the "Skin": Embodied Inter-subjectivity, "Prosthetic Memory" and Witnessing in Almodóvar's *La mala educación*' in *A Companion to Almodóvar*, ed. Marvin D'Lugo and Kathleen Vernon, Malden and Oxford: Blackwell (2013b), pp. 322–44. Finally, parts of Chapter 4 were published as an article in Spanish, 'La piel del horror, el horror en la piel. Poder, violencia y trauma en el cuerpo (post)humano en *La piel que habito*', *The Journal of Spanish Cultural Studies*, 14.1 (2013c), 70–85. I would like to thank Claire Taylor, Editor of the *Bulletin of Hispanic Studies*, Laurence Goodchild, Managing Editor of Area Studies at Taylor & Francis Group, and Rebecca Harkin, Editor at Wiley Blackwell, for permission to publish substantial revisions of these pieces in this book. Revising these earlier pieces has enabled me to rethink my own perspective on Almodóvar. I would also like to express my sincere thanks to El Deseo, Almodóvar's film company, especially Emmanuelle Depaix, Agustín and Pedro Almodóvar, for permission to use the still from *La mala educación* on the book's cover and the reproductions and illustrations throughout the book. Gillian Leslie and Richard Strachan at Edinburgh University Press deserve my deepest thanks. Their support and help throughout the process of bringing this book to completion have been invaluable.

Finally, I am fortunate to share my life with Eduardo Leonardi, who designed this book cover, and Lilly Hannah. I thank them for their emotional support and patience throughout the challenging and yet stimulating process of bringing this book to completion. During the writing of this book, I had to deal with one of the most difficult and painful experiences that one has to face in one's lifetime: the unexpected illness and recent death of my mother, Leovigilda Albilla López. The traces of her presence are felt in every single sentence that I articulate here, as if writing were a form that inscribes all the affects and emotions of a subject who transmits to the readers his own fragility and vulnerability to the internal and external forces that are part of one's existence. Like any mother, I assume, mine believed in me more than I possibly could do. The love, education and wise advice she offered me as well as the passion for work she inculcated in me when she was alive, even during the last months of her life, will always remain in me. Honouring her legacy gives me the emotional strength to keep going on a personal and professional level. This book is dedicated to her.

Introduction:
Encountering the Trace

This stain reveals itself only in the precarious opening of the becoming visible; it is deployed only as a closing of signification, a closing to signification. It says nothing. It doesn't seem made to be understood [. . .] It seems to arise from pure contingency. It tells nothing in itself about its origin. Would segmenting or scanning it give it meaning? Yet it appears to be outside the bounds of scansion or any sort of narrativity. It is only a chain of non-mimetic, chance occurrences, neither imperceptible nor yet perceptible as figures. (Didi-Huberman 1984: 65–6)

How does a concern with trauma and memory offer a different and more profound way of engaging with the work of Pedro Almodóvar, one of the world's most critically acclaimed and commercially successful filmmakers? And what can Almodóvar's aesthetic practice offer ethically and politically to 'post-traumatic' cultures,[1] both nationally and globally – given that his work has been called 'apolitical' or 'ahistorical' (Smith 2014: 2)?[2] This book provides a critical and theoretical reformulation of a neglected aspect of Almodóvar's cinema: its engagement with the traumatic past, subjective and collective memory, and the ethical and political meanings that result from this engagement. I focus on close readings of Almodóvar's films from the 1990s and 2000s, *Volver* (2006), *Todo sobre mi madre* (*All About My Mother*, 1999), *La mala educación* (*Bad Education*, 2004) and *La piel que habito* (*The Skin I Live In*, 2011), in order to explore how his cinema mourns and witnesses the traces of trauma and fragments of memory. This book pays attention to the toxic effects of these traces, as well as the transformative potential of encountering them in the present.

I begin with the aesthetic and psychic economy of the trace.[3] As Georges Didi-Huberman's reflection in my epigraph shows, the trace establishes a productive tension between visibility and invisibility, between the intelligible and unintelligible. The trace stands at an ambivalent point. It is both silent and a remainder of that which cannot be signified. It points to the primal other, a pre- or post-symbolic Other, what Parveen Adams calls the other of language and representation (Adams 1991: 93). Although the trace points to that which is simultaneously present and absent, it is not only the *index* of the unsymbolisable traumatic event; the indexical trace is the traumatic event itself. It probes the boundaries of subjectivity and representation, pointing to the absence of referents around which the otherwise unsymbolisable traumatic event can become precariously present.

For Jacques Derrida, the trace points to the absolute beginning, while also indicating the impossibility of finding any sign of an absolute origin – so it indexes the origin's disappearance. Derrida defines the 'arche-trace' as the trace that is felt as it erases itself: 'As a mark that makes itself present through its erasure the trace is the origin of sense, the "différance" that opens appearance and signification' (1998 [1967]: 65).[4] However, he suggests that the trace also indexes the non-disappearance of the origin, as it was constituted by a non-origin. So the trace is the 'origin of the origin'. But, while the trace functions as Derrida's alternative to 'presence', it is not merely the inscription of the absence of other presences. The trace is both origin and absence.[5] My theoretical concern with the relation between aesthetics, ethics and trauma in Almodóvar's cinema is rooted in this aspect of the trace: the multiple, paradoxical connections, disconnections or displacements through which the trace is precariously and belatedly present or deferred, repetitively erased and absent, non-represented and transformed – and through which it inscribes and transmits signification.

This book does not focus on reductive biographical readings of Almodóvar's cinema, but, as Dona M. Kercher argues, some 'biographical details already participate forcefully in the cultural discourse' (2015: 95) – in this case, the filmmaker's much-quoted statement that he started making films as if Franco, who may be seen as the 'origin of the origin', had never existed, as if the 'intoxicating trace' had erased itself (McDaniel 1994). Almodóvar's claim must be seen in the context of Spanish debates about memory and amnesia.

In 2007, the Spanish parliament approved the *Ley de memoria histórica* (Law of Historical Memory) proposed by the former Socialist government of José Luis Rodríguez Zapatero. This legislation was a response to what many historians and cultural critics have identified as the process of political, social and cultural mourning, abreaction and healing. This process was violently repressed under Franco, consciously silenced during the political transition from dictatorship to democracy and historically negated by the political Right. The new law afforded moral and symbolic recognition and extended rights to those who suffered persecution and violence during the Spanish Civil War and under Franco – but it did not take legal action against the perpetrators. For some, the attempt to restore legal rights to Franco's victims and to normalise historical inquiry showed the health and strength of Spain's democracy. But, as Stephanie Golob argues, the law also generated a range of controversial public statements – by politicians, judges and representatives of historical memory associations – concerning the implications and efficacy of the legislation, which was seen as anti-punitive (Golob 2008).

Many filmmakers and spectators in Spain are committed to using film as a way to confront and work through the personal and collective memories of Spain's historical traumas: the silencing, persecution, execution, exile and exclusion of Franco's victims and the victims of the Civil War. The memory debates have certainly been ideologically instrumentalised and commodified by the Spanish cultural industry (Estrada 2013), but this has only given greater significance to the commitment of filmmakers and spectators. In the absence of institutionalised transitional justice, and the ambiguities of the memory debates, filmmakers have become important political and ethical figures.

The debates on historical memory have now been eclipsed, however, by the economic crisis, and they have been completely excluded from the political agenda of the Conservative government since its return to power in 2011. That does not mean, though, that the traces of the traumatic past have stopped affecting us, subjectively or collectively. Given these continued effects, we need to keep reflecting on how the terms of the debate can be defined, historically and theoretically, so we can see how the traces of trauma and fragments of memory function as an intervention in the neoliberal present. The current socio-economic conditions threaten the subject of neoliberal democracy (as Estrada contends in her study of Spanish documentary filmmaking); could that threat itself be a perpetuation of, or succumbing to, the dark shadows of the spectral past? Or could the fragments of memory, to the contrary, help us to a brighter future? This book is then, in part, a contribution to scholarship on how memory debates have shaped cultural production and reception in Spain for the last few decades.[6]

More specifically, I focus on the aesthetic, ethical and potential political implications of our affective and interpretive encounter with memory in Almodóvar's film, whether that memory be subjective, shared or both.[7] I ask: to what extent in Almodóvar's work do we encounter or avoid subjective and shared traces of trauma and fragments of memory associated with, for example, state terror or patriarchal violence? Are these traces and fragments inscribed in his films, transmitted via the medium of film and actualised in our body's memory? To what extent are we ethically and politically transformed by such encounters, or missed encounters, with the belated traces of trauma and fragments of memory?[8] Do we remain afflicted by this experience of trauma? To what extent can we recuperate and re-inscribe in the present what was there before the trauma, to paraphrase Suely Rolnik (2008a), and so overcome the toxic effects inscribed in the body's memory, without submitting to a reductive teleology of resolution or cure? The remainder of this introduction offers an explanation of the theoretical concepts underpinning the book's argument, but not so that I can apply an existing body of theoretical work to a particular case. The point is rather to explore how Almodóvar's films both illustrate and push back against these theoretical concerns.

Spectres of Francoism?

In both the Spanish and the Anglo-American academy, previous scholarship has considered Almodóvar to be the most modern (or (post) modern) of Spanish filmmakers. Cristina Moreiras proposes that his films – particularly those of the 1980s – have consistently contributed to the image of Madrid as a city of desire and tolerance. They present the city as one of Europe's most modern capitals, and Spain as a modern nation, throughout the post-Franco period. He is thus open to criticism for contributing to the culture of amnesia favoured by many Spanish institutions, because this culture itself was deemed necessary to create a modern, Europeanised phase in Spain's history (2002: 28). Accordingly, Moreiras notes that Almodóvar participated 'in an image of a democratic Spain that privileged subjects alienated by the spectacle of reality, oblivious to political processes, sceptical of any type of ideology (except that of the market), excluded from their own collective history, and exclusively immersed in an apparent superficiality and banality' (2002: 65, my translation).[9] Moreiras' rigorous attention to Spain's disavowal of the past, as made manifest in Almodóvar's 1980s cinema, raises very important questions. In Chapter 1, I will consider two possibilities. First, whether the celebratory embrace of (post)modernity on the part of Almodóvar (and of Spanish society as a whole) was a release from the psychic and social burdens of the recent past; and second, whether this embrace can be theorised in terms of trauma at the heart of everyday life in the (post)modern condition – which David Harvey, in a broader context, has associated with the advent of flexible capitalism and increasingly uneven economic development (1990).[10]

Almodóvar's career (1980–present) began five years after the start of Spain's post-Franco, democratic period,[11] and scholars often argue that there is a clear distinction between Almodóvar's early films, which show a lack of political commitment, and his latest films, which contain more explicit allusions to politics and to Spain's traumatic past.[12] According to Adrián Pérez Melgosa,

> the Civil War and Franco's dictatorship [are] two historical periods which Almodóvar had insistently declared to be located outside of his interests, but which have progressively gained a larger presence in his work, either tangentially through allusion, as part of the films' backdrops, or through direct political statements. (2013: 177)[13]

But, in line with Paul Julian Smith's argument (2014), Pérez Melgosa problematises the idea that Almodóvar's cinema was ever 'apolitical'. Rather, he argues, Almodóvar has been concerned with Spain's social, cultural, economic and political transformations since he started making films. This requires a critical reappraisal of his oeuvre, which may 'register the presence of a quest that traverses all of his films, one that joins the personal and the political in the right embrace of the aftermath of a traumatic experience' (Pérez Melgosa 2013: 178). So the apparent distinction between an apolitical early period and an increasingly political later period overlooks the ways in which the past has irrupted, been evoked, or been registered, albeit obliquely, throughout Almodóvar's career.

For instance, Alejandro Varderi rightly suggests that Almodóvar successfully integrated the traditional *castizo* (authentic) culture into a (post)modern aesthetic through the use of camp and kitsch. Varderi calls Almodóvar's an 'estética heteróclita' (heteroclite aesthetics) (1996). It incorporates elements of popular Spanish culture, and reworks familiar styles and genres from Hollywood into a kind of artistic pastiche. Almodóvar's characteristic collage appears as a clash of visual quotations, resulting in a cinema that cuts across genres and modes. Similarly, Alejandro Yarza focuses on Almodóvar's recycling of national stereotypes, such as bullfighting or flamenco, in order to rescue them from their reactionary Francoist connotations (1999). But Almodóvar's disavowal of the Francoist past could also be read symptomatically as the foreclosure of the symbolic order. Almodóvar's reinterpretation of reality, with a different kind of meaning outside the symbolic order, would then manifest that foreclosure. Could such a reinterpretation of reality palliate the disastrous effects of the foreclosure?[14]

I am not offering a psychological history of Almodóvar – one that rediscovers in the films the hidden truths of Almodóvar's unconscious. Nor am I approaching the relationship between aesthetics, ethics and trauma in Almodóvar's cinema by focusing on his conscious intention or ethical and political commitments; this book is not an auteurist argument. Despite the fact that Almodóvar's authorial signature (a concept that I problematise in Chapter 3) is predicated on his appropriation and subversion of popular cinematic genres, auteurism remains the most common scholarly approach to Almodóvar's work. This can be explained by Almodóvar's 'determination from the very beginning to devote as much time to promotion as to production' (Smith 2014: 5). This study departs from a conventional auteurist approach; it thinks with, rather than about, Almodóvar.

But am I trying to perpetuate a psychoanalytically inflected understanding of contemporary Spanish society as haunted by the spectres of Francoism? My focus on trauma and memory might seem to be in line with the work of Hispanists whose sophisticated focus on hauntology has enabled them to engage productively with historical memory in Spain, by exploring how the spectres of Francoism belatedly return as residues of the collective amnesia, the erasure of subjective and collective traumatic memories, that characterised the Spanish transition from dictatorship to democracy.[15] In this case, my emphasis on the spectral past could limit my reading of Almodóvar's films to a continuous backward glance; back to mourning, to the traumas of the historical past and the memory of the Franco dictatorship. My use of hauntology could seem to neglect the complex theoretical implications underpinning the concept of hauntology itself – spectrality as constitutive of the film medium, the vicissitudes of the present, or the promise of an incalculable future.[16]

I raise these points because a psychoanalytically inflected approach to contemporary Spanish culture has already encountered some scepticism, if not outright hostility. In Jo Labanyi's seminal issue of the *Journal of Spanish Cultural Studies* dedicated to the politics of memory, Ángel Loureiro questions the value of trauma theory and psychoanalysis in work on the historical specificity of the Spanish context, hence establishing a division between the psychic and the political, or between subjective and shared experiences. The distinction between structural trauma, which is caused by psychic events, and historical trauma, which is caused by external events, is attributed to psychoanalysis itself. The latter is understood as a science or epistemology that focuses on individual subjectivity at the cost of collective history. Loureiro argues that cultural critics who use psychoanalysis run the risk of resorting to simplistic metaphors of physical and psychical pathologies which, he claims, fail to take into consideration the complexity of social, political, cultural or historical processes (2008: 225).

However, Mignon Nixon reminds us that psychoanalysis cannot be dissociated from traumatic historical events. The theory itself is inextricably linked to historical trauma and to the exploration of the impact of traumatic events upon the self (2007). For instance, Freud's 1920 'Beyond the Pleasure Principle', which is a crucial source for trauma studies, was stimulated by the destruction that Europe suffered during the First World

War. Freud's work continued to consider questions of collective, historical trauma, as in his 1933 correspondence with Albert Einstein, published as *Why War?* (Nixon 2007). *Moses and Monotheism* (1964 [1937–9]) is another critical reference for the study of trauma. Freud established an analogy between the effects of trauma on the individual and the collective guilt at the core of Jewish culture due to the event of the murder of Moses, the founder and giver of Jewish culture and laws (Luckhurst 2008; Gutiérrez-Albilla 2011a).

More specifically, *Moses and Monotheism* is a source for Derrida's conceptualisation of the archive, which Griselda Pollock calls 'the textualisation of cultural memory populated by our own ghostly projections and phantasies, the encryption of both a conscious record and an unconscious impression' (2013b: 12). Derrida questions the historian of psychoanalysis Josef Hayim Yerushalmi's lack of engagement with psychoanalysis in a study devoted, paradoxically, to the founder of psychoanalysis. In this argument, the archive both perpetuates authority and questions it. For Derrida, Freud's theory that compulsive repetitions are caused by the death drive is the condition for the possibility of the creation of the archive; the archive either records and preserves information, or erases it. Implicitly evoking the figure of the *marrano*, who carries with him an inaccessible secret larger than himself and that can never be revealed,[17] Derrida situates the archive at a tensional point between monumentalising and documenting the past, and revealing the haunting traces of the past. Even though they may be effaced from the archive, these traces carry the promise of a hidden secret in an unpredictable *futurity* (1995b).[18]

Given this, and following Jeffrey Skoller, I ask: does not psychoanalysis enable us to think about how our underlying unconscious structures impact the present at both a subjective and collective level, thereby becoming an important element in the production of the social field (2005: xviii)? From this perspective, as Joshua Hirsch has put it,

> the application of trauma theory to culture may offer at least one method of bridging the apparent gaps between a historical approach to culture and a textual approach; between a focus on the past signified by a historical text and a focus on the text's work of signification in the present; between documentary and fictional modes of representing history; and between individual and collective experiences of history. (2001: 9)

Pollock reminds us that, for Derrida, culture, history and tradition always already depend on the way spectres inhabit the archive. Psychoanalysis, as both a clinical and an epistemological practice, conceives the psyche as a kind of archive of the archaic (past) desires and fears that, as inaccessible spectres encrypted or carved in our psyche, unconsciously determine our present and future (Pollock 2013b: 11). Such underlying, unconscious mechanisms are extracted through repetition in the psychoanalytic encounter.

My emphasis is not on a detached scientific method that attempts to find the historical truth from an outside position. I want to pay attention to the traces, the affects or, to use Derrida's term, the impression of history and memory inscribed precariously in subjectivity and leaving its (invisible) mark on the body. These traces are, I argue, extracted through our encounter with Almodóvar's cinema in an already 'out-of-joint' present, and brought into a presence that cannot be reified beyond signification.[19] So, despite Spanish film studies' retreat from critical theory and psychoanalysis, I hope to demonstrate that psychoanalysis remains a promising epistemological framework and critical resource for thinking about traumas, both subjective and shared, in relation to the film medium. As Kristeva argues, psychoanalysis presents 'the only modern interpretative theory to hypothesize the heterogeneous in meaning'. In psychoanalysis, this heterogeneity is 'so interdependent with language and thought as to be its very condition, indeed, its driving force' (cited in Pollock 2013b: 10).

At the same time, it is important to underscore Almodóvar's own ambivalent position vis-à-vis psychoanalysis. This is manifest, for instance, in the way his films depict psychoanalysts, psychologists or psychiatrists. *Laberinto de pasiones* (*Labyrinths of Passions*, 1982) parodies Lacanian psychoanalysis in the figure of an Argentinian analyst who can only offer a facile explanation of the main female character's obsessive sexual addiction.[20] In *¿Qué he hecho yo para merecer esto?* (*What Have I Done to Deserve This?*, 1984), the psychoanalyst, whose house is cleaned by the main female protagonist (Carmen Maura), is portrayed as unprofessional, dysfunctional and apathetic, while in *Hable con ella* (*Talk to Her*, 2001), Alicia's psychiatrist father reduces the main character's emotional, social and affective problems to a symptom of his closeted homosexuality. Yet, in *Matador* (1986), the female psychologist (Carmen Maura) *responds* to the main character's traumatic experiences in an intimate, compassionate manner; she is an effective witness to the unknown other's painful experiences.

Of course, Almodóvar's engagement with psychoanalysis cannot be reduced to a simple discussion of how characters associated with this profession are positively or negatively represented in his films. Psychoanalysis is part of the dramatic, or anti-dramatic, construction of his films, and a theoretical resource for thinking about his films, even when those films problematise psychoanalysis as an effective epistemological discourse. I contend, rather, that my use of trauma theory and psychoanalysis is not an instance of nostalgia or melancholy over the obsolescence of psychoanalysis in Spanish film studies and film studies in general. Instead, it embraces and replicates Almodóvar's own ambivalent attitude towards psychoanalysis, as well as the (unfulfilled) promises of psychoanalytic study for an incalculable and unpredictable *futurity* in the field of Spanish film studies, and film studies and the humanities more broadly.

Encountering Fragments

Psychoanalysis considers fragments in order to find meaning in, or identify symptoms of unconscious structures. My critical interpretation of Almodóvar's cinema is teased out from a close textual analysis of selected scenes (or fragments) that may or may not be supplementary, marginal or decentred in relation to the film as a whole. Laura Mulvey has persuasively argued that, although one has to pay attention to the specificity of each artistic practice, Roland Barthes' notion of the *punctum* in the photograph can be helpful to think about other media, including film (2006). Mulvey is concerned with an 'aesthetic of delay' based on repetition and return, which can be located in the process of perception and interpretation. Mulvey notes how the shift from celluloid to the new moving image technologies, including the electronic and the digital, has transformed the way spectators engage with film. For instance, Mulvey is very interested in delaying images, 'returning to and repeating certain moments' or rupturing the linearity of narrative continuity, all techniques that put pressure on analytical categories conventionally used to discuss film *dispositif* (2006: 183). Mulvey argues that interrupting the flow of film breaks the different levels of time that usually coalesce. With these interruptions to the film's continuum, fragments acquire a new resonance that would otherwise not emerge, because the continuum is, of course, constitutive of the film medium (2006: 192). In this context, Mulvey tells us, the spectator can attribute to fragments an unexpected significance because they delay fiction. Likewise, this mode of engaging with the film, by focusing on interruptions to the film's flow, points self-reflexively to the way the ontology of film is predicated on the relationship between stillness and movement, as I will discuss in Chapter 1. Mulvey famously drew on psychoanalysis to lay bare the voyeuristic and fetishistic mechanisms underpinning the scopic economy in Hollywood cinema. By contrast, in her recent work Mulvey argues that a slow, delayed engagement with fragments in film is the condition for the possibility of activation in the 'pensive spectator', 'the disturbing sense of reality that belongs to Roland Barthes' concept of the *punctum*' (2006: 195, emphasis in original).

In line with Mulvey's work, I focus on fragments in Almodóvar's cinema, while remaining aware that any critical reading of a film is always already predicated on a violent fragmentation of it. Fragments encapsulate the allegory of perceptual, affective, interpretive engagement with Almodóvar's cinema. Jean-Claude Seguin (2009) advocates just such a methodological approach if one wants to apprehend, rather than understand, Almodóvar's cinema. His is a work made through creative attention to details, and the critic must work with just such attention. I propose, then, that the fragment establishes a significant relationship between the spectator and the cinematic image, thus enhancing the contingent relationship between the aesthetic/cinematic practice and the viewing/aesthetic experience. Sarah Cooper also notes that the construction of a film always already depends on the relationship between representation or mediation and the viewing encounter (2006: 7). In similar terms, Vivian Sobchack explains that, although certain cinematic conventions may lend themselves to or condition a specific form of identification of the spectator with films, these processes of identification cannot be pre-established. They are produced in the contingent viewing experience (1999). Such a phenomenological, affective and interpretive encounter between the cinematic image and the spectator always depends on conscious intentions and unconscious structures. As Michael Renov suggests in the context of documentary filmmaking, our encounter with the cinematic image is motivated by curiosity, which is a conscious intention, and by our unconscious desires or fears (2004: 101). Gilles Deleuze tells us that 'learning takes place not in the relation between a representation and an action (reproduction of the Same) but in the relation between a sign and a response' (1994 [1968]: 22). Our process of 'learning' Almodóvar's cinema, to use Deleuze's term, implies a 'depersonalisation through love', which replicates Almodóvar's own 'depersonalisation through love' of cinema as an analogical medium (I will come back to this point in Chapter 3). Following Seguin's privileging of 'apprehension' over 'understanding', I suggest that a contingent encounter with the other (in this case, Almodóvar's cinema) does not exclusively lead to the acquisition of knowledge, that is, recognition by means of pre-established categories. Our contingent encounter with the fragments of his cinema generates a process of thinking that retrospectively evokes the past and opens onto the future, thereby evoking an endless becoming.[21]

Repetition and Difference

Any reading of Almodóvar's cinema must pay attention to the idea that some of the formal and thematic concerns and *leitmotifs* in his latest films may have originated in and developed from those of his early films – without thereby implying a straightforward, linear approach. Marsha Kinder has described this organic, creative arc in Almodóvar's cinema and the practice of reading his films with the term 'retroseriality'. Kinder explains:

> I am using the term 'retroseriality' to describe both an aspect of Almodóvar's films and a method of reading them. I am not suggesting that his work is regressive or nostalgic; nor am I referring to his thematic of a 'return', which can be found in many of his films, as well as in the title of the recent *Volver* (2006). Rather, I am arguing that his films increasingly perform an evocation of earlier works (both his own and intertexts of others) that leads us to read them as an ongoing saga and to regroup them into networked clusters. (2009: 269)

Kinder here responds to critics who practise a 'hermeneutics of suspicion', searching for repetitive elements in Almodóvar's films, including implicit and explicit reference to cinematic intertexts, and who identify these as creative shortcuts. More importantly, the notion of 'retroseriality' offers a more theoretically sophisticated interpretation of a repetition that moves away from 'compulsive repetition' to the generation of differences within repetition in Almodóvar's cinema. This concept can be used to bring Almodóvar's films into conversation with Deleuze's philosophical reflections on repetition and difference, and difference within repetition, hence underscoring the ontological and epistemological complexity of these concepts in Almodóvar's cinema.[22]

Francisco José Martínez Martínez describes Deleuze's work as an interrogation of the Platonic distinction between the Idea (intelligible essences) and the copy (sensible appearances). Deleuze argues that, instead, one should pay attention to the concept of the simulacrum. The copy and the simulacrum are not synonymous. Both look like Ideas, but the simulacrum subverts the logic underpinning the distinction between Idea and copy, rejecting the hierarchy that is established in it. Deleuze then introduces the concept of the phantasm, which is constituted through the repetition of several simulacra, between which resonances are established and repetition becomes creative. For Deleuze, the phantasm is not a repetition of a past event, but the relationship that is established between an actual and a virtual event, which takes place in the present without having existed in the past. As Martínez Martínez shows, for Deleuze repetition is not merely repetition of the Same. It is a creative power, which produces difference. The actual simulacrum is not, then, the repetition of a past simulacrum, but the actualisation of a virtual simulacrum that has not yet existed.[23] But, Martínez Martínez asks, is this difference still circumscribed by the concept of representation? Deleuze explains that 'representation was defined by certain elements: identity with regard to concepts, opposition with regard to judgement, resemblance with regard to objects. The identity of the unspecified concept constitutes the form of the Same with regard to recognition' (1994 [1968]): 137). Martínez Martínez goes on to explain that Deleuze distinguishes between a representation that is limited to the finite and a representation that opens onto the infinite, either that which is infinitely minute or that which is infinitely immense. However, for Martínez Martínez, neither concept of representation points to an irreducible and non-mediated difference. He distinguishes between a repetition defined as a repetition of the Same – in other words the copy of the original – and a repetition which affirms a difference, one that opens onto the new, the irreducible, the irreplaceable, the unique, the singular. This difference without a concept exceeds the Idea; it cannot be contained within representation or mediation. Repetition becomes the eternal return of a heterogeneous difference, and points to a virtual future.

Our encounter with Almodóvar's repetitive, yet different, films thus points to what is beyond representation and mediation (I will come back to this point shortly): an affirmation of alterity; different intensities, multiplicities, qualities and potentialities, by which 'thought comes to us' (Deleuze 1994 [1968]: 144); the formulation of questions instead of finding solutions; the virtual instead of the possible; the Real instead of the actual. The films, too, help us to think about the relationship between repetition and difference beyond a framework or logic associated with the thought of the Same. Particularly in his later films, such as *La mala educación* or *La piel que habito*,[24] our encounter with Almodóvar leads us to reflect more explicitly on the way the cinematic image witnesses and re-experiences the traces of the traumatic past, and mediates between or encounters individual and shared experiences in the complex relationship between aesthetics, ethics and trauma.

Macro- and Micro-politics

Other useful Deleuzean distinctions for my work are those between the molecular and the molar, and between the micro- and macro-political. As Patricia Pisters notes, the molar is associated with the logic of identity within a representational mode of thinking based on binary oppositions.

Such a dialectical thought structures social organisation. The molecular plane, however, points to lines of flight or ruptures within the molar system. For Pisters, these two planes are in a constant negotiation of de-territorialised and re-territorialised forces (2001). The spectator encounters these traces of trauma and fragments of memory on a micro-political and macro-political level. For Rolnik, both macro- and micro-politics may reinforce or overcome repression at the molecular or molar level. Rolnik goes on to say that such immanent and transcendent interventions in us potentially transform perceptible and imperceptible reality, either reinforcing repression and control (micro-fascisms), or producing resist-ant forces of creation and differentiation for the possibility of becoming. Rolnik argues that the macro-political level points to the 'conflictual ten-sions in the cartography of visible and speakable reality [. . .] It is the plane of stratification that outlines subjects and objects, as well as the relation between them and their respective representations' (2008a: 135). Rolnik goes on to explain that '[w]ith micropolitics, we are confronted by the tensions between this plane [the macro-political level] and what is already announced in the diagram of the sensed reality, invisible and unspeakable (a domain of fluxes, intensities, sensations, and becomings)' (2008a: 135).

In line with Rolnik's attention to the tensions between the macro- and micro-political, which constantly traverse each other, my study is con-cerned with how we can derive meaning from representations that are already projections of the forms associated with our conception of the world. I explore how our senses are affected by the resonance of the world conceived as a diagram of forces that escape symbolic representation (Rolnik 2008a: 135). By paying attention to the connections between the molecular and the molar, the immanent and the transcendent, the micro-political and the macro-political planes, we can explore how Almodóvar's work offers a flexible and complex cartography of the forces operative in subjectivation in the social field (Rolnik 2008a: 136).

Mimesis and Aisthesis

Another aspect of this book is how Almodóvar's recent films negotiate cinema's mimetic properties and its affective properties. According to Jill Bennett, these are associated with art as a 'means of apprehending the world via sense-based and affective processes – processes that touch bodies intimately and directly' (2012: 3). I am not, however, interested in whether Almodóvar's work can be recognised as belonging to a particular genre (for instance, melodrama), if it is a 'good' or 'bad' reflection of reality, if it properly establishes a division between what can be represented and non-represented, or if it respects the principles of verisimilitude. Following Rancière, these questions follow the criteria of Aristotelian mimesis, which is predicated on intellectual recognition and articulated emotion (Rancière 2008: 3).[25] Rancière offers a more nuanced and complex understanding of mimesis:

> [M]imesis means: the concordance between the complex of sensory signs in which the process of *poiesis* [making] is displayed and the complex of the forms of perception and emotion through which it is felt and understood – two processes which are united by a Greek word: *aisthesis*. *Mimesis* first means the correspondence between *poiesis* and *aisthesis*. (2008: 6, emphasis in original)

Against this mimetic regime, Rancière describes a politically emancipatory regime. This 'aesthetic regime' problematises the relationship between *poiesis* and *aisthesis*, between cause and effect, between representational mediation and ethical immediacy. He argues that it creates a 'new sensory fabric' by producing a rupture in the affections and perceptions through which the fabric of common experience is constituted. Such a change in the cartography of the feasible, the perceptible and the thinkable could lead to the articulation of political subjectivities.

Rancière criticises Jean-François Lyotard's emphasis on the inability of art to capture the (traumatic) event through his concept of the 'différend'. For Lyotard, the Shoah produced both a rupture with humanity and with the existing means of representation and cognition. Hence, any attempt at suturing the gaps and holes through a finite form of representation would imply a betrayal, a form of violence or a reduction of the complexity of the traumatic experience. Rancière argues that Lyotard's concept of the 'différend' subjugates the aesthetic regime to the ethical dimension:

> Thus, in Lyotard in particular, the existence of events that exceed what can be thought calls for an art that witnesses to the unthinkable in general, to the essential discrepancy between what affects us and such of it as our thinking can master. It is then the peculiarity of a new mode of art – sublime art – to record the trace of the unthinkable. (2007: 111)

Since Rancière is interested in the affirmation of new forms of political subjectivities, he objects to what he considers Lyotard's (and, more broadly, (post)modernism's) ethical turn. He sees this as disallowing the possibility of thinking aesthetics in relation to unpredictable, emancipating political actions in the future.

Although this study shares Rancière's emphasis on art's potential to transform our affects and perceptions through the 'redistribution of the sensible', I do not limit such a transformative potential to the spheres of the 'thinkable, the feasible or the perceptible'. Instead, like Pollock, I conceive subjectivity as determined by the relationship between language and what escapes linguistic symbolisation. Again like Pollock, I identify the 'aesthetic' as a process of knowing beyond cognition and as a sensorial process beyond perception (2013b: 12). So, by focusing on perceptible and imperceptible traces, I associate Almodóvar's cinema with a cinematic/aesthetic practice that

> pays tribute to the shattering of existing means of comprehension and representation resulting from real historical outrages by a constant fidelity, by working towards a phrasing – not merely linguistic, but gestural, sonic or graphic – a touching or encountering of some affective elements capable of shifting us both subjectively and collectively that do not arrive at containing the event in finite forms. (Pollock 2013a: 26–7)

In addition, I am inspired by Bracha Ettinger's emphasis on a 'matrixial' psychic resource which may or may not be used to think about *response-ability*: our ability to respond to the suffering of the other (I shall come back to this point later on). In other words, the trans-subjective pre-conditions of our subjectivation, which in Ettinger are associated with our 'intimated co-human-subjectivity' (cited in Pollock 2013b: 16), may potentially lead to our ethical way of being in a tangible world inhabited by a plurality of beings. Instead of overlooking the political, whether the macro- or micro-political levels, I emphasise the transformations of our perceptions through the aesthetic experience, and of our ethical way of relating to irreducible others. Such transformations at the unconscious, micro-political level may potentially lead to macro-political, conscious, yet incalculable political decisions and actions in an unpredictable future. Our engagement with Almodóvar's films evokes the traces of trauma and fragments of memory by provoking a reverberation in our subjectivities and bodies, without making us succumb to an over-identification with others' suffering.

One of the reasons for putting Rolnik's (see above) and Ettinger's work into conversation is that both of them are interested in how artworks, which can be understood as processes rather than objects, mobilise bodily and psychic forces that provoke in us a fragilisation of the self, without assuming a previous sovereign 'I', or assuming that fragilisation (which implies some loss of one's boundaries) leads to psychosis. The fragilisation of the self is caused by the poignant impact of our (prolonged) encounter with an aesthetic practice on our thought and body. We may miss such an encounter, as this is always already a contingent event. But the fragilisation of the self is a condition of possibility for a movement beyond ourselves, in which we can be affected by and perceive the visible and invisible traces of the irreducible other, as they are imprinted in and transmitted through the artwork.

Rolnik foregrounds the embodied and cognitive processes through which we experience the work of art to think about the force of desire in the reconfiguration of a new politics of subjectivation in the social field. Ettinger uses the artwork as a way of accessing the 'matrixial borderspace', in which a shift from subjectivity and intersubjectivity to trans-subjective encounters takes place. Ettinger articulates a syntactical structuration of the psyche that undoes psychoanalysis from within, provoking an aesthetic transformation and a transformation of our ethical way of relating to others. This new relationship cannot be accounted for by the (pre)dominant psychoanalytic and philosophical focus on the individual subject, or on endless multiplicity.

In sum, both theorists describe the realm of art as a space of potential transformation, in which we can move beyond the psychic and social limitations that underpin the symbolic structures sustaining our 'being-in-the-world' with others. I am not, of course, simply 'applying' these theories to Almodóvar's films. Instead, I conceptualise Almodóvar's cinema as a 'theoretical object', to use Mieke Bal's term (1999), which both articulates and puts pressure on Rolnik's and Ettinger's aesthetic, ethical and political propositions. This will highlight the complexity of Almodóvar's cinema in relation to theoretical debates on trauma and memory.[26]

Trans-forming Trauma via the Aesthetic

Beyond the distinction between an early, supposedly apolitical period and a later, more political period in Almodóvar's work, some critics have associated Almodóvar's early period with eccentric and spontaneous filmmaking, explicit gay thematics and a hedonistic vision of Madrid as the city of desire (Smith 2003: 150). By contrast, Smith informs us, Almodóvar's recent cinema has been associated with austere and experienced filmmaking, a mastery of narrative and cinematic form, heterosexual thematics and a more sombre vision of the city as marked by social alienation and violence, disease and death (2003: 150). Drawing on Pierre Bourdieu's work on distinction, Smith suggests that Almodóvar's cinema has moved into a higher cultural register by displaying increasing formal perfection, thematic seriousness and social prestige (2003: 153).

Almodóvar's integration of literary or performance pieces, such as, for instance, Pina Bausch's dance pieces in *Hable con ella*, can be associated with what Saša Markuš has defined as Almodóvar's 'etapa de sublimación' (period of sublimation). This period is characterised by the integration of various poetic experiences that are less clashing than in his earlier work (2001). Although Almodóvar does not dismiss popular autochthonous cultural expressions, this integration of literary and performance pieces could reveal a desire to embrace modernity and high – in other words, European – culture. Although, as I have said above, this book is not an auteurist study, it is important to underscore that Almodóvar's embrace of European culture both reflects and contributes to his international status as one of the last European 'grands auteurs'. As is well known, Almodóvar was denied the status of an artist in Spain until his cinema had become commercially successful and critically acclaimed on a global level.

Smith accordingly identifies Almodóvar as the only remaining European auteur who balances critical and commercial success (2003: 153). However, he notes, there is a continuity in Almodóvar's cinema. Almodóvar's early cinema focused on the impossibility of love, the irrevocable nature of loss and the persistence of traumatic experiences that resulted in the death and/or loss for his characters (2003: 150). By contrast, Smith rightly suggests that some of his latest films, such as *Todo sobre mi madre* and *Hable con ella*, focus optimistically on the possibility of redemption (2003: 150–1). Smith also suggests that *Hable con ella*, 'apparently so straight in its premise of twin heterosexual couples, does continue Almodóvar's oblique investigation of queer sexualities' (2014: 175). By contrast, some critics have seen the recent *La piel que habito* (the focus of Chapter 4) as evidence of a distinct break. They read it as symptomatic of Almodóvar's increasing alienation from social reality, and an increasing obsession with his own cinematic oeuvre and formalist concerns. This study, to the contrary, proposes that Almodóvar's increasing self-reflexivity (and thus apparent withdrawal from social concerns) actually encourages the spectator to ponder how the fragments and traces of memory and history endure in the present. I draw on Rancière's aesthetic theory in my argument that Almodóvar's cinema paradoxically embraces a modernist conception of autonomous art *as well as* a heteronomous conception of art. In other words, his art intervenes in life while maintaining its distinctiveness as art.

Almodóvar's cinema sits between mainstream and art cinema, between genre cinema and auteur cinema. Instead of perpetuating a conservative nostalgia for utopian modernism, his work underscores the ethical and potential political implications of aesthetic practices and experiences. Nelly Richard argues that the aesthetic

> deploys as marks of production, circulation and inscription of images that distinguish aesthetic forms from other signifying practices in order to establish a valorative

distinction between the respective *motivations* and *accomplishments* of meaning, between different reading *experiences* that mark each practice. (2013: 140, emphasis in original, my translation)

Almodóvar's cinema is an aesthetic practice in which the traumatic event may or may not reverberate in our subjectivity and body, by means of our affective and interpretive encounter with the traces of the irreducible other (see Ettinger 2000). It shows how traces of trauma and fragments of memory 'impinge upon concrete reality, but also upon [. . .] intangible reality' (Rolnik 2008b: 155), and affect us on a spectral and material level.

Mourning and Melancholia

This book attempts to enrich our reading of Almodóvar's films by paying attention to recent arguments about 'the recuperation of historical memory', and I reconceptualise some of the debates on trauma and memory. For instance, the Franco regime changed dramatically over its life. Yet, using Rolnik's theory, we can still insist that there is almost no space, physical or symbolic, that can escape the omnipresence of a military dictatorship. Such a regime restrains almost any 'vital movement [. . .]', creates 'a state of permanent alert [. . .]' and an almost 'total impossibility of rest [. . .]' (Rolnik 2008a: 134). The state terror that characterised the Franco regime for much of its existence imposed itself onto almost every space and the subjectivity of almost every agent. Given this, I argue that trauma can be a useful concept for thinking about how the sensory mark or effects of trauma – as well as its traces and fragments of its memory – can be actualised in our bodies and psyches, without necessarily perpetuating a melancholic repetition of traumatic symptoms or leading to a closure of the past after the process of working through.

Freud distinguished between mourning, in which the subject suffers the loss of the object, and the more pathological state of melancholia, which takes place within the realm of narcissism. Mourning and melancholia both result in a 'loss of interest in the outside world – in so far as it does not recall him [the lost object] – the same loss of capacity to adopt any new object of love (which would mean replacing him) and the same turning away from any activity that is not connected with thoughts of him' (2009 [1917]: 45). But mourning is a process of working through the loss, so that the subject can eventually sever the attachments to the lost object. In melancholia, on the other hand, the lost object is incorporated into the subject, so the loss of the object is internalised, without the loss being mediated by consciousness.

Although Freud's distinction between mourning and melancholia seems to imply a teleological 'cure', Tammy Clewell argues that we can undercut such a distinction. For her, the loss of the loved object and the traumatic impact of the event leaves a residue in the subject, who is thus inhabited by a radical alterity. The residue, the alterity, makes it impossible to completely work through a trauma.[27] And the presence of alterity is often argued to be the precondition of subjectivation. Darian Leader, for instance, argues that 'the very process by which Freud characterized melancholic identification was later used to describe the actual constitution of the human self. Our egos, he wrote, are made up of all the leftover traces of our abandoned relationships' (2008: 55). Leader enables us to think of the constitution of subjectivity through our experience and registering of loss.

Idelber Avelar applies the distinction between melancholy and mourning, and the problematic presence of a residue, to the context of post-dictatorship Latin America. He argues that mourning implies an active forgetting, as the subject carries out a 'metaphorical operation whereby the lost object is subsumed under a newly found object of affection' (1999: 4). Avelar is highly critical of this process. He sees this subsumption as a pathological symptom of the post-dictatorial society's passive forgetting. The current neoliberal order, implemented by the dictatorships themselves, is predicated on forgetting the past, and life in a perpetual present. But successful and complete mourning is (or should be) an impossible task. For Avelar, literature reveals the residue or trace left behind in the substitution of new for absent objects, and in doing so reveals the ethical and political potentialities of mourning.

This is not to say that my book will instrumentalise traumatic events or advocate a depressive, melancholic position – one that would imply remaining immobilised by the impact of traumatic events, whose untransformed effects are buried or encrypted in the psyche or the body (Abraham and Torok 1994). In their study of 'encrypted identification', Abraham and Torok use the concept of the 'phantom' to explore how traumatic events remain buried (encrypted) in the psyche without the subject being able to process them cognitively, thus producing painful, untransformed, affective and sensorial effects in the damaged ego (1994). Past traumatic experiences are inscribed on our body, and leave an invisible yet indelible mark in the psyche. The concept of 'encrypted trauma' does not relegate trauma to oblivion, however. Instead, traumatic encryption implies that the traumatic experience remains entombed, frozen, untransformed in our psyche. When the crypt collapses, the affective intensity of trauma disintegrates the structure in which we had tried to contain the traumatic experience. Instead, I want to foreground the impossibility of complete working through in order to articulate an affirmation of the ethical and political potential of mourning, both subjectively and socially. The traumatic event can be transformed aesthetically in and through Almodóvar's cinema without forming a fiction of redemption. Rather, in his work the perceptible and imperceptible affects and effects of the traumatic event become an inassimilable, radical alterity. This alterity resists the commodification of memory, as, for instance, in commemoration, to which Estrada (2013) refers; it also threatens the obfuscation of the past. And such an obfuscation is what our current neoliberal order, and the political agenda of Spain's conservative government, in particular, is predicated on. The neoliberal order in Spain can be seen as one of the consequences of the Franco dictatorship's 'stabilisation plan' of 1959, a series of economic policies that paved the way for the political transition to democracy in the 1970s.[28] The transition is often understood as a grand success in economic, cultural and political terms; the state moved from an economically backward, politically authoritarian and isolated country to a democratic nation fully integrated into the European Union and global capitalism. But, as Txetxu Aguado notes, 'the past did not exist, it should not have existed, because all it could do was intrude with its demands for reparation, the paying-off of debts and the undertaking of justice' (2009: 27, my translation). In this context, memories that cannot be commodified are simply ignored.

Hospitality

My study's emphasis on psychoanalytic time – what Freud called *Nachträglichkeit* (Laplanche 1999) – may appear to overlook more historically focused accounts of power. Instead of emphasising historical time – a linear conception of homogeneous time that implies unidirectional historical development – I focus on how some of the horrors of the past inform and are translated into forms of violence inherent to modern sovereign power. But does this approach reduce complex, multi-layered and contentious historical, social and cultural processes to a single category of trauma? Does such a reduction preclude the critical recognition and understanding of the historical past and run the risk of translating individual into collective trauma?

Thinking of the imbrication of the individual with the collective, Pollock and Silverman argue that 'the magnification of individually experienced trauma [. . .] can lead to collectively shared experience' (2011b: 30). Pollock notes that a focus on trauma allows us to understand how traumatic events take place without us fully registering or processing them, due to a lack of representational and cognitive resources. Yet, whether we have participated or suffered from those traumatic events or not, we may collectively and belatedly re-engage with the residues of such painful experiences. Here, the distinction between individual and collective experiences is undercut. After all, individual traumas are transmitted by collective culture, while, on the other hand, the collective legacy of traumatic events impinges on individual subjects.

Trauma's belated nature can be inscribed in the film or transmitted in the encounter with the cinematic/aesthetic practice. Trauma also implies a non-lineal conception of time. Anti-teleological temporality can be understood as a kind of 'palimpsest', which resonates with Deleuze's understanding of the relationship between difference and repetition. Silverman claims that, in the non-lineal temporality of trauma, traces of individual or shared experiences may be confused with latent traces of another, earlier or later event. In this way, 'the whole becomes a superimposition of interconnected traces', of individual and shared experiences of different yet similar events (2011: 206).[29] Hence, approaching the complexity of individual and shared traumatic experiences in and through the cinema of Almodóvar requires that I move beyond a linear narrative of historical progress and a teleological conception of history.

This study is also not an exhaustive survey of the criticism and scholarship on Almodóvar's work. I am aware of the danger of reducing the richness of Almodóvar's cinema to a critical or theoretical framework that may exclude other perspectives. Seguin rightly argues that Almodóvar's films cannot be conceived as structures pointing to a single, foundational centre. Instead, his cinema undercuts any possible homogenisation; it is constantly and endlessly formed and de-formed of heterogeneous fragments in a state of suspension and becoming (2009: 9). Seguin suggests that Almodóvar 'rejects in some ways any structuring proposition – any structure contains in its genesis its fascisms and dictatorships [. . .] [Almodóvar] escapes from certitudes to open up a space for fluidity, margins, borders, fringes or frontiers' (2009: 10, my translation). Pérez Melgosa insists that we should not let memory and trauma 'become the master signifiers through which Almodóvar's work must be interpreted', but rather 'add these concepts to the multiple layers of interpretation that his films instigate' (2013: 181). In line with Melgosa, I hope to establish productive connections and tensions between my methodologies and Almodóvar's cinematic practice in order to show how Almodóvar's cinema offers a reflection on, pushes back against or moves beyond the theoretical debates on the relationship between ethics, aesthetics and trauma.

For instance, connecting theories of trauma and Almodóvar's cinema foregrounds the impossible process of working through traumatic events, and an awareness of this impossibility paradoxically becomes the condition of possibility for thinking about the ethical and political transformations in an incalculable future yet to come. Our encounter with the traumatic event through Almodóvar's cinema does not just lead to a calculable, responsible commitment to the past. The relationship between aesthetic practice and aesthetic experience may create the conditions of possibility for *wit(h) nessing* (that is, to witness to and with the other the traces of trauma and fragments of memory) and sharing the suffering of an irreducible other.[30] This bears comparison to Lévinas' and Derrida's concept of hospitality and Ettinger's concept of 'compassionate hospitality'. In hospitality, an autonomous subject does not make a calculable decision on the conditions for receiving the other. Instead, hospitality implies an unconditional openness to the irreducible other. It acknowledges a heterogeneity that cannot be captured within knowledge, and foregrounds the vulnerability of the subject. The irreducible traumatic event vibrates in our bodies and psyche as an index of an 'im-possible' (that is both possible and impossible), unconditional hospitality, which is predicated on respect for the uniqueness and singularity of an incalculable and undetermined event's rupture (Fernández Agis 2009; Raffoul 2007). In the case of Almodóvar's cinema, my book proposes that this openness and hospitality derives from perception and cognition as well as affect and sensation.

Responsibility

Ulrich Winter and Ann Davies warn us that an interest in the representation of memory and trauma might be interpreted as a symptom of cinema's reduction to commemoration, which, as mentioned earlier, contributes to the instrumentalisation of memory and a vacuous commodification of nostalgia (Winter 2006; Davies 2012).[31] But in fact our encounter with Almodóvar's cinema can be, to the contrary, a constitutive force for a rethinking of the effects of the fragments and ruins of the past on the present. I use Benjamin's theory of history as convoluted time (Benjamin 1968) to reconsider how the (historical) unconscious haunts the present on a material and spectral level. This haunting – a form of knowing beyond re-cognition – by traces of the past allows us to engage with an undecidable and infinite form of responsibility and *response-ability*, to use Ettinger's term.

Such responsibility carries the promise of the secret while evoking the transparency of objective knowledge. Derrida associates responsibility with the possibility of responding to the singular call of an irreducible other, who is already in the self, yet inaccessible to the subject. Such a response does not exclude conscious and calculable decision, but goes beyond it. Derrida writes:

> Saying that a responsible decision must be taken on the basis of knowledge seems to define the condition of possibility of responsibility (one can't make a responsible decision without science or conscience, without knowing what one is doing, for what reasons, in view of what and under what conditions), at the same time as it defines the condition of impossibility of this same responsibility (if decision-making is relegated to a knowledge that it is content to follow or to develop, then it is no more a responsible decision, it is the technical deployment of a cognitive apparatus, the simple mechanistic deployment of a theorem). (1995a: 24)

Derrida also suggests that the possibility of responding is predicated on the impossibility of responding to all the other calls of all the others. Hence, Ruedin claims that one would, paradoxically, be responsible by being irresponsible in relation to general ethical laws (2002).

This understanding of responsibility is in productive tension with Ettinger's concept of *response-ability* (the ability to respond to the ethical call). Derrida reflects on the impossible conditions of possibility and possible conditions of impossibility underpinning the concept of responsibility. For Derrida, the source of infinite responsibility is one's secret and mysterious relationship with an irreducible other, who is already in the self (see Derrida 1995a).[32] For Ettinger, however, *response-ability* is connected to the matrixial borderspace, in which an un-cognised 'I' shares the space with a 'non-I' in *distance-in-proximity* and *proximity-in-distance*. Such an intimate yet non-fusional space may or may not become a resource for subsequent ethical and political relations. Our response to the call of the other's suffering allows us to share the traumatic event and to *wit(h) ness*, to use Ettinger's neologism, the traces of trauma and fragments of memory and their uncertain effects, both in the present and for the future. Ettinger's work does not advocate a foundational, theological or psychological essentialism (Pollock 2013b: 16). Instead, as Pollock explains, Ettinger

> introduces into the field of thinking about responsibility (the ethical call) its psychic potentiality or its resources in an earlier psychic disposition, what she calls *response-ability*. She asks: what are the conditions, perhaps already engendered within subjectivity, that might make us able not only able to respond, but yearning to respond to the call of the other in their suffering as if this responsiveness were an originary condition of an already intimated co-human-subjectivity [. . .]? (2013b:16, emphasis in original).

This study uses the proto-ethics (Ettinger); the ethics within and beyond a notion of ethics that implies conscious decision-making (Derrida); and

potentially macro- and micro-politics of trauma (Rolnik), thereby revealing how we *wit(h)ness*, and are affected by, the aesthetic *puissance* borne by
the cinematic image as a kind of after-image. We are affected, bodily and
psychically, by this encounter with the traces of trauma and fragments of
memory – but the rupturing effect of an unpredictable, undetermined,
irreducible event is not pathologised. As Derrida suggests, 'the injunction to
remember' (1995b: 50) in the present may allow us to anticipate or hope for
a promising future that remains virtual and unknown (see Derrida 1995b).
Drawing on theoretical approaches from trauma studies, philosophy, psychoanalysis, film studies and visual studies, I suggest that Almodóvar's
cinema may unintentionally propose an ethics of intersubjective relations,
or, to use Ettinger's concept, trans-subjective transactions. Such encounters are based on our non-antagonistic and com-passionate relation to an
irreducible alterity that can never be fully comprehended or accessed. Such
a relation to otherness, which cannot be based on empathy, becomes the condition of possibility for thinking of our different ways of being in the world.

The Face

This, of course, resonates with Lévinas' notion of the face of the other in
his ethics of alterity. Cooper notes that what Lévinas calls the face of the
other is not a visible or tangible object (2006: 15). Rather, 'the face from
the outset carries meaning over and beyond that of the surface plasticities
which cover it with their presence in perception' (Lévinas 2002: 535),
Thus, Lévinas contests the phenomenal world of objects, images and
appearances. The face goes beyond visual and tactile sensations. However,
our aesthetic encounter with the cinema of Almodóvar (a sensible form) is
not an illustration of Lévinas' work. It is an opening onto his philosophical
reflections on the ethical implications that underpin the encounter with
the other's face. According to James Hatley, for Lévinas, the face manifests
itself through its 'nudity' (that is, its vulnerability to violence). Hatley
explains that 'nudity' for Lévinas means

> [a] non-form, abandon of self, ageing, dying . . . poverty, skin with wrinkles. All of
> these traits do not depend upon the actual violation of the other for their instantia-
> tion but are from the very beginning already a feature of the other's revelation as
> other. The face, and only the face, has already opened up the issue of its violation by
> means of its own vulnerability. (Hatley 2000: 83)

Hence, for Lévinas, ethics precedes ontology. As ontology already and
traumatically implies the violence and aggression of a defensive subject.
As Derrida suggests,

[a]s soon as there is the One, there is murder, wounding, traumatism. *L'Un se garde de l'autre*. The One guards against/keeps some of the other. It protects *itself* from the other, but, in the movement of this jealous violence, it comprises in itself, thus guarding it, the self-otherness or self-difference (the difference from within oneself) which makes it One. (1995b: 51, emphasis in original)

A Lévinasian reading of Almodóvar's cinema allows us to think of the inevitability of the ageing process, accumulation of experience and final succumbing to one's own mortality – that is, our own vulnerability. From this perspective, the face of the irreducible other can be considered an analogy for ourselves, as we constitute the other and, in reciprocity, are constituted on the basis of the perceived behaviour of a body analogous to the one that we inhabit (Lévinas 2002: 434; Hatley 2000: 83). But the suffering encountered in the other cannot be taken as one's own. In fact, we constantly fail to contain or translate the other's 'nudity' into an intentional structure within one's consciousness of the other (Hatley 2000: 84). For Lévinas, the encounter with the face of the other is based on an asymmetrical relation between the self and an irreducible alterity, the latter of which can never be fully comprehended or accessed. Rather, the encounter invokes one's responsibility to the other before making any attempt to grasp the other on a cognitive level. For Cooper, Lévinas leaves us with a quandary: the responsible relation to the irreducible and inaccessible other is incalculable. As we will see in Chapters 3 and 4, especially when I pay attention to the face of the perpetrator, we cannot reverse the dialectics of mastery – Lévinas is interested only in the transcendence of 'the weakest of the weak' (Cooper 2006: 24). This is, perhaps, one of the most challenging and difficult ethical imperatives underpinning Lévinas' logic. In other words, even if we reduce the other to an association with the position of the perpetrator, who certainly fails or has failed to see the other's 'nudity', our ethical encounter with the other's face remains unconditionally predicated on our non-sovereign, un-predetermined, com-passionate hospitality. This leaves us entirely exposed to our shared, yet asymmetrical, vulnerabilities.

Book Outline

This book is, then, about the relationship of aesthetics, ethics and trauma in Almodóvar's cinema. It is in no sense a complete account of his work, and I have no intention of suggesting that there are no other significant thematic and formal concerns in the films of one Spain's most critically acclaimed and commercially successful filmmakers. Most obviously, my focus on trauma means that I will say little about Almodóvar's use of humour or the complex engagement with comic material and modes that characterised his early films. At the same time, I recognise that humour and seriousness are highly imbricated in Almodóvar's work.[33] As Smith notes, 'the seriousness of Almodóvar's commitment to the analysis of social and psychic concerns [. . .] in no way contradicts the brilliance of his comedy [. . .]' (2014: 3). Most obviously, one of his most recent films, *Los amantes pasajeros* (*I'm So Excited*, 2013), draws heavily on comedy in an attempt to return to the outrageous humour that characterised his films of the 1980s; but *Los amantes pasajeros* is also concerned with the fragile, precarious and de-territorialised conditions of existence that characterise our neoliberal culture, suffering as it is from economic and moral crises, at national and global levels. However, this combination of humour and seriousness falls outside the scope of this study.

Instead, I look at Almodóvar's cinema in the light of the relationship between aesthetics, ethics and trauma. In doing so, this book demonstrates that Almodóvar's cinema expands our repertoire of experiences, including those that are painful and traumatic. Almodóvar's work can, perhaps, impel us forward into a more satisfying, unpredictable and incalculable future. I work, particularly, with four films Almodóvar made from the late 1990s to the present that have been called his 'serious' or more 'abstract' films: *Volver, Todo sobre mi madre, La mala educación* and *La piel que habito*. Focusing on this period enables us to explore how Almodóvar's cinema anticipates and responds to, directly or obliquely, the debates on historical memory in Spain, which have intensified since representatives of historical memory associations in the year 2000 undertook the first exhumations of mass graves. I am not trying to impose an artificial periodisation on his oeuvre (because Almodóvar constantly reappraises his cinema) or an arbitrary partial selection of his films; rather, close-readings of these films, based on my own affective and interpretive engagement with them, can provide a productive engagement in theoretical debates about personal and historical trauma and memory, particularly when they are combined with a queer or feminist psychoanalytic perspective. Those debates, in turn, offer us a profound and complex way of perceiving, being affected by and understanding Almodóvar's cinema.

Although each chapter focuses on one of these later films, I also address issues from his earlier work that remain present in the films of the 1990s and 2000s. My study explores how these four films distinctively make manifest the 'after-effects' of traces of trauma and fragments of memory as they surface in the cinematic form. I hope, in particular, that my approach will encourage other scholars to be affected by and to think about the ethical and potentially political implications of their own encounter with the work of Almodóvar, especially when that is an encounter with films beyond the scope of this book. So, each chapter provides a close textual analysis of an individual film. I use these as case studies, through which we can encounter the theoretical framework I have described above. These distinct, yet interrelated chapters combine theoretical engagement with formal explorations, and, in particular, focus on the contradictory relationship between perception and cognition on the one hand, and affect and sensation on the other. Almodóvar's cinema is a mode of witnessing and re-experiencing the traces of the traumatic past, and of mediating between individual and shared experiences. In addition, I find in these films an ethical model based on com-passionate relations.

I have arranged the chapters according to formal and theoretical concerns, rather than strictly by chronology, but still, some thoughts from earlier chapters reappear in later chapters, while some explorations in the later chapters will lead us to reconsider the conclusions of the earlier ones. This structure resonates with Almodóvar's own creative method. I am not the first to notice this as a way of understanding his work: through her notion of 'retroseriality', Kinder has shown that Almodóvar's work invites us to creatively read and re-read his films, even when they are dismissed as meretricious and repetitive. Almodóvar's cinema asks us to keep experiencing and understanding his work in different, productive ways. This structure allows me to underscore the 'asymmetrical', formal and theoretical connections and disconnections between the films. And finally, this structure – which allows for organic connections, but resists linearity and chronology – evokes the structure of the traumatic event itself.

My first chapter, then, is a reading of *Volver*, which shows how Almodóvar's cinema confronts and works through the personal and shared traumas that return to haunt the present. The film is itself a mode of mourning and witnessing, in which both history and the present can only be understood as undergoing a traumatic encounter. More specifically, the film pays attention to how women work through the violence inflicted on them by patriarchy and heteronormativity. These hegemonic ideologies have created conflicts and divisions in both the private and the public sphere, thereby damaging both familial and social relations. The film tries to recuperate a 'utopian', maternal, rural space as an im-possible alternative to the world of these ideologies. 'Utopian' fantasy, of course, can imply nostalgia, and I attempt to disassociate nostalgia from its reactionary connotations. Rather, the film reflects on the incorporation of memory into the present, without disavowing longing or the contradictions of late modernity. *Volver* proposes the concept of a feminine community predicated on an ethics of embracing an irreducible alterity. This would move beyond social and psychic conflicts and aggressive political antagonisms between the defensive self and the unknown other. Sexual difference, as understood in the dominant phallic terms, would not relegate femininity to lack and castration. Finally, *Volver* allows us to think of the film medium itself as an articulation of a notion of history based on the open-ended coexistence of different temporalities, thereby undercutting conventional ways of experiencing and understanding time and space.

My second chapter focuses on the way that *Todo sobre mi madre* engages with trauma, while also reconsidering some of the concepts deployed in the first chapter – here, I discuss at some length the theoretical interconnection between 'matrixial' psychoanalysis and a queer/feminist subjectivity, on which the argument of the book depends. In the light of social, political, historical, physical and emotional injuries, the film proposes a return to the specificity of the feminine in human subjectivity. Drawing on Ettinger's notion of the 'matrixial', I argue that *Todo sobre mi madre* evokes a sub-symbolic psychic sphere. It helps us to shift from a fixation on subjectivity or inter-subjectivity so that we can understand transsubjectivity, or subjectivity itself as an 'encounter at shared borderspaces'. *Todo sobre mi madre* escapes from and resists the ideological and psychic burdens of patriarchy and heteronormativity, holding out the potential trans-formation of the traumas produced by patriarchal and political violence. Finally, I explore the ethical and potentially political implications of *Todo sobre mi madre*'s ethics of motherhood and 'embodied care'. I argue that such an ethics, beyond patriarchal and heterosexist conceptions of maternity and relationality, is based on a com-passionate relationality, thus underscoring the necessity to *wit(h)ness* the traumatic experiences of irreducible others, without falling into a rhetoric of redemption. While I focus on the film's ethical mode of relationality, the second chapter does also pay attention to the spectator's embrace of the ethics of motherhood and 'embodied care' through her or his encounter with the film.

The third chapter focuses on *La mala educación*, one of only two films in which Almodóvar alludes explicitly to the Francoist past.[34] I explore how *La mala educación* reflects on cinema as a mode of witnessing and re-experiencing the traces of the traumatic past, and of mediating between individual and collective experiences. I am particularly interested in the way *La mala educación* conceives the film medium as a generator of 'prosthetic memory' (Landsberg 2004); this opens up an understanding of how traumatic experiences and memories are fragmentarily embodied by and displaced onto those who have not lived them. Almodóvar's emphasis on corporeality allows me to reflect on how the fragments of memory can be rethought in the present. In other words, *La mala educación* asks us to rethink the body as a material force that contains the fragments of memory and history. Spectators who witness the film's obsession with embodiment may themselves engage with fragments of subjective memory. Similarly, subjective memory is aligned with collective memory and history. The film articulates a self-reflexive discourse about the way cinema mediates the traces of trauma, and witnesses the layers of memory that may escape linguistic symbolisation. *La mala educación* unfolds the traces of its characters' personal experiences, in particular Ignacio's, and of particular moments in Spanish history – not by completely reconstructing the past, but by translating past traumatic experiences so that they impinge on our mind and body. In this way, *La mala educación* problematises the logic of the archive, understood as the exclusionary transmitter of the historical past.

The fourth and final chapter focuses on *La piel que habito*. I explore how the film reflects and responds to the vicissitudes and catastrophes of the past and present. Whether they be individual or collective, national or trans-national, they are all inscribed on and irrupt through the surface of the body. This reading encourages spectators to ponder the endurance and actualisation of fragments of memory and history. Developments in biogenetics and biotechnology – one of the main themes in the film – can be read as leading to the infliction of a 'synthetic wounding' on the human body by scientific, technological, political and economic power. This wounding, in turn, obliges us to question and reconceptualise how we understand embodied existence, which leads to a consideration of the ties between science and technology on the one hand, and modern sovereign power and biopolitics, on the other. To question these categories is precisely to show their instability. So, I propose that Dr Ledgard's imprisoning, mutilation and scientific manipulation of Vicente/Vera can evoke broader past historical events. At the same time, I argue that *La piel que habito* evokes a traumatic return to the past by making us aware of the dangers of the 'concentrationary' logic at the core of late-capitalist society. The film ultimately helps us stay hypervigilant in the face of such a 'concentrationary' logic and its toxic effects.

To sum up, then, *Aesthetics, Ethics and Trauma in the Cinema of Pedro Almodóvar* encourages us to embrace an 'ethics of listening and seeing'. In our affective and interpretive engagement with Almodóvar's cinema, spectators become conscious of our position of responsibility. We bear witness to the other's experiences via the cinematic medium; in confronting these films, we are aware not so much of their representational nature, as of the way the cinematic medium itself can performatively interpellate us. This interpellation is the condition of possibility to open up an inter-subjective or trans-subjective transmission of experiences, both subjective and shared. Responsibility is one of the defining criteria of effectively witnessing the other's experiences – it is the way to avoid false witnessing, in which one can slip in and out of the relationship, without being con-scious of the dramatic consequences of this act (J. Hirsch 2001: 21). If the cinematic medium participates in the transformation of our consciousness of reality, an 'ethics of listening and seeing' may help us sustain a variety of human life, a kind of otherness, and encourage us to work towards a national and global culture that pays much deeper attention to caring and com-passion. Only such a culture can sustain the safety and dignity of all others and their different ways of 'being-in-the-world' (Pollock 2008).

I would like to end this introduction by highlighting some scholarship on the cinema of Almodóvar and, more broadly, Spanish literary and cultural studies and film studies. Without this work, I would not have been able to develop the urgency that has prompted me to think about the way aesthetics, ethics and trauma are imbricated in and through the cinema of Almodóvar. Any process of writing is subjective, and therefore, intersubjective. In other words, my research relies on previous studies on Almodóvar and, more broadly, on Spanish literary and cultural studies and film studies – but, I hope, I have not been immobilised by received interpretations.[35] I have inherited much, and I am thankful for it, but this book has also given me the opportunity to articulate my critical and theoretical differences vis-à-vis other scholars.[36] I hope that this book will open my theoretical and critical position here onto other Almodóvar schol-arship. Our encounter with traces of trauma and fragments of memory in and through Almodóvar's cinema allows us to reflect more broadly on the way we are constantly connecting with and disconnecting from ourselves, others and the world, without ever becoming completely disconnected or immobilised. Our encounters are encounters to come – and encounters that have already been. We have been, we are and we will be affected and perhaps transformed by the perceptible and imperceptible traces and fragments of such encounters. This book starts with our encounter with *Volver*.

CHAPTER 1

Im-Possibility of Not-Returning:
Volver

Tombs, Ghosts and Songs

I begin with three sequences of Almodóvar's *Volver*. The film's first sequence starts with a tracking shot of ladies cleaning tombs in a rural cemetery. The soundtrack is a Spanish *zarzuela* song by the late singer Conchita Panadés, which may suggest an idealisation of an anachronistic past. The camera stops, and a static shot shows an almost monochrome grey tombstone of marble or granite on which the title of the film, *Volver*, is superimposed in red. Yet it looks like an inscription. We might associate the opacity of the monochrome with the death or the birth of painting, as the tombstone is a kind of unyielding screen which blocks our field of vision; the red letters 'VOLVER' then refer to a relationship between infinite mourning and cinematic representation or interpretation. Both of these processes, these letters suggest, may involve the endless repetition of what is lost, absent or dead. The repetition would be an attempt to reintegrate it into the present so it can be witnessed through our affective, critical encounter with cinematic practice.[1]

Laura Mulvey has noted, in *Death 24 X a Second* (2006), how the tension between movement and stillness is constitutive of the cinematic medium, which is predicated on the animation of the still frame. According to Mulvey, cinema's relation to movement is accomplished by the camera, editing and ultimately by narrative, cinematic elements that contribute to the repression of the still frame. If the ontology of cinema is, then, predicated on transcending stillness through movement, the medium of film replicates the ontology of modernity, which is itself predicated on a continuous and accelerated mobility.[2]

Bojana Kunst draws on Peter Sloterdijk's concept of 'kinetic modernity' to suggest that the very concept of movement can be instrumentalised, expropriated and appropriated by flexible, neoliberal capitalism. Like capital, subjects are socially divided into those who can move freely across the globe and those who cannot. In the case of refugees and migrants (an important thematic concern in *Volver*), the sense of dislocation and non-belonging caused by the migrant's movement from one place to another may imply a potential transformation of material and symbolic conditions, thereby enabling us to think of migrant subjectivity beyond the category of victimhood. Yet Kunst suggests that movement can also be associated with a form of exclusion and material and psychic dispossession (Kunst 2010, unpaginated). In this context, stillness can be read as an act of resistance. It would, then, not succumb to the flow or temporality of modernity, but nor does it fall into regressive nostalgia. Stillness is a form of enduring time. It deactivates, as Kunst puts it, the cultural 'apparatus (*dispositif*) that regulates and organizes our flexible subjectivities' (2010, unpaginated, emphasis in original).

So Almodóvar's shot of the tombstone is still, held for some seconds, as if time and movement had been placed between brackets to interrupt the kinesis on which the ontology of film is predicated. The non-diegetic song in this opening scene then reinforces our ungovernable affective and well-articulated emotional engagement with the film. But, Kunst argues, bracketing time and movement through stillness can lead us to see time as redundant. Spectators may then be unable to fill the emptiness caused by the interruption of movement with pathos (as in melodrama) or meaning. And the impossibility of emotion or cognition would not empower, but dispossess, our subjectivity.[3] In the context of performance theory, Kunst argues,

> [t]he consequence of such redundancy of time is the dispossession of our subjective inner feeling of time, where our attention is not empowering our subjective experience, but exactly the opposite: we are stuck, duration disables us, it takes over. When we are overwhelmed with a redundancy of time, duration does not stimulate our attention, making our awareness more intense. Attention becomes rather impersonal. (2010: unpaginated)

I suggest, however, that the interruption of movement to lay bare the mechanistic operations of the repression of the stillness underpinning the cinematic medium could in fact be associated with an intensification, rather than a deflation, of our phenomenological and interpretive encounter with the event of cinema – without suggesting full presence.

The shot of the tombstone can be seen as a kind of Deleuzean 'time-image', which implies the autonomy of time in relation to movement, and the suspension of the relationship between cause and effect required to connect actions. Then, stillness in *Volver* can be interpreted as foregrounding the film's theoretical self-consciousness. It becomes, as Rob

Stone suggested in a different context, 'a vehicle for a changing, incomplete consciousness that in a Bergsonian sense expresses something like a moral response that is temporalized and in a constant state of becoming' (2011: 44). By producing, as David Rodowick argues, 'breaks or ruptures in space, irrational intervals that open a direct image of time, that demonstrate the whole is not there, even if continuity is re-established afterwards' (1997: 54), the association of stillness with the 'time-image' in Almodóvar's film expands our perceptual and interpretive encounter with the cinematic experience. It allows for the possibility of a transformation of the aesthetic experience and the ethical relation to the other (the cinematic image) and of a micro-political transformation at the affective and immanent level. As Elena del Rio explains, the 'time-image' articulates a

> *puissance* – the form of power that operates within the virtual plane of consistency – [which] is the kind of power embedded in affect, whereas the concept of power as *pouvoir* operates within the actual plane of organization where subjects dominate or resist one another in some social, ideological, or political relations and systems. (del Rio 2008: 24, emphasis in original)

Stillness can also be associated with a return to an inanimate state, in other words, with the logic of the death drive. Mulvey argues that, even if stillness is understood as a form of re-inscribing death, the cinematic medium itself is always already inhabited and constituted by spectres whose traces undo the dichotomy between presence and absence, thereby resisting the complete phenomenologisation of the cinematic trace. The tombstone and the red title of the film do explicitly evoke death, but death is brought back through the stillness of the shot, thereby provoking in us an epistemological uncertainty about the blurring of the conventional boundaries between life (birth) and death within a linear conception of time.

The camera then cuts to a close-up of two portraits, one of a man and one of a woman, placed on a tombstone. As the camera tracks back, we see three women, the main female characters of the film. They have come to this rural cemetery to repeat the ritual of cleaning their parents' tombstones – the subjects of the portraits. The women speak to Agustina, a neighbour from the village, who is suffering from a terminal illness. Agustina mourns her own mortality and disappearance, her singular finitude that human beings share. Jean-Luc Nancy reflects on a notion of community that is based on what is shared by and what divides singular pluralities that cannot be reduced to essences, substance or common identity. He argues:

> Sharing comes down to this: what community reveals to me, in presenting to me my birth and my death, is my existence outside myself [. . .] *Community itself, in sum,*

is nothing but this exposition. It is the community of finite beings, and as such it is itself a *finite* community. In other words, not a limited community as opposed to an infinite or absolute community, but a community *of* finitude, because finitude 'is' communitarian, and because finitude alone is communitarian. (1991: 26–7, emphasis in original)

For Nancy, one's exposure to the other's death becomes the condition of possibility for one's own process of de-subjectivation, so that one can become a singularity whose finitude is associated with our being in common. Hence, Nancy emphasises our common finitude as the condition of our non-essentialised coexistence, one that does not ever fall back into a fusional community. Agustina has accepted her condition, suspended between life and death. Living, then, in a time that is heterogeneous to a linear conception of chronological time, Agustina has come to the cemetery to clean her own tombstone, as if she wanted to leave everything ready for her life after her imminent, premature death, her dissolution after a life cut short due to her body's internal and long battle with cancer.[4]

The second sequence I will focus on here shows us Raimunda, the female protagonist of the film, who sees through a restaurant's window a group of musicians and singers. They are rehearsing a song that reminds her of her childhood. She has taken charge of the restaurant clandestinely, as a strategy to survive on the periphery of the city. She hides her husband's corpse in its freezer, as if the frozen corpse would remain in a state between life and death. The shot through the window frame is immediately repeated. For Deleuze, as I showed above, repetition is predicated on divergent meanings. It can be associated with a static temporality or, on the contrary, it can relate to the process of becoming.[5] Deleuze explains:

[There are] two types of repetition: one which concerns only the overall, abstract effect, and the other which concerns the acting cause. One is a static repetition, the other is dynamic. One results from the work, but the other is like the 'evolution' of a bodily movement. One refers back to a single concept, which leaves only an external difference between the ordinary instances of a figure; the other is the repetition of an internal difference which it incorporates in each of its movements, and carries from one distinctive point to another. (1994 [1968]: 20)

Hence repetition can be repetition of the Same, which remains within the logic of identity and representation; or, it can be a heterogeneous difference that exceeds the Idea and cannot be subsumed by representation. *Volver* seems to focus on a difference within repetition that can only be mediated by (cinematic) representation; I foreground here the kind of interferences and intersections that Deleuze establishes between repetition and difference (1994 [1968]: 27). The repeated, yet different scene, shows Raimunda in the frame, illustrating how the difference at the core of repetition points to the 'unconscious of representation' (Deleuze 1994 [1968]: 14). The scene is seen from Raimunda's sister's point of view and from Raimunda's daughter's point of view. The sister, Sole, runs an illegal hairdressing salon in her own apartment. The daughter, Paula, was born as a result of their father committing a traumatic, incestuous act on Raimunda. Because the scene is shot from inside the window, we are unable to hear Raimunda's conversation with the musicians. This ambiguity at the enunciative level, however marginal to the film's dramatic structure, undercuts the film's apparent dependence on a conventional narrative structure; the lack of sound points to a gap or fissure in *Volver* that spectators are unable to fill or suture. This is true of our ontological condition as well, based as it is on a structural lack that can never be fully completed.

But we assume that Raimunda has asked them to sing a tango–flamenco song, originally sung by the Argentinean Carlos Gardel, and then by the Spanish flamenco singer Estrella Morente. Music is here associated with one's emotional connections to the realm of the feminine, our relation to one's m/other and to what Didier Anzieu refers to, according to Caryl Flinn, as an '"audiophonic" system of communication that emerges directly out of the body' (1992: 53).[6] In this context, Raimunda's singing allows her to emotionally connect to her daughter and to her supposedly dead mother,[7] who taught her the song when she was a child. Raimunda's singing voice is thus associated 'with the mother and with the prehistory of the subject, referring [. . .] simultaneously to the primordial role played by the mother's voice, face, and breast, and to the psychic and libidinal conditions of early infantile life' (Silverman 1988: 102). This sequence consists of reaction shots of Sole and Paula, as Penélope Cruz lip-synchs the song that gives *Volver* its title, as well as repeated crosscuts between shots of Raimunda's mother, and shots of Raimunda singing, within the diegesis, but looking out of the shot, as if she sees or feels her mother's presence (see Figures 1.1–1.3). The song's lyrics relate both literally and symbolically to the actions and themes of the film: the painful return of the traumatic past to the present; the traumatic return from the present to the painful past; and how our existence is shaped by remembering traumas, by incompatible memories, by forgetting traumas, acting them out, enacting them, or (im-possibly) working through them.

Raimunda's mother is hidden in Sole's car, like a ghost, both present and absent, apparent and disappeared, visible and invisible, neither alive nor dead, so the marks and traces of her presence are infinitely deferred – and also able to possibly reappear, differently, in the future. Like Sophocles'

Figure 1.1 Raimunda, Sole and Paula see a group of musicians

Figure 1.2 Raimunda sings *Volver*

Eurydice, suspended between two deaths, the spectral dead mother stands at an ambivalent point between two mutually exclusive worlds: life and death. According to Diana Taylor, '[m]any cultures are grounded on the notion of a second coming – the Mexica[n], the Christian, the Jewish, the

Figure 1.3 Raimunda feels her mother's presence

Marxist, to name a few. The ghost is by definition a repetition, Derrida's
revenant' (Taylor 1999: 64, my emphasis). Just as the traces of the spectre
may return from the past or the future to haunt us in the present, the
phantasmagorical appearance/disappearance of Raimunda's mother is
constantly made manifest, repeated, *revenant*, to use Derrida's term,
throughout the film (see Figures 1.4–1.5). These repetitions point to
Volver's conceptual, ethical and political concern with the experience
of spectrality, which is predicated on its im-possibility. In other words,
when we are haunted by the irreducible alterity of the spectral, we open
ourselves onto 'the passive movement of an apprehension' (Derrida, cited
in Critchley 1995: 18).

According to Simon Critchley, haunting provokes a rupture in the
homogenous flow of objectivist history in order to produce an 'ethical
history'. The latter is the condition of possibility for infinitely mourning those dead and unborn subjects who are considered the 'losers' of
history. Spectrality, associated with the production of an ethical history,
is thus the condition of possibility for thinking about the time of justice
in an unpredictable future. The time of justice is based on the experience
of a temporality that is 'out of joint', it interrupts the flow of objectivist
history. The present evokes a past that was never present as well as a future
that remains incalculable. Critchley argues that Derrida's concern with
the injunction of justice, the 'un-deconstructable condition of possibility
for deconstruction' (cited in Critchley 1995: 9), depends on one's relation

Figure 1.4 Irene's ghost

Figure 1.5 Irene is suspended between life and death

to an irreducible alterity, which becomes the condition of possibility to think of the concept of difference. Hence, *Volver*'s emphasis on 'the movement of haunting, of the ghost, of the ghosting of the ghost, la revenance du revenant' (Critchley 1995: 18), illustrates the concern with the time of justice in Derrida's conception of the political, which is at the core of deconstruction. The logic of haunting is, for Derrida, the condition of possibility and impossibility for philosophical reflection.[8]

To return to the apparition of the mother: Raimunda's sister Sole has been at their aunt's funeral and has returned from the village through a landscape now populated by high-tech windmills. Kinder observes how 'the camera sweeps across the stark landscape, lingering on the turbine windmills' (2007: 5). Although the film mainly associates rural Spain with a utopian, anachronistic space, this shot shows that much of the countryside is not untouched by or immune to technology and progress. The landscape also forms a passage through which the characters constantly move between rural and urban spaces. Steven Marsh defines the highway as one of the film's 'threshold locations', which also include the airport and the cemetery (2009: 348). They foreground *Volver*'s thematic and formal concern with the juxtaposition of dis-continuous movement across, and the relationship between incompatible spaces, times and subjectivities. The characters themselves are neither rural nor urban, but both; they embody a suspended, 'in-between' existence. They are migrant or exiled subjects whose existence is predicated on a kind of 'undecidability', to use Derrida's term. Hamid Naficy argues that 'the exiles can be both and neither: the pharmacon, meaning both poison and remedy; the hymen, meaning both the membrane and its violation; and the supplement, meaning both addition and replacement' (2006: 113).

For instance, Raimunda visits Sole. We see Raimunda in the bathroom; a close-up of her profile emphasises that she is smelling the spectral presence of her mother, and this gesture resonates with Sole's smelling the bike her mother used (or still uses) earlier in the film – as though the sense of smell were the condition of possibility for triggering memories of the maternal body. We see memory here as a dynamic process generated from the present, rather than a buried substance waiting to be unearthed from the past: the mother has returned from the 'rural past' to the 'urban present' by occupying Sole's truck, as if the truck were a crypt inside which the dead mother is entombed alive.[9] In psychoanalysis, narrative helps patients translate the overwhelming effects of the traumatic event into a cognitive experience, thus integrating it into one's consciousness, so that it can be witnessed in the present (Wong 2007: 174). In this context, Raimunda's mother returns from death without actually having died in order to bear witness and to talk to Raimunda about the latter's trauma. Raimunda may or may not come to terms with or move away from the compulsive repetition that forces her to 'involuntarily and repeatedly relive her trauma' as a belated experience (Guerin and Hallas 2007: 8).

An objective shot of Sole's bedroom shows one of their mother's robes on the bed. The robe is a remnant of the past, a material signifier or a metonymic displacement for the presence of the absent mother. In her discussion of Doris Salcedos's art, Edlie Wong suggests that such material signifiers or metonymic displacements 'impose a relation of silent, yet attentive proximity. This relation maintains the integrity of the dead when it requires the viewer to forgo a vision of the person in favour of a contemplation of a metonymic possession, an object that once characterised the dead' (2007: 177). From this perspective, Irene's robe indexes the absent presence or present absence of the mother, thereby becoming a material inscription and a vehicle of transmission of the positive and negative affects and emotions that sustained the intersubjective relationship between mother and child.

The camera cuts to Irene, Raimunda's mother, who is lying under the bed,[10] again, occupying a phantasmagorical space. This is followed by a shot of Raimunda's feet, seen from Irene's point of view. This partial perception is compensated for by the sound of her steps, as though sound has acquired a relative emancipation from the image. This could be read as a kind of fetishisation of the aural, but sound may also have a corporeal and haptic resonance that resists the psychic mechanisms of fetishism. The emphasis on the sense of hearing here (like that of smelling earlier), points to the implication of the corporeal and the sensorial in the process of perception and cognition, despite the hierarchical privileging of vision over bodily senses. Sound does not only function to compensate for the insufficiency of vision here; as Tom Whittaker has argued in his association of sound with spectrality, sound can also 'undermine the materiality of the image' (2014: 324). Like the figure of the spectre, sound occupies 'a liminal position between life and death, visibility and invisibility, and materiality and immateriality' (Whittaker 2014: 327), between the past, the present and the future, or appearance, reappearance and disappearance. Hence, instead of perpetuating a metaphysics of presence, associated with our phenomenological encounter with the corporeal and haptic resonance of sound, the emphasis on the spectral nature of sound is a haunting force, precariously apprehended in our bodies and psyche in an interrupted or deferred sensation, which cannot be reified – just as our bodily and psychic existence cannot be reified.

To return to the sequence of Cruz's lip-synching of the flamenco-tango song: Raimunda's singing could function as an interruption or suspension of the narrative's linear development, thus acquiring significance as an isolated performance. On the other hand, Ernesto Acevedo-Muñoz has suggested that performative sequences like this one are, to the contrary, linked to the film's actions and themes. Such performances are a supplement to the action or emotion in Almodóvar's films. They transmit ironic messages or are associated with epiphanic moments (2007: 17).[11] As Marvin D'Lugo claims,

> upon closer inspection we note that the tango has been raised to a more prominent textual position as it strategically underscores the film's principal narrative and further serves as a catalyst for action and the transposition of the protagonists' identities within broader social and even political scenarios. (2013: 414)

For D'Lugo, the hybrid tango-flamenco song epitomises the way that *Volver* attempts to forge an affective, transnational community composed of Spanish and Latin Americans. It emphasises an 'auditory culture' that blurs or fuses the cultural and geographical borders between Spain and Latin America. But D'Lugo's emphasis on the blurring or fusing of geographical and cultural boundaries does not reduce this (transnational) community to a logic of common identity and belonging within a transparent social order. Such a logic is predicated on the assimilation or rejection and appropriation of heterogeneous, radical difference. D'Lugo, to the contrary, helps us to think of how Almodóvar's cinema in general advocates a non-sovereign, non-territorially-bounded coexistence with others. Such co-habitation is contingently predicated on difference and 'exposure' to the rupturing effects of the encounter with an irreducible, radical alterity – the ethical requirement for our 'being-in-common' (Oosterling and Plonowska Ziarek 2011: 2). In other words, since our fragile subjectivities are constituted by our own alterity, by a 'strangeness within ourselves', to use Kristeva's phrase,[12] our confrontation with the alterity of the other becomes the recognition of our own strangeness, which lies beneath the surface of the self. Recognition of our own internal fragility may lead us to reinforce our sense of belonging to a common group or nation and to seek out more oppressive and antagonistic ways of relating to others. Yet, by constantly offering antidotes to reality, the cinema of Almodóvar, and *Volver* in particular, helps us to think of community as based less on an essentialised commonality than on singularities sharing a world inhabited by a plurality of beings, in which our relation to irreducible others is based – to evoke Nancy once more – on our common finitude.

To further problematise the hybrid nature of Raimunda's song, I would like to consider Naficy's study of 'accented cinema'. He argues that the dominant cinema, associated mainly with Hollywood, is predicated on the hegemony of the synchronicity of sound and a rigid alignment of speaker and speech (2006: 120). Accented films, on the other hand, particularly with those of exiled filmmakers, tend to de-emphasise or break the synchronicity of sound and to foreground the speakers' accented pronunciation (2006: 120) as a counter-hegemonic formal and ideological self-affirmation of the liminal subjectivity that these film practices deploy. Such a formal strategy articulated in opposition to the hegemonic runs the risk of simply inverting the terms of the dichotomy, and leaving the logic of binary oppositions intact. But Naficy's attention to such formal strategies enables us to suggest that, although Raimunda sings within the diegesis, Cruz's lip-synching is akin to the lack of synchronisation in accented film. It creates a slippage between voice and speaker, acknowledging how subjectivity and our relations to others are always already constituted by an irreducible alterity. From this perspective, the film's concern with migrant or exiled subjectivities, and the experiences of migration and exile associated with loss, dislocation or displacement is made manifest not only through its explicit theme, but also through the poetics and materiality of the cinematic form.[13] The slippage between voice and speaker in *Volver* is associated with an auditory, haptic scar, which reveals how the residues of a lost physical and symbolic space are transmitted through the language of the exile and the migrant. Haunted by the interference of another language or accent, the language of the exile or the migrant is semantically, phonetically and syntactically structured as a previous language, or accent is disintegrated or interferes, thereby indexing the textual inscription of those traces in the unconscious. These traces are precariously present, repetitively erased, endlessly transformed or intermittently inscribed in signification and representation.[14]

Such an articulation of migration or exile through the film's materiality and poetics foregrounds what Bal defines as migratory aesthetics (2011). The spectator is affected bodily by the sound of the traces of exile and migration, which become imprinted in our own subjectivity and body, without reducing, fully understanding, assimilating or over-identifying with the experiences or suffering of an irreducible, migrant or exiled other. In addition, this act enhances the emotional and affective connections of the characters and our own emotional and affective engagement with the cinematic image and experience, thereby foregrounding our bodily and psychic vulnerability in the process of encountering the film. Engaging with the film in this way does not keep us from engaging with it from a more distanced position or on a more rational level. Rather, our affective and emotional engagement helps us to think about how our trans-subjective encounters with the traces of the other, inscribed in the film and transmitted through the cinematic experience, enhances our participatory engagement with the medium. Raimunda's performance helps us to witness how memory, often conceived as an immaterial trace, 'becomes a physical experience', which is both felt and visible in her 'changing expressions and body movements' (Skoller 2005: xliv). In addition, the use of crosscutting in this sequence emphasises the way in which, as I shall explain later, the film registers, celebrates and embrace trans-subjective, co-affective encounters predicated on 'hospitable memory' (Derrida, cited in Marsh 2009: 349) and the possibility of a feminine transgenerational community.

The Politics of Memory

These three sequences in *Volver* suggest that the film deals with the way that we confront loss in personal and collective history; how that loss is constitutive of our subjective and shared experiences; the inevitability or epistemological uncertainty of death; and the desire or anxiety involved in returning from and to past times, spaces and subjects. Those subjects themselves confronted loss in personal and collective history, and their traces point to the visibility of the mark of their absence, or to the invisibility of the mark of their presence. The film also engages with the return to and from the personal and shared traumas and incompatible memories that exceed the boundaries of the visible and representable, but which, as indelible, haunting forces in our psyches and bodies, nonetheless have an effect on our current existence (Skoller 2005: xiv). Just as the spectre of the mother occupies liminal physical spaces, and makes her presence felt through spectral traces and her absence felt through material traces, the traces of subjective and shared traumas and fragments of incompatible memories are inscribed in the interstices of the dominant teleological narrative of history. They, too, constantly haunt, intoxicate and, perhaps, transform the present and the undetermined future by evoking how different temporalities and memories 'commingle, inscribe, and inflect each other' (Skoller 2005: xv).

According to D'Lugo, 'Almodóvar's early characters' motivations were simple, uncomplicated, and nearly always rooted in the here and now' (2006: 9). D'Lugo's point about Almodóvar's focus on the present in his early films is corroborated by Moreiras' recent analysis of *Laberinto de pasiones*. Moreiras suggests:

> The film appears at a time when the cultural production, modes of behaviour and, especially, its processes of identification, show an *apparently* de-ideologised and fundamentally de-historicised attitude (only the present is of interest, which is experienced from a relational emptiness vis-à-vis historical temporality), precisely as a reaction to the disenchantment caused by political and social processes. (2014: 139, emphasis in original, my translation.)

From this perspective, as I explained in the Introduction, Almodóvar's early cinema would seem to emphasise and celebrate the (post)modern present of 1980s Spain's democratic, consumer-orientated society – a society predicated on the disavowal of the spectres of the traumatic past. Yet, rethinking her early (2002) reading of *Laberinto de pasiones* in *Cultura herida*, Moreiras problematises the association of Almodóvar's early films with the disavowal of the traumatic past. She thus shifts the focus from 'synchronic time', which Critchley defines as 'a linear, infinite series of punctual moments spread along the axes of past, present and future', to 'diachronic time', based on the collapse of time, including 'the present falling out of phase with itself' (Critchley 1995: 13). Moreiras argues that the traumatic past, even when rendered parodically or ironically, does emerge in an oblique and suggestive manner in the earlier films. They reveal the horrors to which national identity was subjected under Francoism, and attempts to liberate such a cultural history from the Francoist ideological connotations (2014: 140).

Volver, for instance, relies, at least on a surface level, on a conventional narrative structure to produce movements through time that are perfectly sutured, rather than presenting the kind of fragmented narrative structure associated with what Janet Walker refers to as 'trauma cinema'.[15] I contend, however, that *Volver* attempts to act out and/or to im-possibly work through personal traumas perpetrated by dead paternal figures (Raimunda's father and husband), or, in a more suggestive and oblique manner, the collective traumas perpetrated by the Francoist regime. Marsh establishes a connection between the physical bodies or subjective experiences of the characters and the symbolic body of Spain, or the shared experiences of the Spanish nation, and argues that

> in a film whose on-screen narrative progression is linear rather than retrospective and circular [. . .], an otherwise straightforward female genealogical chain, marked not just by emotional and bodily violation but also by murder and ghostly returns, *disturbs* rather than reinforces any neat unfolding of time. (2009: 342, emphasis in original)

Marsh emphasises the complex imbrication of the personal with the collective and the disruption of the apparently linear progress of the narrative by paying attention to the folds, breaks and gaps of/in time in *Volver*. This enables us to read the personal traumas in the film – Raimunda's rape by her father, or her husband's failed attempt to rape Raimunda's daughter – as, in addition, suggestive and oblique signs of the bodily and psychic wound perpetrated on Spain by Franco's regime. The regime is embodied by Paco, whose presence in the film suggests that Francoism is, in a sense, still present as the dominant patriarchal ideology of Spanish society.[16] The subjective and collective encounter with traces of the traumatic past produces in us 'the sense of the belated experience [. . .] that crosses generations without ever [explicitly] referencing the event itself' (Skoller 2005: xliii). It is interesting to note that Raimunda's husband is called Francisco, echoing the dictator's name, and suggesting that the nation is still re-enacting the traumatic intoxication of totalitarian power. These silent, powerful cultural symptoms affect our present at a micro-political level, precisely because they exceed linguistic articulation and escape from direct representation.

My interpretation of *Volver* relies on the context of the macro-politics of memory in contemporary Spain, and it is important to note that this politics remains a point of contention among cultural historians. But we can say that social and political mourning were repressed under Franco's regime, and disavowed during the political transition from dictatorship to democracy. The Moncloa Pact and Constitution of 1978 were predicated on the silence of parties across the political spectrum, which had all participated in negotiations over them. The 'Amnesty Law' of 1977 implicitly exonerated representatives of Francoism. Post-dictatorship Spain was then characterised by an illusory sense of reconciliation. In this macro-political context, a number of important cinematic practices, particularly documentary films, engaged with the politics of memory. Joan Ramón Resina argues that the false reconciliation anticipated the concern with 'historical recuperation' in the 1990s debates over history memory (2000: 104) – though of course this debate took place in a very different ideological and historical context. Memories of state terror are still negated by the political Right, which does not officially accept its responsibility for or complicity in the crimes of the Franco regime, even though it is incapable of distancing itself from its fascist antecedents on a moral level (Resina 2000: 106). Antonio Monegal has described the popular, pseudohistorical revisionist works of César Vidal and Pío Mora, which attempt to show that the Republic provoked the Civil War in order to justify the military coup d'état and the dictatorial regime (2008: 249).

The attempt to come to terms with Spain's traumatic past is related to an increasing interest in the macro-politics of memory at a transnational level. Andreas Huyssen advocates a political and public role for artistic practices, including film, in the context of the transnational attention to crimes against humanity (2001: 9). He contends that the singular and exceptional experience of the Holocaust should not function as a model that is uncritically translated into historically and politically incompatible realities. Rather, he suggests, the Holocaust is a prism that energises other discourses about collective traumatic experiences 'both in their legal and commemorative aspects' (2001: 9). Similarly, I contend that the theoretical debates on the Shoah offer a productive source of tropes, images, ethical and political questions or conceptual parameters through which we can reflect on the relationship between aesthetics, ethics and trauma in the cinema of Almodóvar.

From this perspective, I interpret *Volver* as participating in public debates on the macro-politics of memory. It uncovers individual and shared traumatic memories and experiences in a suggestive and oblique manner, which forces the spectator to establish connections between the text and the national context as a condition of possibility for effective witnessing. To put it differently, Labanyi has argued that most of the cinematic and literary re-creations of the Civil War and the Franco regime since the 1990s have been realistic or documentary accounts of the events, which misleadingly transport us into the past. But verisimilitudinous representations of the past have 'the effect of reinforcing the difference of the past from the present with the result that, at the end of the viewing or reading process, we feel a sense of relief on returning to a present free from such barbarism' (Labanyi 2007: 103). To avoid this problem, Labanyi identifies the horror film, and its trope of haunting, as the most effective cinematic genre for the representation of the violence of the Spanish Civil War and for Franco's totalitarian regime: horror suggests obliquely rather than stating directly. Haunting reveals the spectral past's intoxicating effects in the present, forcing us to see how memory is transmitted across generations and making us aware that it is impossible to completely recuperate the past. We can relate to it only through fragments and traces.

Labanyi's argument is suggestive, and it does not limit spectrality to a particular genre or film. Film is always already a spectral medium. And horror tends to instrumentalise and reify haunting for entertainment rather than for macro- or micro-political purposes. Labanyi enables us to think that, rather than being present in the film itself, the important effects of haunting emerge only in the spectator's affective, emotional, critical, contingent encounter with cinematic practice. Only then can haunting become an ethical and macro- or micro-political demand that may potentially transform us. Following Labanyi's line of thought, I suggest that Almodóvar's film works in what Skoller calls a cinematic mode of historiography (2005). As such, the film unfolds the traces of these moments in Spanish history through an oblique suggestion of past traumatic experiences that affect our mind and body, without allowing us to succumb to an unreflective empathy that ignores the impossibility of experiencing the other's suffering as if it were our own (Hatley 2000: 5).

So Almodóvar's film echoes the nation's preoccupation with burials (Agustina's mother, Raimunda's mother and father), exhumations (Paco's corpse in the freezer)[17] and reburials (Paco's corpse in the river). Raimunda and Regina, the Latin American prostitute, eventually bury Paco's corpse – drawing on Carla Marcantonio's work, we can see that the physical effort they have to make to bury the dead patriarchal figure can be associated with the emotional and psychological effort that women have to make to work through the violence inflicted upon them by the dominant patriarchal ideology and, historically, by the Francoist regime (2006).[18] Here, we see that subjective and shared trauma is imbricated with the question of sexual and gender difference. Authoritarianism, in the private or the public sphere, deforms our subjectivities and our familial and social relations.

Traumatic Modernity

In addition, *Volver* shows how some of the traumatic consequences of post-Francoist Spain's rapid, belated modernisation are intensified by the characteristics of (post)modernism.[19] These include (1) the dislocating effects of late modernity on the subject (Kaplan and Wang 2003: 3), (2) an increasing sense of alienation both within oneself and from the collective, and (3) the marginalisation of migrant peoples – such as Regina, who inhabits 'the graffiti-scarred barrios' (Smith 2006b: 16) on Madrid's periphery. The migrant remains in a state of suspension, denied legal residency or citizenship, a state that Regina denounces.[20] In other words, while Spain has become a destination for immigrants – as Isabel Santaolalla has pointed out (2005), it is a utopian place for other nations – it has also perpetuated towards migrants the discrimination and marginalisation that Spaniards suffered in Europe decades ago.

Repeated panning shots of these 'graffiti-scarred' barrios suggests that these peripheral areas of Madrid scratch, stab, slash or fissure the cosmetic façade of late modernity (see Figure 1.6). Graffiti 'divide[s] the mythical presence of the autographic gesture with an irreconcilable split [. . .] [thereby instantiating] a presence under erasure' (White 2008: 109). It is a scar, a cut on the cosmetic façade of late modernity, but it is increasingly threatening. It generates horror and anxiety. I associate these neighbourhoods in *Volver* with a rupture or injury on the 'skin' of late modernity (Fer 1997: 149). Following Briony Fer's engagement with Lacan's psychoanalytic concepts in a different context, I suggest that these cuts or scratches add a phantasmatic dimension to the juxtaposition or ambivalent point where two mutually exclusive meanings converge and cannot be distinguished. Just as the anamorphic skull in Hans Holbein's

Figure 1.6 'Graffiti-scarred' barrios on Madrid's outskirts

The Ambassadors (1533) haunts and threatens the existence of the painting's affluent male figures, while producing a disturbance in our field of vision, the fissure of graffiti foregrounds a void by recovering the precarious material conditions of existence. For instance, the peeling walls of the building where Sole lives break into the cosmetic façade of late modernity. Fer explains that the empty object, what Lacan calls *l'extimité*, points 'to that which is neither exterior nor interior but which breaks the continuous skin to reveal the empty centre, the space of the Real' (Fer 1997: 148). The scar produced by the graffiti or the apartment blocks' peeling walls can be associated with the Lacanian Real, and *Volver* thus reveals, uncovers or lays bare the late modern city's defensive strategies of protection or postponement. They are 'played out on the border between inside and outside' in order to cover or defer the encounter with the void (Fer 1997: 149).

In addition, migrants like Regina coexist with working-class Spaniards, like Raimunda and Sole, who have also left their villages for the liminal and precarious spaces between the countryside and the city. Although they belong to a subsequent generation, Raimunda's and Sole's condition as emigrants to the Spanish capital evokes, albeit anachronistically, some of the consequences of the massive structural changes of the 1960s. These included mass emigration from rural to urban spaces as a result of the Franco regime's 'Stabilisation Plan' of 1959, which marked the beginning of the so-called 'development years' (Ross 2004: 119). The rural 'past' and urban 'present' often had tremendously different material conditions. Sole tells Paula that Raimunda had to urinate and defecate in the run where they kept the hens because they had no bathroom in their house when they were children. Sole's memory of Spain's underdeveloped rural areas refers more to Almodóvar's generation – that of Raimunda and Sole's parents (the late Franco period) – than to her own (the film is noticeably set in the present (it shows the new Barajas airport terminal), so Sole and Raimunda would have been children in the 1980s, when most of rural Spain had water and sanitation infrastructures). This anachronism does not, though, invalidate the evocation of the social, cultural and economic inequality and exclusion on which the late Franco period was predicated.

Instead, *Volver* confronts the traumas and memories of rural and migrant subjects, who were constituted through their exclusion, as they are transmitted by and addressed to what Marianne Hirsch has defined as the 'post-memory' generation (1997). 'Post-memory', which Hirsch uses in the context of family history, describes the child's relationship to the traumatic experiences of its parents – events the child did not directly experience, but whose images and narratives shaped its subjectivity (2001: 219). 'Post-memory', Hirsch argues, 'is a powerful form of memory precisely because its connection to its object or source is mediated not through recollection but through representation, projection and creation – often based on silence rather than speech, on the invisible rather than the visible' (2001: 220). My study takes into consideration the transmission of traces of trauma and fragments of memory beyond the family, but I draw here on Hirsch's concept to emphasise that the 'post-memory' generation in Spain (those who have mostly grown up during the post-dictatorship period) still struggles with the uncertainties of the parents' and grandparents' traumatic experiences (Alted 2005: 17).

As is well known, Freud argued that traumatic experiences cannot simply be articulated through language. In therapy, working through requires the patient to articulate events through language in order to detect or bring to the fore those psychic events that escape linguistic articulation. The analysand may become conscious of, and put into language, an event that was not consciously registered when it occurred. Trauma is a case in point: an unknown reality external to the subject that has nevertheless affected the subject without being mediated by consciousness (Freud 2003 [1920]). For Freud, then, working through will cure the patient of these traumatic traces. In this book, however, I emphasise an im-possible process of working through as the condition of possibility for thinking about the ethical and political trans-formative potential of infinite mourning. Seen this way, the 'productive anachronism' in *Volver* helps us think about the extent to which Sole and Raimunda are already constituted by the transmission of memories they have not directly experienced. Yet the collective and cultural traumas *can* be *wit(h)nessed*, and potentially transformed, by later generations who did not suffer them directly. This takes place, as Hirsch has shown, through intersubjective or transgenerational transmissions (Hirsch 2001: 222).

On several occasions in the film, we see the entrance or the courtyard of buildings on the periphery of the city where Sole or Raimunda live. They are adorned with plants, which function, as the terrace of Pepa's luxurious penthouse does in *Mujeres al borde de un ataque de nervios* (*Women on the Verge of a Nervous Breakdown*, 1988): as an indexical trace of the rural in a precarious urban world. A similar effect can be seen in one of the best-known stills of *Volver*, which shows a close-up of Cruz smelling a leaf while she prepares tropical drinks for the film crew members celebrating a farewell party (see Figures 1.7–1.8). D'Lugo argues that Raimunda's restaurant here becomes a 'mythical' space, a 'space of innocence', if not a form of simulacrum; the film 'transpose[s] the Madrid-based action into a hybrid mise en scène filled with Latin American motifs (sultry nights, mojitos, and tango)' (2013: 415). D'Lugo is right to see this as a possible imagining of a new community to come, predicated on hybridity, plurality and difference. But we can add another layer to D'Lugo's argument, if we read Raimunda's smelling a leaf as a kind of remainder of the rural, which evokes and invokes Raimunda actualising memories of her rural origins through a sensorial and bodily way of perceiving, apprehending, experiencing and 'being-in-the-world'.

Almodóvar's *¿Qué he hecho yo para merecer esto?* (1984) is also explicitly concerned with migration from the countryside to metropolitan areas in Spain, and with the Spanish migration to Germany.[21] Like the characters in that film, the women in *Volver* furnish their two-bedroom apartments with cheap furniture and consumer goods (as the *mise-en-scène* of the film shows). The question of Spanish migration to Germany has been left unexplored in Almodóvar scholarship.[22] But *¿Qué he hecho yo para merecer esto?* evokes the personal accounts of millions of anonymous Spaniards who left their country in the late Franco period. The economic and political conditions were unable to sustain them in Spain, so they went in search of a better life in Germany. There, they were thrust into the heart of the capitalist industrial complex. We see this through the film's representation of Antonio, Gloria's unsympathetic husband, although he is a fascist sympathiser and embodies the inextricability of Francoism with machismo, whereas many of the Spanish migrants to Germany became politically

Figure 1.7 Raimunda smells a leaf

Figure 1.8 Farewell party at Raimunda's restaurant

conscious and were instrumental in resisting the Franco regime. This was due, in part, to the fact that they lived in a democratic country, and also due to the support their political resistance against Francoism received from an important part of German society – despite the discrimination and marginalisation the Spanish migrants suffered at the hands of the Germans. Indeed, they never truly belonged. But Almodóvar does not perpetuate a logic of clear-cut definitions between victims and perpetrators. He does not simply force us to identify emotionally, or empathise with those we consider victims (I will come back to this issue in Chapters 3 and 4), nor with those we consider perpetrators, as with Antonio – who also becomes a victim, when he is murdered by Gloria. Instead, Almodóvar helps us to see the impossibility of understanding or assimilating the other's irreducible, migratory experiences into our own consciousness when we bear witness to those experiences, whether subjective or shared. This impossibility becomes an ethical quandary, in which we must, still, bear witness to and share the other's experiences. To return to the symbolic significance of the *mise-en-scène* in *Volver*, these inanimate objects, such as the furniture in Raimunda's apartment, become a source and transmitter of pain, thus revealing the way in which the violence of a globalised economic system 'penetrates the intimate [. . .] spaces of the home' (Wong 2007: 176).

E. Ann Kaplan and Ban Wang argue that trauma studies influenced by the poststructuralist and psychoanalytic work of Cathy Caruth have mainly focused on the traumatic event's catastrophic impact on the subject's psyche and body. From this psychoanalytic perspective, they argue, the subject becomes paralysed, unable to articulate or represent the traumatic experience (Kaplan and Wang 2003: 4). The focus on victimhood and the imagining of trauma as an inaccessible experience runs the risk of dissociating trauma from the social context, they argue, and ignores the possibility that working through is a condition of possibility for changing history (2003: 5). History should be integrated into the psyche as a way of understanding that trauma depends on the historical and cultural phenomenon of modernity (2003: 8) – which is not to say that interpretation can have total access to traumatic experiences, or render them transparent. But, as I explained in the Introduction, their distinction between structural and historical trauma does not take into account the complex imbrication of individual and historical traumas, the complex convergence of temporalities or the limitations of a teleological path from pathology to cure. We must acknowledge these if we are to see the effects of trauma and memory in the subject and in society. Still, I agree with Kaplan and Wang that modernity can be defined as a traumatic experience. In this light, I suggest that *Volver* shows us late modernity experienced as traumatic. Such an experience is obviously related to the identification of nations as on the periphery of modernity, including Spain and Latin American countries – which both suffered a decelerated process of industrialisation

(D'Lugo 2013). One of the causes or consequences of 'uneven development' is the juxtaposition of incompatible temporalities in Spanish and
Latin American cultures, which Néstor García Canclini defines as 'mul-
titemporal heterogeneity' (1995). However, modernity itself also becomes
'a shocking assault on existing modes of experience and representation
through consistent industrial and technological change, urbanisation,
transport, military technologies and communication networking that also
register, traumatically, in art's own technologies' (Pollock 2013a: xxix).

From this perspective, the film reveals the symptoms, the 'blind spots',
which show how late modernity in Spain is predicated on a heterogeneous
temporality that undercuts the teleological conception of history associated with the Western epistemological tradition and the Enlightenment.
The latter requires the repudiation, repression or exclusion of the
incalculable or heterogeneous elements that reveal the always already
failing mechanistic operations of the ideology of modern culture. Mladen
Dolar explains: '[I]deology perhaps basically consists of a social attempt
to integrate the uncanny, to make it bearable, to assign it a place, and the
criticism of ideology is caught in the same framework if it tries to reduce it
to another kind of content or to make the content conscious and explicit'
(1991: 19). For Slavoj Žižek, 'blind spots' articulate or materialise the
surplus, the residue, the remnant that effectively escapes or cannot be
located in the mechanistic operations of the modern bourgeois social and
symbolic order (1991). The intellectual legacy of the Enlightenment has
demonstrated that scientific knowledge and technology can be instrumentalised to produce a violent and unequal social system and destroy humanity.[23] As Pollock explains: 'Modernity's self-image as a rational progress
towards humanly engineered betterment was shattered by its own deadly
and often dominant forces for exploitation and greed, social inequality
and, above all, violence: technological (in warfare notably) and ultimately
industrially enacted genocidal racism' (2013a: xxix–xxx).

Economic and technological globalisation in Spain has attempted
to obliterate the 'rural past', as a kind of '*desecho histórico*' (historical
residue), and to disavow urban poverty in Spain. But this system is,
paradoxically, predicated on social inequality. *Volver* lays bare the uneven
process of development of late modernity and its discontinuous collapse
into forgotten liminal spaces, like the outskirts of Madrid. *Volver* makes us
think about how progress and modernisation coexist with urban poverty
and rural 'anachronism'. And about the cosmetic façade of late modernity,
with its phantasmatic spectres returning from the past or future, which
reveal the shattered fragments and ruins of the present to haunt and
fissure the linear narrative of historical progress.

The Maternal and Feminine Rural Space:
Nostalgia and Utopia

Volver is highly influenced by Italian neorealism and Hollywood melodramas, particularly Michael Curtiz's *Mildred Pierce* (1945), and melodrama is often seen as symptomatic of a culture's need to disavow traumatic events, while paradoxically dealing with them in an oblique or allegorical form (Kaplan and Wang 2003: 9). It does this through, for instance, the *mise-en-scène*, as if the latter were the traces or the fragments of the traumatic historical past in the present. Should *Volver* be thought of as melodrama – strictly defined by the genre's conventions, thereby commodifying the cultural symptoms that the genre packages to manipulate the spectators' emotional responses? Almodóvar's film could then be dismissed as a 'nostalgia film', which encourages the spectator to consume, be entertained by, or think of the 'rural past' only through facile, glossy images detached from historical referent (Nagib 2007: xvii). This is associated with 'a postmodern political cynicism' that leaves us 'in a disempowered state, where resistance and struggle seem pointless and futile' (Elsaesser 1994: 23). And we could perhaps read *Volver* as succumbing to a nostalgic and romanticised vision of the past. Raimunda, for instance, might be associated with a copy of an image of Sophia Loren or Anna Magnani. The film would just be part of the culture industry of nostalgia, which ignores the complexity of collective history, trivialises unresolved, painful past events, emphasises superficial commemoration, or disavows the intoxicating effects in the present of traumatic events. Identifying our interest in history as a mere desire for consuming a commodified image of the past, Fredric Jameson has argued, 'we also universally diagnose contemporary culture as irredeemably historicist, in the bad sense of an omnipresent and indiscriminate appetite for dead styles and fashions; indeed, for all the styles and fashions of a dead past' (1991: 286).

This would, of course, be antithetical to my argument that our contingent encounter with the film produces ungoverned affects. I would argue instead, though, that one of the most salient characteristics of Almodóvar's cinema is the way it recycles Spanish cultural referents that Francoism instrumentalised. Almodóvar uses camp in this way, for instance (Yarza 1999).[24] Camp invades and subverts cultural referents through pastiche, parody and exaggeration, without completely erasing the way in which these cultural referents were instrumentalised by Francoism. Almodóvar uses a camp aesthetics to foreground the coexistence of divergent, incompatible or mutually exclusive meanings. He thus hybridises popular Spanish cultural referents associated with Francoism. Undercutting a logic of identity based on depth, origin or authenticity, Almodóvar's emphasis on the parody and mimicry of identity removes the interiority of identity, so that it emerges to the surface. As Jonathan Dollimore has suggested, '[t]he hollowing-out of the deep self is pure pleasure, a release from the subjective correlatives of the dominant morality (normality, authenticity etc.)' (1991: 311). Almodóvar's deployment of camp allows for the coexistence of mutually exclusive meanings, thereby undercutting the logic of binary oppositions, in which one term is privileged over the other, so that authenticity, mimicry, irony or depth are brought to the same level. *Volver* attempts to re-imagine, to re-inhabit, to recuperate or to reappropriate a rural space that becomes utopian, maternal and feminine. It resists heteronormative and patriarchal ideology, and the latter's association with Francoism, as well as the traumatic effects of late modernity on subject and society.

In this utopian maternal space, houses, such as that of Raimunda's elderly aunt, are furnished with old furniture and artefacts, some mass-produced and others manufactured by craft, thereby transforming village houses into sites of inscription and the transmission of the memories of an anachronistic world threatened by the forces of late capitalism. The camera lingers on the artefacts that decorate Raimunda's elderly aunt's house. Pérez Melgosa draws on the art historical concept of 'rhopography' to think about the symbolic significance of these apparently trivial objects. He points out that

> we find in his movies a plethora of instants when the camera looks attentively at the most humble details of everyday existence, those things, spaces, or actions that display the material supports of our lives and render visible the limitations of our bodies, institutions, and technologies. (2013: 187)

We can think of these objects as material signifiers that transparently or opaquely, manifestly or latently, point to the traumatic event, or the screening memory of it. They are associated with the fragile subject's struggle against external forces that both threaten, and are the condition of possibility for, her/his existence.[25] Smith, following Martha Nussbaum, defines these emotional objects as being not 'intentional but rather as embodying ways of seeing, beliefs, and the attribution of values' (2004a: 373). Similarly, I contend that these artefacts – the antique dolls, or Aunt Paula's jewellery box in the suitcase that is brought from the rural space to the city – are material traces of memory, leftovers associated with both the anxiety caused by succumbing to the destructive and generative forces of late modernity, and the pleasures of re-inhabiting a maternal, feminine, rural space. We can see this latter effect in Melgosa's suggestion that 'the pantry in *Volver* [. . .] presents food as a restorative gift, a message from a loving [present/absent] mother, and a support for affective memory' (2013:192). But thinking of our material and psychic existence as untouched by the process of modernisation is a provisional fantasy of liberation – a point to which I shall return shortly. If these objects are inserted into the logics of both the commodity and affective memory, one cannot neglect the fact that Almodóvar's rendering of these inanimate objects is mediated by the language of advertising, as Melgosa points out (2013: 192). But Almodóvar's emphasis on these resonant objects should make us rethink or re-imagine our social subjectivity as resisting the traumas associated with the violence of a Spanish society that believed it could be 'comfortably' inserted into the (masculinist) modern process of global capitalism. As Kaplan and Wang suggest, our globalised economic system 'has plunged different cultures and regions into painful, bloody paths of modernisation, development and revolution, and has forced them to search for alternatives to survive in the modern world' (2003: 16).

As already mentioned, *Volver* relies on a conventional narrative structure, which could imply a way of 'reducing the messy and ungovernable feminine elements to apparently rational control through the masterful use of a conventional cinematic narrative' (Smith 2004a: 365). This conventional structure is often associated with the kind of fiction used by hegemonic social groups to control the historical archive. This would repress the opacities, folds or symptoms of the spectres that point to the structural lack and incompleteness at the core of the totalising, linear, dominant narrative of history (Menard 2015: 73). The superstitions in the film are associated with the survival and the honouring of the remnants of the dead. The film celebrates superstitious beliefs, for instance, which are conventionally associated with the feminine. It shows them as a legitimate epistemological framework, thereby challenging the realm of the rational and the scientific, which are associated with patriarchal epistemology and the Enlightenment's legacy. Almodóvar's film thus foregrounds the survival of the residues that modernity has repressed and destroyed. Labanyi explains that popular superstition has been repressed by 'the official discourses of the modern nation-state [. . .] in their imposition of a uniform model of bourgeois culture' (Labanyi 2002: 2). That is not to say that the film reifies or romanticises superstition, as if the latter were a more authentic epistemological framework than the patriarchal, bourgeois epistemological tradition. Instead, *Volver* emphasises superstition as a way of complicating the dominant historical archive and the uniform model of bourgeois culture, by interrupting it with heterogeneous and hetero-

Figure 1.9 Agustina appears on a TV talk show

chronic ghost stories of the anachronistic rural past and survivors in the late modern city.

The film thus celebrates or complicates the binary opposition between the supernatural and superstitious, and the rational and empirical. Yet, the presenter of the TV talk show on which Agustina appears ridicules these beliefs (see Figure 1.9). The presenter suggests that Agustina's home village is mostly populated by mad people, rather than seeing superstition as an alternative cognitive system for subjects without access to the normative modes associated with logical reason.[26] Agustina goes on the show to talk about the connection between her mother's disappearance and the death of Raimunda's parents; in exchange, she has been promised money for treatment of her terminal cancer. For Agustina, this is only available in Houston, Texas. In the imaginary of the Spanish audience, Houston is where popular celebrities (i.e. the folk singer Rocío Jurado) go for treatment, rather than use the universal health system in Spain – as if an expensive, private hospital in the United States could magically cure a terminal disease.[27]

Mark Allinson and Smith have both dealt extensively with the way television is often associated with sensationalism in Almodóvar's cinema.[28] When Agustina leaves the talk show, we see reaction shots of Raimunda, who is disgusted. Raimunda watches the TV show in Sole's apartment: we see her react to the grotesque situation the presenter provokes. This scene has comic overtones, but Raimunda's negative reaction does illustrate how Almodóvar satirises and criticises television, the dominant mass medium in Spain, for creating false witnesses who do not respect the integrity or silence of the fragile subject, such as Agustina. They inevitably fail to bear witness, respond or share traumas com-passionately.[29] Similarly, Melgosa suggests that the traumatic effects of the rape in *Kika* (1993) are provoked less by the action of being raped than by the subsequent broadcast of the rape by a national TV programme: 'the broadcasting of the event in a television program, the opening of her private life to the scrutiny of the public [. . .] will render Kika, for a short time, into a defenceless victim' (2013: 197). Along similar lines, Agustina suffers both from a terminal illness and from mass media manipulation. She is made to believe in the power of money and fame, even for treating terminal illnesses – a belief that contributes to a hierarchical distinction between worthy and disposable subjects, depending on their economic and social status. Here, television commodifies and instrumentalises memory. It uses the emotional responses of spectators to entertain and to encourage consumption, and attempts to neutralise the ungoverned affective responses that may potentially function as a heterogeneous form of resistance at the micro-political level.[30]

However, neither Almodóvar's cinema in general, nor *Volver* in particular, entirely reject the possibility that the mass media can function positively by mediating our subjective and shared experiences. D'Lugo argues that the mass media are part of the textual construction of *Volver*; it is, for instance, influenced by radio and apolitical television soap operas. So they could function 'as the filter through which the characters and eventually the audience are brought to understand their world' (2013: 421), and potentially help creating cultural affinities across different 'Hispanic' audiences. But I contend that Almodóvar's inclusion of such a sensationalist TV programme in *Volver* and the explicit dismissal of the value of TV in the film's dialogue can be interpreted as condemnation of mass media's function and influence in Spanish society. The film's dialogue explicitly refers to TV as a trash cultural form, as an inefficient vehicle for denouncing Agustina's mother's disappearance and as an inappropriate place to come to terms with these female subjective and shared experiences. But this need not entirely contradict D'Lugo's interpretation, because Almodóvar's position is an ambivalent one. He both relies on and undercuts the way in which mass media produce and package reality and memory. So the explicit condemnation of mass media in *Volver*, which is most obvious in the talk show scene, could also be interpreted as an example of Almodóvar's ethical and political concern with imagining the im-possible reconstitution of a psychic and social being in a utopian, yet non-totalising, rural, maternal space, which is not affected by, or in which one can resist or dissolve, the symptoms of late modernity. And this can be done, paradoxically, through the modern technology of cinema.

The utopia, then, would be the rural, feminine, maternal space as an 'im-possible return', which can only take place via the cinema. Michel Foucault explains:

> Utopias are sites with no real place. They are sites that have a general relation of direct or inverted analogy with the real space of [s]ociety. They present society itself in a perfected form, or else society turned upside down, but in any case these utopias are fundamentally unreal spaces. (1984: 3)

But Almodóvar's film resists the totalising, anticipatory and liberating implications underpinning the concept of utopia. *Volver* redefines the concept by thinking of the disruptive, heterogeneous and disturbing temporal and spatial implications underpinning Foucault's concept of heterotopia. The latter, which provisionally opens and closes itself to the social and symbolic order that produces it, suggests that utopia cannot be a space to think or feel beyond hegemonic ideological and conceptual frameworks. Heterotopias ambivalently juxtapose incompatible times and spaces in a single space, which, for Foucault, suggests the possibility of transforming social and symbolic structures. Heterotopias are not subjugated to a promising, hopeful, resistant or liberating calculable space (Johnson 2006). Instead, heterotopias

> function in relation to all the space that remains. This function unfolds between two extreme poles. Either their role is to create a space of illusion that exposes every real space, all the sites inside of which human life is partitioned, as still more illusory [. . .]. Or else, on the contrary, their role is to create a space that is other, another real space, as perfect, as meticulous, as well arranged as ours is messy, ill constructed, and jumbled. (1984: 8)

Therefore, although the maternal, feminine, rural space in *Volver* is an 'unreal place', which could be defined as utopian, it simultaneously undercuts the conventional attributes of utopia. In this context, the maternal, feminine, rural space in the film produces the disruptive material and symbolic effects that Foucault would associate with heterotopia. As I mentioned above, for Foucault heterotopic spaces are 'other' spaces, 'other' textual sites that open and close themselves to the world; they are produced in that world in order to provoke ruptures from within the dominant ideological structures. By imagining an im-possible maternal, feminine, rural space, Almodóvar conceives the medium of film itself as a heterotopic site, a linguistic space, which momentarily and radically disturbs, undoes or goes beyond the established categories within the dominant social and symbolic order.

On the other hand, Almodóvar pays tribute to the European auteurist cinema of Luchino Visconti through a television intersection. Near the end of the film, we see Irene watching *Bellissima* (1951) on TV in Agustina's house. We see Anna Magnani, as it were, reanimated, brought back to life by cinema (just as *Volver*'s opening shot of a tombstone brought death back into cinema). This could be read as Almodóvar's attempt to revive the cult of European auteurist cinema (Italian neorealism), and as an allusion to the way in which the ontology of cinema is based on bringing death back to cinema and on bringing the dead back to life through the dialectical relationship between stillness and movement. But, more interestingly, Irene's image is reflected on the screen, and merges with that of Magnani. So the screen functions as a mirror in which the image of Magnani seems like a reflection of that of Carmen Maura. The merging and mirroring of these images establishes a connection between these two great actresses and, by extension, between Almodóvar and Visconti. By identifying himself with Visconti, Almodóvar inserts himself into the canon of European film auteurs. As I will explain in Chapter 3, such an emphasis on inscribing his authorial signature partakes of the im-possibility of relating the cinematic text back to the author as the transcendental signified.

Volver is above all the film in which Almodóvar returns to his rural origins in La Mancha. Though of course this return resonates with that of Leo, the protagonist in *La flor de mi secreto* (*The Flower of My Secret*, 1995) (played by Marisa Paredes). Leo must return to her native village to escape from the present, associated with the modern city, and to reconnect nostalgically with her mother after a failed heterosexual relationship. To problematise further my deployment of the concept of utopia in this chapter, I should ask whether this kind of utopian return to and idealisation of a lost maternal, feminine, rural space could be motivated by nostalgia for the 'anachronistic' rural space and the 'archaic' maternal figure. Does the insistence on establishing a continuous connection to the rural past, as if it remained immobilised, unconsciously reinforce the dichotomy of city versus country in conservative ideology? After all, this opposition resonates with Franco's rhetoric during the almost four decades of his dictatorship. Before, and even after, the stabilisation plan, he figured the rural as offering a more authentic, communal life and more exemplary moral values than the city. *Zarzuela* music, like that played in *Volver*'s opening credits, was heavily promoted during the Franco regime.[31] In addition, Mercedes Camino argues that an emphasis on maternity runs the risk of perpetuating Francoist National Catholic gender politics, with its dichotomy of the 'good woman', the self-abnegating maternal figure, and the 'bad woman', the unfeminine or sexually promiscuous woman (2010: 641). With reference to the genre of melodrama, from which Almodóvar draws and from which my interpretation distances itself, Linda Williams argues that it often starts and ends in a 'space of innocence' and nostalgia (1998: 65), and includes a moment in which 'virtue is taking pleasure in itself' (1998: 65). Such a 'space of innocence' is always an old one, so melodrama is quintessentially conservative (1998: 65). Williams argues that 'the most classic forms of the mode are often suffused with nostalgia for rural and maternal origins that are forever lost yet – hope against hope – refound, reestablished, or, if permanently lost, sorrowfully lamented' (1998: 65).

Moreover, subjectivity is always already implicated in and contingent upon how the subject experiences space and place, as Doreen Massey has argued (1994). Given that, the film's nostalgic idealisation of an archaic pre-Oedipal subjectivity would disavow the fact that psychic relations between the child and the archaic mother is predicated on a painful and chaotic experience. Elisabeth Bronfen has argued that the nostalgic subject is unable to distinguish between her/his lived experiences and the phantasies that screen those experiences. Suffering from a feeling of dislocation, not belonging or displacement, the nostalgic subject needs to screen or dissociate herself/himself from painful feelings by inventing memories that produce pleasure in her/his consciousness and idealise her/his place of origin. For Bronfen, such screening phantasies point to the way that the subject needs to find mechanisms to protect herself/himself from the overwhelming gap between traumatic experiences and their representation. Those screening phantasies lay bare the violence associated with the place of origin (1998: 278). This study problematises the distinction between mourning – the process of coming to terms with the loss of the loved object, so that the loss can be integrated into the present – and melancholia. But Bronfen's reflection on nostalgic subjectivity can be fruitfully associated with the traditional idea that the melancholic subject is unable to come to terms with the loss of the loved object or place, so that the loss becomes pathologically felt as a loss of and in the self.

Svetlana Boym, however, associates nostalgia with mourning, rather than melancholia, particularly when mourning is undertaken to come to terms with the displacement, fragmentation and temporal irreversibility induced by the process of modernisation. Boym makes a clear-cut distinction between 'restorative nostalgia' and 'reflective nostalgia'. 'Restorative nostalgia' implies a reactionary, if not delusional, belief in recovering the lost place of origin and the past – this can be seen, for instance, in nationalist nostalgia. By contrast, 'reflective nostalgia' implies a shared desire to integrate the shattered fragments of memory into the present. 'Reflective nostalgia' does not disavow the fact that such a shared desire for integration is always already an ambivalent process. Instead, Boym argues that 'reflective nostalgia' acknowledges different temporalities and multiple ways of being conscious of the world in the present, as the condition of possibility for establishing more com-passionate human relations. 'Reflective nostalgia' thus becomes a form of resistance to the belief that the past can be totally recovered, and the amnesia on which late modernity is predicated. So, as Peter Glazer suggests, 'reflective nostalgia' can be associated with progressive politics when it integrates human longing into critical thinking and acknowledging, rather than disavowing, the contradictions that underpin late modernity (Glazer 2005: 8).

In this theoretical context, I contend that the maternal, feminine, rural space in *Volver* is neither a (post)modern, apolitical simulacrum, of the type that Nagib describes, nor the perpetuation of the traditional social structure seen in the 'black legend of Spanish ruralism, steeped in reaction and repression' (Smith 2006b: 16). It is, instead, a way of embracing a 'heterosocial' conception of community, which struggles against and resists late modern amnesia. The film attempts to integrate the fragments of the past into the present as a way of envisioning a better, incalculable future. This heterosocial community points to an alternative ethical model of relationality and sociality based on the solidarity within a group of heterogeneous and transgenerational women who can act out and/or work through their personal and shared traumas and incompatible memories, thereby 'transforming an unequal self–other dyad into a relation of coexistence, where self and other meet "eye to eye" (and I to I) to become mutually affirming subjects' (Huffer 1998: 27). Fragments of memories and traces of trauma evoke the traumatic past associated with the Francoist regime and patriarchal law – but also a feminine, transgenerational affective and 'hospitable memory'. Such a memory helps to forge transsubjective ethical relations between women, producing relations based on an asymmetrical yet mutual recognition as subjects, or imagining a shared space where different and singular subjectivities can com-passionately coexist. The women in *Volver* thus form an alternative social space, a radical critique of the dominant heterosexual and patriarchal paradigm.[32] They share experiences and memories and establish alternative 'structures of feeling', to use Ann Cvetkovich's term, that can envision an alternative feminine community that is yet to come (2003: 12).

Figure 1.10 Mothers, sisters and daughters talking in the kitchen

One of the film's final sequences shows the women in the village house's kitchen talking about whether Raimunda has had cosmetic surgery to make her breasts bigger (see Figure 1.10). But here the breast is not an object of the heteroxexual male's fetishistic desire, nor the phantasmatic partial object that the infant considers to be part of himself and fears losing in the pre-Oedipal stage of subjectivity. The re-signification of the breast in Almodóvar's film, although such a foreclosure of the phallic signifier is associated with a psychotic structure, departs from or problematises fixed ideas of male and female subjectivities within the patriarchal and symbolic order, in which, as I will discuss in Chapter 2, femininity can only be associated with lack and castration.[33] The kitchen scene notably contrasts with other scenes in the film that include overhead shots of Raimunda's cleavage, as if her body were trapped in the logic of patriarchy, inscribing her in traumatic domesticity and feminine heterosexuality. In her description of the scene showing Raimunda with her parasite husband in the bedroom, Kinder notes that the intercut between the close-ups of Raimunda and Paco ends with a static shot of an exhausted, upset and annoyed Raimunda (she is crying for her Aunt Paula) – while we hear Paco climaxing after masturbating (2007). Raimunda's rejection of sex, which epitomises the film's insistence on the failure of patriarchal and heteronormative relationships, symbolises the impossibility of a sexual relation which is always already mediated by the phallic signifier in the symbolic order. The off-screen sounds emphasise the violence at the core of non-reciprocal sexual relationships. Even more clearly, the violence on which non-reciprocal sexual relations rest is made even more apparent, although this action is not graphically shown, when Paco attempts to rape his adopted daughter. This results in his death.

By contrast, one of the film's final scenes shows Irene looking after and comforting Agustina, who lies in bed. Agustina seems like a child, fusing again with the maternal body, conveying the symbiotic relationship between mother and child. In this psychic, pre-Oedipal stage of subjectivity, sexual difference (predicated on abjecting the maternal body) has not yet been articulated. This pre-Oedipal subjectivity is prior to castration and the phallic signifier as the condition of possibility for the constitution of subjectivity. The film thus imagines an intersubjective relation that is anterior to Oedipal identification – even as the latter is necessary for entry into the symbolic order. Memory of the indexical presence of a maternal, feminine, transgenerational encounter is also inscribed on Agustina's bed through the temporal cycles of life and death. More interestingly, this scene does not allegorise a delusional return to a stage of subjectivity that is not mediated by lack or castration associated with the maternal body and pre-Oedipality. Instead, this scene allegorises the women's ethical responsibility to bodily care for others; their interdependence as preceding their ontological condition of subjectivity (I will come back to this point in Chapter 4). This mode of relating to others bodily, then, foregrounds a (foreclosed) feminine, 'matrixial borderspace' within the symbolic order: the focus of the next chapter. The subject is constituted beyond a logic of 'me' and 'not me', without falling into complete fusion between mother and self, and without disavowing one's constitution by and relation to an irreducible alterity. Such a bodily mode of relationality helps us to reflect on how the matrixial borderspace is associated with a movement towards, and encounter with an irreducible other, thereby fragilising one's individual psychic boundaries as the condition of possibility for a trans-subjective encounter with a radical, irreducible difference. The act of caring for others is associated with a feminine ethics predicated on one's responsibility to the 'bodily conditions of life', to use Judith Butler's term (I will discuss this point further in the final chapter).[34] The traces of the memory of the archaic mother become a potential resource for engaging in com-passionate, trans-subjective relations in the present and for the incalculable future. The focus on the maternal in *Volver* helps us to imagine a feminine community embracing the dead, the living, and the soon to die. It would be an alternative to the patriarchal, heteronormative order based on violent, non-reciprocal sexual and antagonistic social relations between the masculine self and the feminine other. Here, sexual difference (understood within phallic or Oedipal terms) does not relegate feminine subjectivity to an association with lack and castration.

So *Volver* does not advocate reactionary discourses against the (post) modern transformation of Spain. Instead Almodóvar helps us to reflect on our disorientating present, and offers us resources to rethink the vicissitudes of (post)modern transformation of Spanish society as well as the scars of the past. Through our affective, critical and com-passionate encounter, *Volver* becomes an effective mode of witnessing the traces of trauma and fragments of memory. The film offers us resources to transform our ethical and political consciousness of reality through a re-articulation of our affections and perceptions. In the scene of Irene and Agustina, we see the film encouraging us to embrace a feminine ethics of embodied care, so that we might start – as the ad on the red bus that we see throughout the film says – '*volver a sentir*' (feeling again). The monochromatic tombstone at the start of the film interrupts movement to explore the micro-political potential of stillness. Similarly, the film offers a 'return' to the maternal, feminine, rural space not as a form of nostalgic paralysis, but as an interruption, digression or rupture of the flow of late modernity. It thereby undercuts 'the ontological or economic notion of time and history that reduces and reifies individuals, determining them in terms of their works, relations of exchanges and productivity' (Critchley 1995: 12). Such a maternal, feminine, rural space could be considered a utopian fantasy of impenetrability, and returning to it will always remain an im-possible, incalculable and unpredictable ethical and political action beyond a metaphysics of presence.

In the next chapter, I will consider how Ettinger's concept of 'matrixial subjectivity' contributes to the imbrication of aesthetics, ethics and trauma in Almodóvar's cinema, in general. I will focus particularly, however, on reading *Todo sobre mi madre* from within a queer/feminine psychoanalytic epistemological framework.

CHAPTER 2

Im-Possibility of Not-Sharing:
Todo sobre mi madre

This chapter explores the ways in which Pedro Almodóvar's 1999 film *Todo sobre mi madre* lends itself to interpretation through, or intersects with, concepts in queer theory and queer film theory. I will specifically explore three concepts: first, the supposition that sex and gender are performative, multiple, interchangeable and transmissible embodiments of feminine and masculine identity, subjectivity, and desire beyond patriarchal, heteronormative psychic and ideological frameworks; second, a 'heterosocial' notion of community, referred to in Chapter 1 as an alternative ethical model based on solidarity between a heterogeneous, transgenerational group of women;[1] and third, and most importantly, the idea of becoming a mother beyond biological, heterosexual reproduction and the Oedipal, nuclear, heteronormative family.

I am not the first to pursue these issues in relation to this film (Maddison 2000; Martin-Márquez 2004; Bersani and Dutoit 2004; 2009). I hope to add to the discussion, first, an exploration of the film's representation of femininity in the light of Ettinger's concept of the 'matrixial' (2006a); and second, a reflection on the film's relationship to critical theory and psychoanalysis. In stressing the intersections and productive tensions between cinema and theory, I aim to move beyond the interpretative and epistemological limitations of simply 'applying' theory to cinematic practices. In particular, I think about the film's theoretical self-consciousness, opening it up to a reflection on the interpretive and affective demands produced in spectators by the film's aesthetic and ethical potentialities. I move between a focus on the film's textual signification and a focus on how the spectator may experience the film as a more porous space between the viewing subject and the projection screen.

My interpretation is based on my reading of three sequences: Esteban's fatal accident, Agrado's monologue and Manuela's journey from Madrid to Barcelona. I investigate the ways in which the film represents 'queer motherhood', and propose that it produces in the spectator the notion of becoming a 'queer (m)other'. The notion that sex and gender[2] are performative – as theorised by queer theory, particularly in the early work of Butler – enables us to reflect on how, in *Todo sobre mi madre*, sex and gendered subjectivity are articulated through iteration and imitation (repetition), as well as becoming (difference). This reconceptualisation of sex and gendered subjectivity must take into consideration both the material and the discursive elements that constitute our embodied condition,[3] and in doing so, it challenges or destabilises heteronormative or phallocentric understandings of sex and gender as natural. Sexuality, gender and subjectivity are redefined in our encounter with *Todo sobre mi madre*, but not in overtly critical or political resistances. Rather, we move away from the dialectical opposition of femininity and masculinity, and emphasise the transformative and expansive potential in thinking about gendered subjectivity as a becoming or an opening onto the still incalculable.

Todo sobre mi madre engages with subjective and shared traumas of patriarchal absence, abandonment and domination; with the traces of national and trans-national political repression; with loss, death, bereavement, AIDS, social alienation and marginalisation – to name just a few. In the context of this book's main thesis, then, this chapter is concerned with what Sudeep Dasgupta calls the 'resonances and disjunctions' (2009a) of queer theory and matrixial psychoanalysis, and with the connection between trauma studies, matrixial psychoanalysis and a queer/feminist subjectivity. I argue that the film proposes a complex return to the specificity of the feminine in human subjectivity, which does not replace, but lies beyond and beside patriarchal, heteronormative and phallic conceptions of subjectivity. In doing so, it evokes a sub-symbolic psychic sphere in which, instead of using a psychoanalytic language based on objects and discrete subjects, we can explore how the 'I and non-I are crossprinting psychic traces in one another and continuously transform their shareable threads and sphere' (Ettinger 2005: 704). Ettinger's contribution to debates on historical and personal trauma helps us to explore how *Todo sobre mi madre* offers an antidote to phallocentrism, patriarchy and heteronormativity, and a potential trans-formation of the traumas of patriarchal and political violence.

Finally, I explore the ethical and potential political implications underpinning *Todo sobre mi madre*'s emphasis on motherhood and 'embodied care' (a theme, also, in Chapter 1). I argue that an ethics of motherhood and 'embodied care', beyond patriarchal, phallic and heteronormative conceptions of maternal relationality, is based on a com-passionate relationship that derives from our 'joining-in-difference with others in transference relations' (Ettinger 2006a: 143). Without perpetuating a narrative of redemption, the film calls on us to *wit(h)ness* the subjective and shared traumatic experiences of irreducible others. My focus is on the ethical mode of maternal relationality in the film, but I also pay attention to the way in which the spectator, produced in/within the feminine via the cinematic medium, embraces the ethics of queer motherhood and 'embodied care' through the affective, interpretive, trans-subjective encounter with the film medium. Reading *Todo sobre mi madre* in the light of psychoanalysis and queer/feminist methodologies helps us to think about the 'im-possibility of not-sharing' the traces of trauma and fragments of memory of irreducible others via the cinematic medium.

Repetition of the Loss

I begin with an early scene: Esteban II's fatal accident (see Figures 2.1–2.2). The camera pulls away from Manuela and a shot from her point of view shows Esteban running along a wet street. He is following Huma's taxi to ask her for an autograph. A shot from an unidentified driver's point of view cuts to a close-up of Manuela, whose facial expression seems to anticipate a tragedy. A shot from inside a car shows someone getting hit

Figure 2.1 Esteban and Manuela before Esteban runs along a wet street

Figure 2.2 The camera pulls away from Manuela

by it; we assume this is Esteban. The shattered glass of the windshield produces a disturbing opacity in our field of vision and reflects the pain that Esteban must be suffering as he confronts the im-possible experience of death (I will return to this point in Chapter 3). The disturbing opacity produced by the shattered glass of the windshield, which is always already a trace of looking, also anticipates Manuela's emotional pain at the sight of her son's struggle with death.

Emma Wilson describes the next sequence: 'disconcertingly, the film cuts to Esteban's point of view as we suddenly view the scene tip sideways, upset from its axis [. . .]. We see Manuela's legs as she runs towards him [. . .]. The scene closes with her screams' (2003: 71). Manuela's emotional pain is also reflected by the lack of synchronisation between her image and her screams, and in her involuntary gestures and expression that visually register the inscription of her suffering. This disruption between sound and image emphasises both Esteban's perception of his grieving mother's screams and the shattering of Manuela's subjectivity. It creates a rift between voice and speaker, and a painful resonance in our own body and subjectivity, as if our corporeal engagement is needed to complete the meaning of the scene – a meaning that resides in the interstices of language and representation,[4] or as if our corporeal engagement were the condition of possibility for com-passionately bearing witness (or *wit(h)ness*) to the suffering of the other without attempting to understand or empathise with

Figure 2.3 Manuela plays the pregnant Estella in Tennessee Williams' play

the other's pain. In other words, the film visually underscores the fact that, despite the resonance the sound produces in our bodies, the signification of the other's pain remains opaque.

The scene also reminds us of the simulation in which Manuela plays the part of a widow during a seminar on organ donation – a part Manuela must play in a 'real' situation after Esteban's death within the diegetic reality of the film. Like the spectator in Barthes' study of photography and mourning, Manuela will 'shudder . . . over a catastrophe which has already occurred' (1984: 96). This foregrounds the coexistence of different temporalities, the present opening onto the past and the past onto the future that always already projects one's singular yet shared finitude. This kind of repetition occurs in the film on several occasions. A television intertext for instance, shows the scene in Joseph L. Mankiewicz's *All About Eve* (1950) when Margo (Bette Davis) accuses Eve Harrington (Anne Baxter) of wanting to take her place, and later in *Todo sobre mi madre*, Nina accuses Manuela of wanting to take her place as Estella in Tennessee Williams' *A Streetcar Named Desire* (1947). Likewise, Manuela's 'real' weeping over the death of Esteban is repeated differently when she plays the pregnant Estella in Williams' play (see Figure 2.3). The corporeal resonance of Manuela's weeping in labour reminds us of her cries at the sight of Esteban's death, and Manuela's performance could be interpreted

Figure 2.4 Huma plays the grieving mother in Lorca's play

as a compulsive re-enactment of the earlier traumatic experience. This would point beyond linguistic articulation to the 'unbound affects', to use Pollock's phrase, and the overwhelming effects of her encrypted and entombed trauma, which remains unspoken and untransformed, but leaks from her nonetheless.[5] In another instance, Huma's rehearsal of a scene in Federico García Lorca's *Bodas de sangre* (*Blood Wedding*, 1932) can be read as a different repetition of the previous catastrophe – she plays a mother mourning her murdered son (see Figure 2.4). In psychoanalytic terms this emphasis on repetition,

> involves articulating art [cinema] with trauma and its foreclosure, around the impossibility of accessing a psychic Thing and a psychic Event, encapsulated out-of-sight in a kind of outside that is captured inside – in an 'extimate', nonconscious space unreachable by memory. The Thing, veiled by originary repression [. . .], and the Event, forsaken, are traumatic and tormenting, but I do not know that they hurt, nor where they hurt because I have no memory of them, for they are out of 'my' Time and Space. The Thing struggles unsuccessfully for memory, but finds only momentary relief in symptomatic repetitions. (Ettinger 2006a: 163)

The resonances and reverberations within the film, foresights or reminiscences of other scenes, emphasise how the belated, un-cognised experience of trauma is inserted into other temporalities as an inassimilable excess. The traumatic event's unbound affects are unconsciously repeated, and intensified. Pollock explains:

> If there is a gap of latency, there is also always the return. Since trauma does not occur in its own moment, the unbound affects generated by traumatic impact, [. . .] can be inherited by later events, similar or associated. A later occurrence [. . .] can trigger the displacement of the unassimilated anxiety which surcharges the second-ary event with more intensity that [sic] it itself warrants. By the same token, there can be a certain capture in the second event of that which resonates as the unknown affects of originary trauma which can be structured into a representation of another event that is at once not the trauma itself and the secondary but initial experiential site of its *encounter*. (2013a: 9, emphasis in original)

Todo sobre mi madre shows how the belated and un-cognised traumatic experience may be partially contained within language. But the trauma-tised subject constantly enacts a repetitive return of the absent object, the traumatic Real, to use Lacan's term, that has been effaced by or is an excess of language.[6] Lacan explains: 'The real is beyond the *automaton*, the return, the coming-back, the insistence of the signs, by which we see ourselves governed by the pleasure principle. The real is that which always lies behind the automaton' (1998: 53–4, emphasis in original). The belated experience of trauma thus points to that which remains unrepre-sentable.[7] Almodóvar's film reveals that the psychic economy of trauma cannot be entirely captured by the imaginary (our phantasmatic relation to the external world through the misrecognition of images) or the sym-bolic (the registration of signifiers in the unconscious as the condition of possibility for conscious thinking) registers, which constitute subjectiv-ity.[8] In other words, instead of effacing or foreclosing the traumatic Real, *Todo sobre mi madre* problematises the relationship between repetition and representation in order to confront the void or excess of language. *Todo sobre mi madre*'s concern with repetition or the 'unconscious of represen-tation', to use Deleuze's term, has to do not with veiling, but unveiling, the traumatic Real. The emergence of the latter destabilises the field of representation; the film's repetitions symptomatically point to the leakage of the traumatic Real beyond language and representation, the void or excess that symbolic representation tries, but fails, to contain within its structures.[9]

The film's intra-diegetic sequences also interact with scenes from *A Streetcar Named Desire*, *Bodas de sangre* and *All About Eve*, emphasising how anxieties and desires, or fantasies and realities, move across psychic and physical thresholds. They cannot be contained within a single sub-jectivity, temporality, space or place. These intertextualities register the slippage or collapse of visual and textual registers, blurring any distinction between the 'fictionalised' space and time associated with theatre, and the 'real' space and time associated with the characters' ordinary lives. We can think about these features of the film productively through Christine Buci-Glucksmann's invocation of Benjamin's definition of the 'image-thought' as partaking of 'a multitude of signs and planes [that] melt into a kind of suspension – a gauze veil – or into a reflexive musical mirror with its resonances' (cited in Pollock 2010: 866). She emphasises the superimposition of images and thoughts in Ettinger's paintings, which can also be seen in Almodóvar's work. Similarly, Deleuze advocates the production of affective movement, that is, a movement that touches us immediately, not through representation. He explains: 'it is a question of making movement itself a work, without interposition; of substituting direct signs for mediate representations; of inventing vibrations, rotations, whirlings, gravitations, dances or leaps which directly touch the mind' (Deleuze 1994 [1968]: 8). *Todo sobre mi madre* consists of permutations or conflations of textual references, images, dialogues, characters, scenes, actions and voices. This 'theatre of repetition', to use Deleuze's term, produces a precarious space in which multiple, interchangeable, transmissible textualities coexist, as do – of particular importance to my discussion here – identities and subjectivities.[10]

Becoming (An)Other

The convergence and interaction of diegetic reality and the reality of the theatrical pieces contained in the film can be seen when Agrado, recalling the *gracioso* of Spanish Golden Age drama (the character who provides comic relief), steps away from the theatre to interact with the audience, even though she is about to perform a monologue.[11] Unmotivated by plot,[12] a panning shot of the theatre's red velvet curtain avoids depth of field, rendering the image an almost monochromatic abstract red, as if colour became a fundamental element for the registration of experience (Fer 2004: 172). Yet, as Fer suggests in relation to Michelangelo Antonioni's *Red Desert* (1964), 'a dialectic between colour and monochromy becomes the motor of a poetics of cinema' (2004: 172). This unyielding but mobile surface fills the spectator's field of vision, creates an overproximity to the object on screen, and thereby produces in the spectator a feeling of dislocation. Despite this, the spectator can haptically perceive the velvet's texture and the tonal differences within the surface:[13] the dark folds interrupt the uniformity of red.

The camera moves rightward, a close-up of Agrado's profile being followed by a quick subjective shot, from her point of view, of the theatre audience. At this point, a beam of light, which we assume comes from a spotlight, fills the cinema screen to such an extent that, instead of illuminating, it blinds us – while also inscribing the dialectic between opacity and transparency as the condition of possibility for visual perception. The blinding light resonates with a scene from *Laberinto de pasiones*: Toraya sadistically reflects the sun's light into Sexilia's eyes (played by Cecilia Roth, who plays Manuela in *Todo sobre mi madre*) with a mirror so that Sexilia must, involuntarily, re-enact her childhood traumatic experiences.[14] It is as if, like Toraya, Almodóvar wants to perpetrate such sadism on the spectators in *Todo sobre mi madre*.

On the other hand, in *Los abrazos rotos* (*Broken Embraces*, 2009) Almodóvar's thematic and poetic concern with visual impairment is the condition of possibility for Harry Caine restoring a damaged, unsuccessful film and engaging with the cinematic image – the arrested, grainy image of his beloved, deceased Lena (Penelope Cruz, who plays Rosa in *Todo sobre mi madre*), though his interaction with her is less visual than haptic.[15] This scene points to the dialectical relationship between visibility and invisibility at the core of cinematic representation. As Brad Epps puts it in his discussion of *Matador*, '[t]he interplays of light and darkness, sight, insight, and blindness, continuity and discontinuity, plenitude and lack, are rich in *Matador*, but they are also [. . .] a fundamental part of cinema in its fractured entirety' (2009: 318). More importantly, Caine's use of the sense of touch here alludes to one's corporeal implication in cinematic perception without succeeding in a total phenomenologisation of the cinematic image. In *Los abrazos rotos*, Caine is, of course, able to move towards the other (Lena), even if Lena is already a spectral figure who can only appear and disappear as a cinematic trace – and who thus points to the spectrality of the cinematic medium. By contrast, in this scene of *Todo sobre mi madre*, we see a connection between the impossibility of moving towards the cinematic image, which is inherent in the poetics of the cinematic form, and the impossibility of relating to the other as a symptom of the dysfunctions underlying the phallic structures of a patriarchal society, as represented in Rosa's father. Rosa's father embodies patriarchal abandonment; he cannot connect with his daughter, cannot move towards her on a physical, affective or emotional level – an inability that underscores the film's concern with how the patriarchal and phallic social and symbolic orders fail to allow for any ethical relation to the other predicated on the opening of one out onto the other. The father's failure to open himself allegorises the negation, and irrevocable disconnection from the other, on which patriarchal society is predicated. The father here cannot offer the mutual security and protection that is the condition of possibility for an asymmetrical yet reciprocal ethical relation.

After the light, there is a long shot of Agrado announcing the cancellation of the play and offering, instead, to tell the narrative of her life. She begins her story, and the camera moves towards the stage until Agrado is seen in medium shot. The subject of Agrado's monologue seems to be the process of becoming (an)other. Crosscutting between shots of Agrado and reaction shots of a predominantly sympathetic audience, the film focuses on how the narrative of Agrado's life is based on a repetitive series of cosmetic surgeries, which allow her to feel the 'emancipatory', yet non-redemptive potential, in the process of becoming a transitional/transgendered, embodied feminine subject.

Agrado's transformed, 'artificial' body can be related to Almodóvar's preoccupation with surface and style (a reading that need not invalidate the ethical and political concern with one's constitution by and compassionate relation to irreducible alterity and radical difference that underpins the film, as Smith rightly points out (2014: 168)).[16] The film's *mise-en-scène*, too, emphasises costumes, the blonde and red wigs worn by Huma, and the interior design of both bourgeois Catalan households (Sister Rosa's mother's Gaudiesque apartment) and more modest homes (Agrado's and Manuela's apartments). All of these are so artificial that they seem almost as theatrical as the sets for the plays seen in the film. The film thus reinforces a kind of hyperbolic engagement with characters, whether cisgender or transgender women, as well as objects like clothes or décor. The boundary between 'artificiality' and 'naturalness' is also problematised by the film's association of a 'real' baby – Sister Rosa's child, Esteban III – with the baby doll that Nina and Agrado hold during the staging of *A Streetcar Named Desire* (see Figures 2.5–2.6). Just as Agrado's monologue emphasises the process of becoming (an)other, rather than the final product of the change (Weidner-Maluf 2005: 11), the uncanny confusion between the baby, Esteban III, and the doll blurs the distinction between 'one' and 'another'.

We can read *Todo sobre mi madre* as advocating for the subject positions excluded from and articulated beyond the dominant social and symbolic order. This is most obvious in Agrado's transgendered, embodied feminine subjectivity, and can be seen, too, in the representation of Lola as a transgendered mother and/or father, despite Lola's embodiment of the patriarchal violence and domination that Manuela denounces in a conversation with Rosa. Agrado's excessive libidinal investment in the performativity of her feminine identity challenges the 'naturalness' of gender and sexuality, undoing essentialist notions of identities and

Figure 2.5 Nina holds a baby doll

Figure 2.6 Lola holds Esteban III

gendered subjectivities within phallocentrism and heteronormativity. The latter, as Butler suggests, is itself an effect of mimetically repeating its own idealisation (1999: 338). The characters' transgendered subjectivity undoes, through a process of citation, the conventional binary opposition between an original gender and a copied gender. For Butler, the performativity of sex and gender cannot be interpreted as an intentional action on the part of the subject since, she argues, what is before us and outside us already constitutes the subject (2004: 3). Thus, the subject can only displace or subversively resignify the social and cultural norms that already precede, constrain and exceed subjectivity (Harris 1999). Butler's focus on the body's contingent construction in relation to social and cultural discourses seems to eclipse the materiality and the expressiveness of the body as a formative element of the self, even if she does pay attention to the relationship between the material and discursive conditions of the body (see Pollock et al. 1995).[17] In addition, although Butler reflects on the production of new meanings through reiterative or repetitive actions, her emphasis on improvisational possibility as always predicated on the cultural and social norms that constrain subjectivity seems to neglect the 'potential process of radical emergence, of becoming [. . .], of creative evolution' (Tuhkanen 2009: 21).

Shifting the emphasis from iteration and imitation to becoming, I contend that Agrado's and Lola's transgendered embodied feminine subjectivities are articulated between the folds of subject positions at the molecular level, rather than through a fixed notion of masculine or feminine identity at the molar level.[18] This underscores a subjective process of becoming what is still incalculable and points to the transformative potential of 'in-between' bodies and subjectivities.[19] A major concern in queer theory has been to undercut the stability of molar identities and to point to the failure of representation to account for heterogeneity and opacity as constituent elements of subjectivity. For instance, Dasgupta argues that queer theory advocates a 'politics before the subject, including the queer subject' (2009b: 2), and a conception of sexuality as a 'destabilizing structure' in a subject already marked by 'indeterminacy', rather than 'a substantive core to the subject's being' (2009b: 9). So 'queer difference' cannot be entirely captured within a concept of identity predicated on a logic of exclusion and inclusion – that would ignore the heterogeneous constituents of subjectivity. In effect, queerness is not an essential constituent of subjectivity, but an oblique and elastic process of reading and 'writing' through which one can spatialise and temporalise the unrepresented, unexpected destabilisation of normative representations and interpretations, and, more broadly, of the social and symbolic order. As Eve Kosofsky Sedgwick claims, 'queer' can refer to 'the open mesh of possibilities, gaps, overlaps, dissonances and resonances, lapses and excesses of meaning when the constituent elements of anyone's gender, of anyone's sexuality aren't made (or *can't* be made) to signify monolithically' (1993: 8, emphasis in original). Similarly, Chris Perriam associates the unfixed and 'undecidable' term 'queer' with a 'mode of interpretation [. . .], formed around an odd, heterogeneous and anti-heteronormative, structurally imperfect and inconclusive experience of viewing' (2013: 10). A queer practice or subjective position undercuts 'normative knowledges and identities' precisely because it is unfixed, shifting and diffuse (2013: 10).

Todo sobre mi madre thus undercuts an emphasis on the beginning and end points in the shift from one subject position to another. Although Agrado embraces cosmetic surgery, she tells Nina that she resists sex change surgery, that her femininity is contingent upon holding onto her phallus. This stance subverts the medical, if not the biopolitical, interventions on the body, which are based on a teleological move from an 'abnormal' subject position to a 'normative' one – a move that would perpetuate the binary thinking of patriarchal and heteronormative ideology. Almodóvar's film shows how traces of one body move or remain in another body, and vice versa, raising the ambivalences, instabilities, indeterminacies, incompletenesses and multiplicities that are beyond dialectical modes of thinking. *Todo sobre mi madre* can be interpreted as a cinematic articulation of queer theory's concern with 'not delineating a subject where the body incarnates an identity but the *jeu-croisé* of bodies, words, and images before-the-subject that "happily never arrives"' (Dasgupta 2009b: 8, emphasis in original). Queer subjectivity in *Todo sobre mi madre* cannot be reified. It points towards a micro-political form of a becoming subjectivity at the molecular level that moves beyond a representational form of politics and the logic of identity at the molar level. Pollock rightly suggests that:

> [t]he formation of subjectivity is never achieved by arrival at a destined point: the adult. The illusory ego is trying to be in charge of the various elements of subjectivity. The ego does function as a regulatory agency but it is the continuous plaything of the other two thirds of the subjective iceberg, the unconscious and its time-reversing or even timeless processes layered into that which constitutes the subject. Subjectivity is, therefore, not identity. Identity (as man or woman, for instance) [. . .] is shown by psychoanalysis constantly to fail. (2013b: 19–20)

The subject can never reify her/his identity. Unlike the sovereign subject, the un-reconstituted subject emerging here is always contingent upon the impossibility of reifying her/his own presence.[20]

Trans-subjective Encounters/Events

Agrado and Lola engage in an endless, incomplete process of 'becoming' another by altering their material bodies. But we can also read *Todo sobre mi madre* for the way the film itself produces in the viewer's body and psyche the effect of occupying, however impossibly, another space: the body of the film. After Esteban's death in Madrid, Manuela goes back to Barcelona to search for Esteban's absent father. Esteban longs for the latter, but he epitomises an irrevocable absence that Esteban can only spatialise and temporalise by writing in his confessional diary – a creative activity that transports the unbound affects induced by his loss to the diary itself (see Figure 2.7). Esteban's diary becomes the locus of the inscription of Esteban's encrypted trauma, which is associated with paternal absence and abandonment,[21] and the creative process of writing structures and potentially trans-forms, without being able to cure, the traces of Esteban's constitutive emptiness and loss. This occurs due to the ambivalent association of linguistic symbolisation and artistic formulation. This association is articulated in cinematic terms, for instance, at the beginning of the film. A subjective shot from Esteban's point of view shows him writing in his diary. This cuts to a subjective shot from the diary's point of view – hence anthropomorphising it. Instead of an opaque piece of paper, Esteban

Figure 2.7 Esteban writes in his diary

is writing on a transparent surface, as if he were writing on the camera itself. The letters he produces are invisible to the spectator; we see only Esteban's hand and pencil moving across the transparent surface, as if the symbolic but also physical action of writing were associated with the process of Esteban moving corporeally across the transparent surface, more than with the inscription of the indexical traces of Esteban's hand's movement across the sheet of paper. This, then, detaches language from its condition as a signifying system.[22] We assume that the sentence written in his diary gives the film its title (*All About My Mother*), as the latter appears and disappears in the next scene. The title is shown in red between Esteban and Manuela, as if the scene of Esteban writing in his diary could not contain the expression of Esteban's affective experiences, and the linguistic articulation had to be displaced into the next scene. To return to the scene of Esteban writing, however: the shadow of Esteban's hand, the hand itself and the pencil produce an 'otherwise than writing', which obstructs our field of vision. Their opacity interrupts the transparent surface. From this perspective, Esteban's act of writing creates a liminal space, in which signification can take place only through and in the unstable and slippery interstices of language and vision. This scene invites us to pay more attention to the 'texture of the event', to use Rancière's phrase (2011), than to the (invisible) letters as units of signification. This emphasis on the destabilisation of the field of representation potentially transforms our affective and perceptive relation to the cinematic image.

As we later learn, Esteban's father is the transgendered, HIV positive Lola (Esteban I). He has had a sexual relationship with Sister Rosa, which results in her tragic death from childbirth-related complications, exacerbated by the HIV that he has given her (see Figure 2.8). Queer theorists have recently discussed the rectum and the sexual practice of barebacking, as can be seen for example in Bersani and Adam Phillips (2008) or Tim Dean (2009). Here, barebacking becomes a mode of relationality based on an impersonal intimacy not only between the passive subject and the active subject, but also between the passive subject and all those who have previously established an impersonal intimacy with the one penetrating him (Dasgupta 2009a: 3). Rather than being seen in the context of 'social intelligibility', then, barebacking becomes a mode of trans-subjective relationality that is based on the way in which 'the self plunges himself into non-meaning and a self-shattering', by carrying in her or his own organism the infectious traces of another's organism transmitted trans-subjectively (Dasgupta 2009a: 2). Rosa's generous gesture of looking after Lola and receiving Lola in her body during unprotected sex leads to her death. When Manuela re-encounters Lola at Rosa's funeral, she blames

Figure 2.8 Lola waits for Manuela and her/his child

Lola for Rosa's undeserved and premature death, identifies Lola as an 'epidemic', an 'infecting pathogen', to use Dean Allbritton's term (2013). This potentially perpetuates the stereotypical image of the queer subject as the monster who can infect harmonious, heteronormative society with his poisonous blood (Bersani 1987; Watney 1997). Manuela's initial identification of Lola as a monstrous sexual outlaw who needs to be expelled from society – an association also drawn by Rosa's mother after Manuela and Lola re-establish their emotional bond – in conjunction with the film's tragic rendering of Rosa's living with and dying from HIV complications, may be interpreted, on one level, as a moralising attitude on the part of Almodóvar towards those infected by HIV (Rosa) and those who transmit the HIV virus to others (Lola). This would certainly, if unconsciously, perpetuate the dominant, negative and discriminatory cultural discourses and representations of AIDS and the AIDS epidemic.

Yet, Almodóvar arguably offers an effective antidote to the prejudices and preconceptions of these dominant representations and discourses. We can read the film as redefining and complicating 'concepts of mortality, gender, and well-being' (Allbritton 2013: 233). It can, then, be read as resisting and undoing, as Allbritton suggests, 'normative notions of identity and health while producing radical new forms of personhood based on illness and mortality' (2013: 226). In addition, the film's apparently moralising attitude towards AIDS can be further problematised if we pay closer attention to the generative, as well as the shattering, effects on Rosa of her encounter with Lola. On the one hand, Rosa's unprotected intimacy with Lola and with all those who had previously had sex or shared needles with Lola is an action or event with catastrophic consequences. On the other hand, however, this relationship can be seen as the condition of possibility for Rosa giving birth to a child who will live on after her, who will succeed, however implausibly, in completely neutralising the HIV virus at the end of the film.[23] To connect this with the theories mentioned earlier: Bersani and Dean emphasise the rectum as the place for conceiving death, which looks like the first reading of this event, while Allbritton stresses the generative possibilities of sickness, death and masculinity – a perspective that looks like the second reading.

I suggest that the transformative potential of sickness, masculinity, death (finitude) is always predicated on its interferences and intersections with natality, health, maternity and femininity. In his cinema generally, and in this film in particular, Almodóvar complicates, redefines, resists and undoes the notions of femininity and maternity that are or have become conventional in heteronormative, patriarchal and phallocentric culture. Allbritton explains:

> In short-circuiting a normative idea of masculinity within the film's male characters, *Todo sobre mi madre* highlights the feminine while at the same time stressing its intimate connection with masculinity, and vice versa. In doing so, in building a world that is bolstered by death just as it is by life, one that finds femininity and masculinity similarly in flux, this child [Esteban III] escapes from the bad legacies of the past even while he must live within and because of them. (2013: 235)

Seen from this perspective, Esteban is always conditioned by Manuela's promise to Sister Rosa that she will not conceal the past from him, and so he is still within the economy of exchange. But, at the same time, Sister Rosa offers him to Manuela as a generous and altruistic gift, a replacement or substitute for her own dead child. Just as the trans-sexual Tina (played by Maura) becomes Ada's daughter's adoptive mother (Ada is played by the trans-sexual Bibiana Fernández) in *La ley del deseo* (*Law of Desire*, 1987), Manuela is transformed from a biological to an adoptive mother, a point to which I shall return shortly. She had already performed this ethical and potentially political gesture by taking 'embodied care' of Sister Rosa during her pregnancy, though that ended with the latter encountering death, her singular finitude, just as she brought Esteban III to life. On the one hand, Sister Rosa's death symbolises the inevitable, inexorable process of succumbing to the vulnerability, perishability and ephemerality of our bodies, to life beyond us and without us – even if, to paraphrase Freud (1918), the unconscious is unable to imagine one's own mortality. On the other hand, Esteban's birth inserts his being into time and the 'human condition', to use Hannah Arendt's phrase (1958). This human natality provides the possibility of unpredictable political actions that may transform and contribute to a world inhabited by plurality. Perhaps Esteban's implausible neutralisation of the HIV virus could be read as precisely such a political action, given that, for Arendt, such political 'action [. . .] looks like a miracle' (1958: 246), precisely because one's capacity for transformative, unpredictable action, is, for Arendt, ontologically linked to natality – which she sees as the possibility of starting something genuinely new.

As a nun and social worker (as Manuela defines her during a visit to the gynaecologist), Sister Rosa spends her life helping those who have been either expelled from or aggressively assimilated into the body of Spanish society in the late 1990s: prostitutes, transgendered subjects and illegal immigrants (a theme tackled in Chapter 1). Faceless, nameless, voiceless African immigrants figure periodically in the film – they populate the Raval neighbourhood where Agrado lives, and stand behind Sister Rosa and Manuela during their visit to the Hospital del Mar. Although they could seem merely to fulfil the function of *figurants* (extras), to use Didi-Huberman's term (2009), the presence of disenfranchised, socially alienated and marginalised non-citizens forces the spectator to confront the existence of the irreducible other. As previously explained, Rosa's father was unable to move towards his own daughter, thus severing all the possible emotional bonds he may have had with her daughter. Likewise, although Rosa's biological mother, who embodies a conventional notion of maternity within a patriarchal, bourgeois, heteronormative social and symbolic order, eventually attempts to restore her physical and emotional connection with her daughter, she also constantly fails to provide protection to or respect her own daughter's irreducible alterity and experiences. Unlike these failures of relating, Almodóvar's attention, albeit oblique, to the voiceless, nameless, faceless immigrant subjects enables us to *wit(h)ness* their experiences through an affective encounter with the irreducible other, as transmitted via the film medium, rather than through straightforward communication. Such an encounter is the condition of possibility for generating a trans-subjective relation, which is central to the act of *wit(h)nessing*. From this perspective, the impression of the traces of the other's presence, achieved through the spectator's im-possible apprehension of the traces of the other's corporeal inscription in the film, potentially enhances our encounter with the other – even though these African subjects are in some sense relegated to the position of the *figurant*.[24]

It is important to note that the use of the *figurant* as a way of encouraging an affective response on the part of the spectator, even if well intentioned, could be seen as a kind of injustice towards the other. Bennett suggests that such a strategy runs the risk of failing to respect the dignity, integrity and agency of the other, reducing the other 'to a cipher of victimhood and thereby enacting a further form of colonization' (2005: 64). In a different context, Antonio Gómez argues that the association of alterity with victimhood contributes to a false feeling of uncritical solidarity with the irreducible other, which does not require a questioning of the social, historical, economic, political or cultural contingencies that condition and determine the individual and shared experiences of the marginal subject or subjects represented in film. Drawing on Wendy Brown's political theories, Gómez suggests that such a feeling of immediate and uncritical protection of and solidarity with a defenceless, powerless, innocent other makes it impossible to think politically about the film medium. For Gómez, the concept of the political is defined as the negotiation of social conflicts and the tensions that exist between socially antagonistic subjects as a way of working towards a more democratic and equal society (Gómez 2006: 105).

I offer here a more 'reparative' reading, to use Kosofsky Sedgwick's term (2003), of the association of alterity with victimhood. I propose that our spectatorial attention to the irreducible other becomes the condition of possibility for a com-passionate trans-subjective encounter, which acknowledges one's *response-ability* to the singular call of the other. This takes place beyond a concept of the political based on antagonisms and beyond any emphasis on the autonomy of the subject. I should also emphasise that Almodóvar's attention to socially marginalised subjects does not perpetuate an unproductive and unreflective sympathy or empathy for a reified 'victim'. Unlike the destructive effects produced by the blinding bright light hitherto described, which frustrated our inclination to move towards the cinematic image, our cinematic confrontation with the other in this film enables us to *wit(h)ness* beyond re-cognition the other's irreducible experiences, even if we cannot understand them. From this perspective, the spectator is encouraged to adopt a non-phallic mode of seeing and relating to the other, which can embrace radical difference and alterity instead of repudiating it, destroying it, or assimilating or appropriating the experiences of the irreducible other (Bennett 2005: 105).

We are first introduced to Sister Rosa when Manuela is in a taxi, looking for Lola in Barcelona. The taxi drives around an area outside the city where, as Smith aptly describes it, 'cars slowly cruise prostitutes as if in some lower circle of suburban hell' (1999: 29); a subjective shot from Manuela's point of view shows Sister Rosa giving something to two transgendered prostitutes. But that scene is the end of a journey that has already brought Manuela from Madrid to Barcelona, in search of Esteban's father – which is also the start of a journey into her individual and shared past. In an earlier scene, we see Manuela's face, her head resting on what is recognisably the seat of a train. In off-screen oral testimony, she states that her trip to Barcelona is a *different* repetition of an event seventeen years ago, when Manuela escaped from Lola, while pregnant with Lola's child – in that case, moving from Barcelona to Madrid.

Considering the imbrication of personal with collective history, I suggest that Manuela's journey into her personal past (her flight from Barcelona seventeen years ago) obliquely refers to the counter-cultural movement of the *Movida*, to which Almodóvar belonged, during Spain's transition from dictatorship to democracy. As is well known, before its official institutionalisation, instrumentalisation across the political spectrum and ultimately commercial neutralisation,[25] the *Movida* celebrated experimentation in artistic expression and in micro-political social and sexual subjectivities – even though Spanish society as a whole was intoxicated by the legacy of political violence and seemed about to succumb to fascism at the micro- and macro-political level.[26] Interestingly, the oblique evocation of the period of the Spanish political transition coincides with the film's allusion to the military repression and state terrorism in Argentina during the 1970s and early 1980s, which resulted in the murder or disappearance of many Argentine citizens. This history is evoked by *Todo sobre mi madre*'s use of tango music in the soundtrack, Almodóvar's casting of an Argentine actress to play an Argentine character and by explicit references in the film's dialogue to General Videla's incarceration. In this context, *Todo sobre mi madre* seems to point to the way in which the individual and shared process of enacting, abreacting, im-possibly working through or remembering the traumas of post-dictatorial societies takes place at a national, as well as trans-national level:[27] Almodóvar enables us to think about the interweaving of the traces of trauma and fragments of memory associated with the legacies of state terror in Argentina and Spain. *Todo sobre mi madre* thus explores how different layers of memories associated with political violence coexist or are juxtaposed, tangibly and intangibly, explicitly and implicitly. The juxtaposition of similar, yet different historical events enhances the connections between Spain and Latin America, but it does not eschew the ontological and historical differences between them. Rather, the film reflects on how the memory of some traumatic historical events is animated and reshaped by the transmission of memories of other similar, yet different, traumatic events. The film's complex rethinking of how the historical unconscious haunts the present may enable us to confront our own complicity and to understand our ethical and potentially political *response-ability* for the effects of the traumatic past, both Argentine and Spanish, both in our own 'post-traumatic era' and for the unpredictable future.

In addition, the film's Argentine allusions are an example of Almodóvar's concern with historical memory and his technique of inscribing references, both direct and oblique, in his films. With regard to the specific Spanish context, instead of celebrating the optimistic, radical and transgressive social, cultural and sexual attitudes associated with the multiple subjectivities of the *Movida*, *Todo sobre mi madre* revisits the period to foreground the dramatic effects that the 'excesses' of such liberating attitudes – such as drug addiction and multiple forms of sexual expression[28] – have had in the present. This points to the failure of the social and micro-political promises that were once associated with the counter-cultural movement, despite the fact that the *Movida* has largely been perceived as a frivolous, apolitical movement. But nostalgic mourning for what the *Movida* could have been or became does not necessarily lead to a feeling of failure, paralysis, resignation or loss, nor a wish to return to the *Movida*. Instead, *Todo sobre mi madre* can enable us to reflect on how we might embrace, that is, remain faithful to the event of, the *Movida*, and how we might critically evaluate the contradictions and failures and the dramatic, if not traumatic, consequences of the *Movida* – not in order to feel melancholic over the movement's obsolescence, nor to fetishise it by disavowing its contradictions, but rather to defer the *Movida*'s unfulfilled promises of what Rancière calls the 'non-anticipated' micro-political, social, cultural and sexual transformation in an incalculable future yet to come (2011).[29]

In this sequence, we can see a symbolic relationship between the spatial movement of trains and the temporal return to the past, as though the movement of the train is the condition of possibility for the triggering of the effects of Manuela's memories of dislocation, abandonment, loss, or displacement in the present. Here we can see that movement, which is at the core of the experience of displacement and dislocation, is always already constitutive of memory. In other words, memory is always already a process of displacement and dislocation, through which another temporality and spatiality emerges, virtually and materially, and is transmitted across spaces, times and subjectivities. Manuela's past becomes accessible to us not in a transparent account of the past, but by our witnessing how her experiences resonate in the present and by the film's allusion to those events in a suggestive rather than direct manner. Instead of a conventional image of a train cutting across the cinematic screen, which could be symbolically associated with phallic penetration (Acevedo-Muñoz 2004: 29), Almodóvar shows us the inside of a long, dark tunnel, drained of colour but not affective resonance. This is seen from the camera's, and thus the director's, point of view, not Manuela's. The soundtrack to this shot is 'Tajabone', sung by the Senegalese Ismaël Lô. Kathleen Vernon characterises the song as a 'mixture of "exotic" African words and familiar musical gestures [. . .] The song's musical hybridization acknowledges the mixed identities and hybrid bodies on display in the film' (2009: 55). This understanding of the song as uncanny – both strange and familiar – does not imply that the difference in question must be objectified, tamed, or mastered by relegating it to the realm of the exotic or translating it into a familiar structure within our own consciousness. Rather, it emphasises the ambivalent and 'undecidable' nature of musical sound in Almodóvar's cinema. Vernon implicitly argues that our encounter with the 'otherness' of musical sound is predicated on an asymmetry between the self and the other. Such an asymmetrical encounter with the other will always escape total comprehension, but without perpetuating the phallic rejection, destruction or forced appropriation of heterogeneous difference. Similarly, I suggest that Lô's song emphasises our affective encounter with radical alterity through the sense of hearing. The process of listening is transformed into an immersive but also alienating, an empowering but also fragilising, embodied experience.

As previously noted, the sequence that shows Esteban's death is seen from his point of view. In that scene, the spectator's point of view merges with that of the dead Esteban. In that scene and in the subjective shot from the point of view of Esteban's diary, the principle of suture – the process through which the subject disavows the mediation of the camera to identify with the point of view of a film character (Silverman 1983) – is unveiled. Martin-Márquez suggests that the subjective shot from Esteban's point of view could imply that the film's narrative is told from beyond the grave and that, from this 'particular frame, the narrative that follows centers on Manuela as ur-mother' (2004: 502). This raises a crucial issue for spectatorship theory: Martin-Márquez implicitly reflects on the way in which the spectator is the receptor as well as the producer of the text, which challenges a unidirectional mode of looking at the screen (Kuhn 2009: 7). We would then think of film spectatorship as an always already interactive experience, but one in which the spectator never completely apprehends the cinematic image.

Based on this more interactive and participatory mode of spectatorship, I suggest that the dislocating shot of the long, dark train tunnel makes us feel, however implausibly, as if our bodies were entering, or were located in the space of the film – or as if the film itself were coming out of frame and entering the spectator's space. As Tanya Leighton puts it in a different context, the film might point to 'the illusory dissolution of the boundary between the viewing subject and the projection screen, [opening] up a new psychological space for a more inclusive sensory environment' (2008: 33). Writing on the great possibilities of 3D cinema, Akira Lippit has argued that 'the appearance of 3D cinema offered an opportunity to bring film closer to that destiny [that is, to transgressing the limitations of the apparatus itself], to touch the site of the real, as Kracauer imagines, like an "umbilical cord"' (1999: 215). *Todo sobre mi madre* is, of course, not a 3D film, and it is totally circumscribed by the limitations of the apparatus, the conditions of possibility for the reproducibility of the cinematic work. But it seems as if Almodóvar wants us to feel a direct connection to the film medium itself.[30] This direct connection is always already predicated on a temporality that remains 'out-of-joint', so it would not perpetuate a metaphysics of presence. Instead, *Todo sobre mi madre* reconfigures the spectator's affections and perceptions, without reconciling the contradictions between our perceptions' failures or excesses and our consciousness of our embodied spectatorial position, which is the condition of possibility for some kind of awareness of our 'self-presence' (O'Bryan 2005: xvi).

Manuela repeatedly travels between Madrid and Barcelona, moving towards and away from the traumatic loss, bereavement, abandonments, dislocations and displacements of the past and the present. Just as Esteban's writing productively transported the traces of trauma and fragments of memory by means of linguistic symbolisation, Manuela's moving from place to place is a form of 'generative repetition', rather than a deadly, compulsive repetition. Her travelling produces the involuntary re-enactment of the traumatic event and potentially allows her to spatialise and temporalise her encrypted trauma. She can thus transport and trans-form the unbound effects of her traumatic experiences into compassionate, 'hospitable memory', without completing a process of working through. As Deleuze explains:

> We are not, therefore, healed by simple anamnesis, any more than we are made ill by amnesia. Here as elsewhere, becoming conscious counts for little. The more theatrical and dramatic operation by which healing takes place – or does not take place – has a name: transference. Now transference is still repetition: above all it is repetition. (1994 [1968]: 19)

Such an imbrication of 'hospitable memory' with the impossibility of completion is made manifest, for instance, at the end of the film, when Manuela returns to Barcelona with Esteban III. They are participating in a

Figure 2.9 Huma shares Manuela's trauma of bereaved motherhood

medical seminar about Esteban's neutralisation of the HIV virus. Manuela appears to be 'cured', to have completed the process of working through, but we are soon disabused. She goes to a theatre's dressing room to visit her friends, Agrado and Huma. The three friends happily celebrate their reunion and Esteban's success, but, as they do so, a photograph of Nina, and one of Esteban II, which has circulated among several characters throughout the film, ends up with Huma. It is as if Manuela's traumatic memories had been transferred onto her friend (see Figure 2.9).

Huma's performance of the grieving mother in Lorca's play could thus be interpreted as Huma's spatialisation and temporalisation, within her own psyche through aesthetic, creative practice, of the inscription of Manuela's traumatic loss. A static camera showing Huma on the left side of the frame and Manuela on the right cuts to a close-up showing the two photographs, with that of Esteban more prominent. As the camera tilts up, we see Manuela's reaction to the photographic image of her dead child through her reflection in the mirror. Similarly, we see that Huma is still upset by the memory of Nina – the final medium close-up emphasises her apprehensive expression. The photographs of Nina and Esteban, and the characters' memories of them, become traces (material and immaterial respectively) of traumatic experiences that will keep affecting them at a trans-subjective level beyond the individual (I will come back to this point shortly). The photographs and the haunting shadows of Esteban and Nina, which make their absences present, thus become infinite remainders of that which cannot be articulated explicitly. Their indexical and spectral presence lingers uncannily within the characters' field of vision, and in their unconscious. Such traces of trauma and fragments of memory become the condition of possibility for establishing past, current and future affective forms of feminine relationality and sociability, which are based on the shareability of lived experiences and traces imprinted within and beyond the discrete, autonomous subject.

As Joshua Chambers-Letson argues, 'it is by a kind of compensatory growing (which occurs through the sharing out of the experience of the incommunicable with the collective) that we carry our losses within us in order to survive them and build a brighter future' (2014: 14). The final scene seems to point to a conventional closure, which would fix the film's meaning by excluding the infinite possibilities of heterogeneous difference. But instead the photographs and the shadows of Esteban and Nina become signifiers of loss, remnants that return from the Real to destabilise, or perhaps expand, the symbolic order. From this perspective, the indexical presence of Esteban and Nina can be read, through the photographic medium and their spectral presence, as residues, as leftovers that will repetitively but differently return to make us com-passionately embrace the destructive, disruptive and yet potentially generative affects and scattered effects of the traces of traumas and fragments of memory, both subjective and trans-subjective – rather than refuse them. This concept of 'com-passionate memory' enables us to move away from anxiety over the re-enactment of the traumatic event's imprints. But it does not do so in the way of a reductive, therapeutic concern with the complete integration or assimilation of traumatic events into consciousness. Such therapy would resolve the pathological compulsive repetition of the unremembered trauma, would bring it to (narrative) closure and render the trauma either communicable or forgotten. Instead, 'com-passionate memory' allows a community to share residues or traces of personal and collective history, whether they are known or unknown, and to look forward to the unpredictable future. This suggests a potential transformation or reconfiguration, rather than attempting to master the traces, or relegate them to oblivion.

Before I return to the image of the tunnel, it is important to note that the first shot of it cuts to a ravishing aerial shot of Barcelona at dusk. Almodóvar portrays the city as the epitome of a world co-inhabited by plurality and difference. He imagines a Barcelona in which our ethical responsibility to coexist in a pluralistic space cannot be reduced to our calculable choices as autonomous subjects. It is impossible to sovereignly decide whom we can share a world with without destroying the right of the other to exist as such; Almodóvar's representation of Barcelona speaks in favour of a *non*-sovereign ethical relation. As for the tunnel itself, it could be read, along the lines of Kracauer's 'umbilical cord' metaphor, as an image about the cinematic medium's direct connection to the real. This reading would, then, associate the long, dark tunnel with metaphors of the body, particularly of the maternal uterus or womb.[31] But such a metaphorical association identifies the womb as an abjected phobic object. Instead, the shot is better read as enacting particular psychic processes. The repeated scene of the tunnel emphasises the porosity of the boundaries of subjectivities, spaces and times (Dasgupta 2009a: 3), so that the tunnel itself could become a signifier of the shared borderspace that Ettinger associates with our primordial shared site of human becoming. The tunnel can be read, then, as a passage that connects different temporalities, spaces and subjectivities. This underscores the film's concern with the creation of a trans-subjective, affective borderspace in which the traces of trauma and fragments of memory can be shared – without perpetuating an empathic model of relation to the pains of the irreducible other. Such a space does not replace the structures of phallocentrism and molar identities – rather, it takes place beyond them as well as beyond the logics of the molar and the phallocentric, which would police the subject's boundaries, and the psychotic dissolution of them, in the interests of clearly defined identities.[32] The alternative space suggested by the tunnel would stand against all such policing.

From this perspective, I want to suggest that *Todo sobre mi madre* represents and creates several affective relationships and borderspaces of co-emergence and co-affection, within and beyond the diegetic space of the film, thus creating and allegorising trans-subjective encounters between characters in the film as well as between the film and spectators. These spaces can be read as what Ettinger calls the 'matrixial borderspace', to which we can gain access when we fragilise ourselves in our encounters with aesthetic practices – here, of course, the film medium. This encounter would expand or open up the boundaries of the symbolic order itself, so that what was considered to be 'outside' the symbolic order turns out to be, instead, beyond the symbolic order's binary opposition of 'inside' and 'outside'. I want to establish a connection between Ettinger's groundbreaking theory and *Todo sobre mi madre*'s emphasis on trans-subjective encounters. Esteban, for instance, lives on, his heart transplanted into a Galician's body, as Allbritton discusses;[33] he narrates the story and haunts the film's characters beyond the grave, as Martin-Márquez argues; and he is resurrected as Esteban III. As I argued above, we have our own affective encounter with the face of the *figurant*, the marginalised peoples of the film. Sister Rosa carries the traces of Lola's contaminated body in her own.[34] And, as I explained above, Huma registers the traces of Manuela's traumatic experience of bereaved motherhood. A porous intersection between Ettinger's theory and Almodóvar's cinematic practice helps us to explore how *Todo sobre mi madre* points to the productive tensions and interconnections between queer theory's challenge to phallocentric and Oedipal logics on the one hand, and Ettinger's emphasis on the specificity of feminine difference beyond concepts of the feminine as a socially constructed gender or an essential identity based on biological difference.

Ettinger's Theory of the Matrixial Borderspace

In order to better understand how *Todo sobre mi madre* could point to a re-articulation of feminine subjectivity that would be both beside and beyond the patriarchal, heteronormative psychic and ideological framework of the social and symbolic order, I will here engage further with Ettinger's theory. Phallocentric culture has historically excluded, trivialised or misunderstood the feminine. It often reduces the latter, as Pollock suggests, to a naturalised, essential identity, based on biological difference (2009a: 12). The feminine is, thus, the constitutive outside of the phallocentric symbolic order. Ettinger does not simply reverse this formulation. She connects the philosophy of art, her own artistic practice, and psychoanalytic theory, with her personal and shared traumatic experience of the Shoah and feminine difference. She then undoes psychoanalysis from within. Psychoanalysis focuses on subjectivity and intersubjectivity; Ettinger, however, shifts that focus to 'subjectivity as encounter' or trans-subjectivity. In order to think about this more effectively, Ettinger uses a complex alternative language impregnated by neologisms. What she calls psychic borderspaces and trans-subjective, affective transactions relate back to prenatal experiences between the 'becoming-mother' and the 'becoming-infant', and are associated with the realm of the feminine 'm/Other'. But, as Pollock informs us, Ettinger's psychoanalytic theories do not perpetuate 'a theory of essences and origins'. Instead, they propose 'potentialities of event-encounters that, while conditioned by the corpo-Real event, already resonate at the level of human subjectivity' (2006: 16). Ettinger, that is, understands the feminine in human subjectivity as beyond the binary opposition that is asserted within the phallocentric symbolic order. The feminine becomes, in her thought, a supplementary signifier, which enables us to think of the feminine from within the feminine, without foreclosing the symbolic order. The space of co-affection can be re-animated retrospectively, and be symbolically articulated, once the affecting traces of the psychic experiences in the matrixial are phantasised and thought (Pollock 2013b: 169). Ettinger thinks what was previously unthought in the phallocentric psychoanalyses of Freud and Lacan. For them, subjectivity was predicated on the cut from the archaic m/Other (as I mentioned in Chapter 1, a focus on pre-Oedipal plenitude still emphasises a language of objects haunted by their relationship to the cut of castration, for Freud, or to the phallic signifier, for Lacan).[35] Ettinger also moves away from Kristeva's revision of Freud. Kristeva emphasised the maternal body, but still conceived it as an object that the child needs to abject in order to constitute her/his subjectivity as a discrete entity. Kristeva pays attention to the link between the non-visible maternal body and the visible linguistic sign, but her emphasis on the maternal body as an object is still haunted by its relation to the dominant phallic signifier. The latter itself stands for lack, and it is from the place of the phallocentric symbolic order that we can think of lack or impossible plenitude (impossible, because it can only take place as a hallucination in the Real).

For Ettinger, to the contrary, we must think the feminine in human subjectivity from within the feminine, that which is excluded from psychoanalysis's main Oedipal narrative of the constitution of our sexually differentiated subjectivity. We must, that is, think the feminine from within the feminine, from within that which is foreclosed in the phallocentric symbolic order of linguistic signification. As Butler explains: 'the entrance into language comes at a price: the norms that govern the inception of the speaking subject differentiate the subject from the unspeakable, that is, produce an unspeakability as the condition of subject formation' (1997: 135). Ettinger moves beyond the logic of identity, however, not associating the feminine with a particular gender or space of non-identity, nor with the 'unspeakable'. Such an approach would relegate femininity to the realm of the psychotic and leave femininity without a signifier in the Real (Pollock 2010: 83). Instead, Ettinger associates the feminine with a 'subjectivising stratum', a supplementary psychic dimension. This dimension relates to female corpo-Reality; it enables the relation between 'I' and 'non-I' to be rethought beyond and beside Lacan's notion of the phallus.

In her reading of Lacan, Ettinger argues that, for Lacan, the phallus is the original and master signifier. It is the condition of possibility for desire, it is constitutive of subjectivity, and it is the condition of possibility for entering the social and symbolic order. This order is predicated on a binary opposition between the masculine and the feminine, in which the feminine becomes the negative term of a dialectic based on the phallus's phantasmatic absence (lack) or presence. In her foreword to Ettinger's first monograph in English, Butler writes:

> I would even claim that, in her view [Ettinger's], it is not possible to say 'I am femi-
> nine' or 'You are feminine'; the very ontological designations 'I am' and 'you are'
> postdate the space of the matrixial. The matrixial is what we guard against when we
> shore up the claims of identity, when we presume that to recognize each other is to
> know, to name, to distinguish according to the logic of identity. (2006: x–xi)

From this perspective, a supplementary, non-psychotic, sub-symbolic sphere or dimension of the feminine continuously affects the meaning, and expands the boundaries, of the phallocentric symbolic order. This is not the sphere of undifferentiated subjectivity (associated with pre-Oedipality, as I explained in Chapter 1) or of differentiated subjectivity (associated with Oedipality), but a third form, what Ettinger calls 'matrixial subjectivity'. Ettinger moves away from a psychoanalytic language of objects, subjects, lack, presence and repression, and towards one based on threads, strings, partiality, plurality and shareability, in which subjectivity can be best described as an encounter/event between the 'I' and the 'non-I' at shared borderspaces. Instead of endless multiplicity, Ettinger argues that the matrixial borderspace occurs in a cluster of several partial subjects, which are neither in a symbiotic relationship, nor completely separated, neither fully known to each other, nor completely un-cognised. One partial subject neither assimilates, nor fully rejects the other. The partial subjects, Ettinger argues, can best be thought of as borderlinking, becoming vulnerable and fragile in their encounter/event (Ettinger 1996); in the matrixial borderspace '[w]e thus metabolize mental imprints and traces for one another in each matrixial web whose psychic grains, virtual and affective strings and unconscious threads participate in other matrixial webs and transform them by borderlinking in metramorphosis' (2005: 705).

In some ways, Ettinger's emphasis on the effects of another's threads upon one and the effects of one's threads upon the other resonates with the Spinozist and Deleuzean conception of the body as having the potential to affect (affect here does not relate to psychic interiority) and be affected by other bodies. Paola Marrati has read *Todo sobre mi madre* as a cinematic visualisation of Spinoza's and Deleuze's reflections on the unpredictable *puissance* of the body in its encounters with other bodies. She argues that 'the whole universe is like a spider's web in which all threads are somehow related, and what we call individuals are the connections among threads, while, of course, the threads can always be arranged differently' (2006: 315). Although Ettinger works from within psychoanalysis, rather than in a materialist philosophy as in Deleuze, she does conceive the matrixial borderspace as producing a reorganisation in the field shared by the 'I' and the 'non-I'. It transforms limits into thresholds to be transgressed. This, added to the rejection of the common conception of subjectivity as circumscribed by an individual body (Ettinger 1992: 201), provides ethical and politically potential resources for transformation in these com-passionate trans-subjective encounters/events. Pollock argues that the matrix supplements the capacities of phallic logic and 'blunts its ter-rible, paranoid violence by theorizing the psychic resources in hospitality/ compassion for ethical dispositions and political responsibility in the face of violence with real historical conditions but also with imaginary, phantasmatic structurations' (2013b: 189). Such com-passionate trans-subjective encounters with others are predicated on the 'impossibility of not sharing', in co-emergence and co-fading, traces of events of the other that relate to other traces in the 'I', or traces of events of the 'I' that relate to other traces in the other.

In the light of Ettinger's redefinition of 'subjectivity as encounter', we may think of *Todo sobre mi madre* as proposing a similar notion of feminine subjectivity, articulated beyond and beside either a subjectivity founded on the cut of castration (as in Freud and Lacan), or a regression to the pre-Oedipal, archaic psychic stage (Kristeva).[36] Ettinger's emphasis on the specificity of the feminine, and its contribution to human subjectiv-ity, could seem to be antithetical to the discourses within queer theory that I deployed in this chapter. But, as I explained above, queer theory's emphasis on gender performativity advocates a politics of identity beyond gender essentialism, and Ettinger's focus on matrixiality similarly moves beyond a politics of naturalised identity. Her rethinking of the feminine from within the feminine is 'a psychic *event-encounter* understood through such concepts as borderspace, borderlinking' (Pollock 2006: 19, emphasis in original). So, as Dasgupta argues, matrixial psychoanalysis and queer theory 'share a reformulation of subjectivity beyond an enclosed, essen-tialized subject, and suggest a breaking of the boundaries which have circumscribed theories of the subject based primarily on a focus on the phallus and lack' (2009a: 1). From this perspective, if we move beyond the Freudian Oedipal psychoanalytic model, Lacanian phallocentrism and Kristeva's emphasis on pre-Oedipality, we can associate Almodóvar's film with a more complex articulation of the feminine in human subjectivity. This articulation, understood through Ettinger's matrixial paradigm, can be embraced by non-reified queer subjects.

Com-passionate Hospitality

I argue, in the context of Ettinger's thought, that *Todo sobre mi madre*'s emphasis on feminine difference within the feminine is inextricably linked to the com-passionate acts and maternal practices that the characters, whether women or transgendered subjects, adopt, and which form the core of their trans-subjective relationships. Despite Almodóvar's long association with queer politics, he has been extensively criticised for representing women as exaggeratedly emotional, to the point of being hysterical or overly sexual. He seems, in these representations, to be setting himself up as Pygmalion. Is the filmmaker, whether consciously or unconsciously, reinserting motherhood into a patriarchal, heteronormative ideological framework, in which women's virtue is associated with a self-abnegating maternity that in some ways reproduces the traditional National Catholic gender politics advocated by Francoism?[37] Does *Todo sobre mi madre*'s emphasis on maternity perpetuate patriarchal, heteronormative notions of kinship based on biological reproduction and the Oedipal nuclear family, in which the child is simply 'a dense site for the transfer and reproduction of culture' (Butler 2002: 22)?[38]

One simple answer to these questions is to point out that the film presents a wide range of embraces, literally and figuratively maternal, as well as non-maternal embraces: the lesbian Nina ends up in a heterosexual relationship with a biological child and returns to her own village; Manuela raises Esteban II by herself; we see Lola, Esteban III's (female) biological father, cradling the baby after Manuela has been able to feel com-passion towards him; Manuela becomes Esteban III's adoptive mother; she also cares for Sister Rosa, as an adoptive sister; Agrado cares for an actress, Huma; Huma embraces a dead, non-biological child in the form of Esteban II's photograph; Sister Rosa helps the marginalised prostitutes, transgendered subjects and African immigrants. Given this range of com-passionate embraces of the irreducible other, I argue that the film does not simply imagine com-passionate hospitality as a natural or essential female attribute within a patriarchal and heteronormative ideological framework. Rather, com-passionate hospitality is the manifestation of an ethical and potentially political gesture associated with the psychic ability to yearn to respond to the call of the irreducible other (Pollock 2013b: 16). This 'cohabitation without limits', to use Smith's term, is articulated beyond heteronormative and patriarchal conceptions of the family, not in opposition to them or within them, so com-passionate hospitality, associated with the feminine matrixial sphere, can take place beyond the mother and child relationship within and outside the immediate family. The feminine relationality in the film shows how our experience of affective transactions during bodily and psychic encounters with the m/Other can be a psychic resource, fostering com-passionate relations with the irreducible others with whom we coexist and share the world. Ettinger herself has written of matrixial relationships beyond the mother and child, for instance, in her reinterpretation of the story of Isaac and Abraham, where we see a matrixial relation between father and son: '*Isaac was compassionate toward his father, because, as Infant, he had already been compassionate toward his mother, apprehending her compassionate hospitality uncognizingly, and emotionally feel-knowing the trauma he had been to her in her bringing him to life*' (2006b: 124, emphasis in original). So, far from perpetuating heteronormative kinship relations, *Todo sobre mi madre*'s emphasis on the association of com-passionate hospitality with the matrixial borderspace underscores the ethical and political potential of one's relation to radical alterity, without understanding, recognising or empathising with the other's irreducible specificity (Hand 1996: 13). In other words, Almodóvar's emphasis on matrixiality, which relates to our prenatal relations, enables us to think of the unconscious resources that we mobilise in order to be able to respond to the ethical call of the other. Of course, as I explained in the Introduction, such an ethical response always partakes of the undecidability of the concept of responsibility. But Ettinger helps us to pay attention to the feminine's contribution to human subjectivity and to the unconscious's contribution to these complex ethical and philosophical concepts in the social and political field.

Todo sobre mi madre thus proposes that maternity can be associated with a structure of thought (compare Pollock 2007). As I explained in Chapter 1, it can be associated with an ethics of 'embodied care', or an openness to the ethical and potentially political gesture that is adopted by women and transgendered subjects in the film. This gesture involves the fragilisation of our individual psychic boundaries, a fragilisation that is the, or at least a, condition of possibility for creating a social, psychic and affective space in which the other can become – even if, as with Manuela's son or Sister Rosa, there is a risk that the self or the other will not be able to go on living.[39] As Smith puts it, 'this is a kind of open heart cinema in which the way we touch one another is shown to have immediate and mortal effects' (2014:167). Martin-Márquez forcefully argues that the film 'exemplifies an "ethics of care", to remind us that compassionate solicitude is a universally human need, demanding a universally human response' (2004: 497). For Martin-Márquez, the apparent self-sacrifice underpinning this 'ethics of care', which could perpetuate a 'masochistic suffering underlying traditionally-defined practices of maternal benevolence', can 'cycle back to serve self-interests' (2004: 497); she thereby detects an emancipatory potential at the core of this 'ethics of care'. I would like to add to Martin-Márquez's argument that this structure of thought – a maternity that can be adopted by human beings regardless of gendered and sexual subjectivity – is not based on the autonomous subject's egoistic calculations in the service of a narcissistic desire to claim back what has been given away (Pollock 2007). Therefore, a com-passionate gesture – associated with a maternity beyond biological, heterosexual reproduction and the Oedipal nuclear family – is a movement without return, beyond an economy of exchange, in which the irreducible other is allowed to become beyond and beside our non-sovereign self.

In a conversation between Ettinger and Lévinas about the feminine in his philosophical work, Lévinas clarified that he does not associate the feminine exclusively with death (he regrets the fact that others had misunderstood his philosophical notion of the feminine). His thought is rather that, since there will always be the possibility that a woman will die while giving birth, the feminine is associated with the possibility of thinking about life without 'me'. Hence, Lévinas associates the alterity of the feminine not with death, but with the future yet to come:

> The feminine is the future. The feminine in its feminine phase, in its feminine form certainly may die in bringing life into the world, but – how can I say it to you? – it is not 'dying'; for me, the 'dying' of a woman is certainly unacceptable. I am speaking about the possibility of conceiving that there is meaning without me. I think that the heart of the heart, the deepest of the feminine, is dying in giving life, in bringing life into the world. I am not emphasizing *dying* but, on the contrary, *future*. (Ettinger and Lévinas 2006: 141, emphasis in original)

It is important to re-emphasise this point. The openness to com-passionate hospitality does depend on self-fragilisation as the condition of possibility for remaining trans-connected to, without fusing with or assimilating, the Other into the self. However, it is neither exclusively associated with the biological mother, nor is it fully inserted into an economy of sacrificial disappearance. Ettinger proposes that 'this alterity does not arise from the absolute Other' in the matrixial feminine, 'but from borderlinking with the Other' (2006a: 85). In other words, according to Ettinger, misericord is an emotion associated with the womb for Lévinas. So it does indeed relate hospitality to the alterity of the feminine. The association of hospitality with the infinitely Other and the absolutely future in Lévinas implies that the I's vulnerable proximity to the Other is traumatic, because it is predicated on the passivity and potential self-sacrifice of the feminine-maternal (Ettinger 2006b: 101). For Ettinger, the matrixial psychic sphere is predicated on partiality and in-betweeness. In this sphere, then, compassionate hospitality, which partakes of a non-phallic Eros, is associated less with sacrifice and death than with grace and solace (2006b: 101). Ettinger argues that, in Lévinas, 'womb-misericordiality can't stand for pregnancy where the process of life-giving, the *living* of the m/Other and a *living-with-in and beside* must be articulated. In my matrixial perspective, womb-misericordiality as pregnancy-emotion stands for *com-passionate hospitality in living-inter-with-in the almost Other*' (2006b: 103, emphasis in original). Finally, maternal-matrixial-com-passionate-hospitality does not perpetuate a concept of sexuality reduced to reproduction, even if such hospitality envisions a culture of life, rather than of death, in the unpredictable future.[40] If one can still refer to an emancipatory potential underpinning one's compassionate responsibility for the other, this resides less in its serving our self-interests or calculable choices than in our non-sacrificial com-passionate relationality, which does not reify our own individual existence, but leads us to become more aware of our co-human subjectivity.

The association of maternal relationality with the matrixial borderspace here helps us to think about how unremembered events, which paradoxically cannot be relegated to oblivion, are transmitted at the trans-subjective level. Ettinger argues that, for Abraham and Torok, the concept of the crypt implies an unremembered loss that remains inaccessible to the subject: '[a]s long as the crypt does not collapse, there will be neither melancholy nor a process of mourning: no memory and no forgetting' (2006a: 164). To put it differently, for Abraham and Torok, the subject imprints in his own psyche the traumas of the m/Other, which are placed in a crypt in the unconscious. A phantom inhabits this crypt, but the subject 'has no relation to its secretly crypted phantom that does, however, haunt the transference and countertransference psychoanalytical relations and all other relationships of love' (cited in Pollock 2013a: 20). Yet, Ettinger continues, Abraham and Torok's notion of the crypt, despite pointing to trans-subjective transmission, remains circumscribed by the boundaries of a discrete subject. Through her concept of 'transcryptum', Ettinger emphasises the *transcription* of one's imprints of trauma for the possibility of being remembered by others, and the *transcription* of others' imprints of trauma for the possibility of being remembered by one (Ettinger 2006a). Hence, *Todo sobre mi madre*'s emphasis on the trans-subjective matrixial borderspace, which is inextricably linked to maternal relationality, opens 'the possibilities of passages through which the blocked, repressed and repeating voids are transformed at a borderspace where translation may occur' (Pollock 2013a: 343).

I want to end this second chapter by proposing that we think of *Todo sobre mi madre* in terms of the work it performs in producing a particular kind of spectator. That is, the film invites the spectator to become a 'queer (m)other', through the affective encounter with, and interpretation of, the film. As I have tried to demonstrate in my description of the film's aesthetics and thematics, and of the effects that it produces in our bodies and psyches, the film could be interpreted as a trans-subjective process that produces the subject, both the filmmaker and the spectator, in the feminine (De Zeguer 1996: 23) – rather than as a text. The production of the subject in the feminine is conceived beyond the dialectical mode of thinking and the logic of identity associated with patriarchy and phallocentrism.[41] The subject in the feminine, as opposed to the feminine subject, is linked to the matrixial gaze, which is 'uncleft yet unfused with the subject or the Other' (Ettinger 2006a: 124). The matrixial gaze coexists with the paranoid gaze (theorised by Lacan), and contributes to the dissipation of the destructive elements of Lacan's persecutory gaze: 'the matrixial gaze doesn't "replace" the phallic gaze but aids in its moving aside from its destructive aspects, a moving which is however a lifelong unending process' (Ettinger 2006b: 111). If the matrixial sphere transgresses the limits of the symbolic order via the aesthetic (cinematic) practice, our trans-subjective encounter with *Todo sobre mi madre* gives us access to the 'matrixial gaze', because, instead of reacting with anxiety or aggression towards the Other, we, willingly or not, fragilise ourselves. This fragilisation is the condition of possibility for cross-inscribing and cross-imprinting the un-known and un-cognised traces of trauma and fragments of experience that are transmitted by irreducible, partial 'Is' and 'non-Is', who are joined in separation and separated in proximity through borderlinking. This ethical, aesthetic and potentially political process of re-accessing the 'matrixial gaze' through the cinematic medium does not imply a rhetoric of redemption, despite the film's emphasis on reconciliation and resurrection. This psychic process can also be traumatising, a negative psychic resource. Ettinger explains:

> The desire to join-in-difference and differentiate-in-co-emerging with the Other does not promise peace and harmony, because joining is first of all a joining with-in the other's trauma that echoes back to my archaic traumas: joining the other matrixially is always joining the m/Other and risking mental fragmentation and vulnerability. A matrixial gaze gives rise to its own desire, which can generate dangerous encounters. (2006a: 147)

Re-accessing the 'matrixial gaze' via the cinematic medium enables us to associate *Todo sobre mi madre* with a theoretical text. Our affective and critical engagement with the film shifts from detached textual analysis to a more physical and more affective exchange with its materiality, thereby enhancing our critical practices.[42] It is from this perspective that I see the spectator becoming a 'queer (m)other', beyond patriarchal and heteronormative conceptions of maternity. The re-conceptualisation of maternity within the notion of becoming a 'queer (m)other' is based on an asymmetry between the 'I' and the irreducible alterity, which can never be fully comprehended or accessed. That alterity evokes one's com-passionate hospitality and responsibility for the irreducible other, in what Pollock calls her/his radical alterity and our own alterity (2009a: 10). Such an ethical, aesthetic and potentially political process of becoming a 'queer (m)other' makes us think of cinema not as a reflection of external reality or of an external referent, but as a means of producing theory itself. Almodóvar's film foregrounds what Bal identifies as both theoretical thinking and the cinematic articulation of that thinking (Bal 1999: 104). From this perspective, through the cinematic medium, individual and collective traces of trauma and fragments of memory are transmitted and com-passionately received at a trans-subjective level as the condition of possibility for trans-formation. Butler explains:

> These become the traces of the other that we retrace, we reregister, to which another form is given. There is a transmutation of trauma that is not the same as its full and knowing articulation. It is a rare event, nearly impossible. It is relived, repeated, as trauma, not precisely 'worked through' in the repetition but nevertheless animated in a new way. (2006: xi)

To sum up, *Todo sobre mi madre*'s emphasis on becoming (an)other, trans-subjective encounters/events, and com-passionate hospitality allows for the possibility of thinking queer/feminine relationality and queer/feminine 'being-in-the-world' in a way that would reverse Tennessee Williams' famous sentence: 'I have always depended on the kindness of strangers' – which is repeated throughout the film during and after the staging of *A Streetcar Named Desire*. On several occasions, Agrado admits that her pseudonym comes from her having attempted, throughout her entire life, to offer kindness and com-passion to others by giving them pleasure and caring for them, even those who were physically violent towards her, as we see when Manuela re-encounters Agrado on the outskirts of Barcelona. Agrado's admission encapsulates the ethical mode of relation underpinning Almodóvar's film. In other words, rather than us depending *on* strangers, our conditions of existence depend on our *com-passionate hospitality to* an irreducible stranger, so that she or he can become beyond and beside us. Finally, just as Huma inscribes and imprints in her partial 'I' the traumas and events of a 'non-I' (Manuela), *Todo sobre mi madre* enables us to think of film as an aesthetic process through which we can com-passionately *wit(h)ness* the irreducible other. We can, perhaps, transport and trans-form the irreducible other's traces of trauma and fragments of memory; can be borderlinked with the other without fusing with, rejecting or assimilating the other in fragilising, yet ethical and potentially political trans-subjective encounters/events. This book now turns to a further reflection on the 'im-possibility of not-sharing' the irreducible other's subjective and shared traumas in *La mala educación*. In the next chapter, I continue my exploration of how Almodóvar's cinema allows us to propose a redefinition of the debates about historical memory from a queer/feminist psychoanalytic perspective.

CHAPTER 3

Im-Possibility of Not-Writing Otherwise:
La mala educación

The third chapter of this book continues to explore how Almodóvar's cinema can function as a mode of witnessing and re-enacting traces of the traumatic past, as well as mediating between individual and shared experiences, through a complex relationship between subjectivity, trauma, memory and the ethical relation between film and the spectator. I am particularly interested in *La mala educación*'s conception of the film medium as a generator of what Allison Landsberg calls 'prosthetic memory' (2004). In line with the previous chapter's arguments about 'the im-possibility of not-sharing' the irreducible other's traces of trauma and fragments of memory, the association of Almodóvar's film with 'prosthetic memory' points to the fragmentary embodiment of traumatic experiences and memories by, and displacement of them onto, those who may not have experienced them. This involves the relating of the self to the bodies and memories of others who are affected by the pains of history – here, in particular, sexual violence and abuse, and political repression during the Franco regime. As I explained in the Introduction, during Spain's political transition to democracy, the processes of mourning, abreaction and healing were forestalled. This had significant effects on the Spanish people's subjectivities and bodies.

I will mainly focus on the way Almodóvar emphasises corporeality in order to reflect on how fragments of memory and traces of trauma affect the present. In other words, *La mala educación* asks us to think of the body as a force that conditions the fragments of subjective and shared memory and history.[1] The film explores how the subject may engage with fragments of subjective memory, associated here with the violence and abuse inflicted on Ignacio's body and subjectivity.[2] On a parallel plane, subjective memory is aligned with collective memory and history, which the film associates with the aggression and repression that was inflicted on the Spanish national body and psyche by the Franco regime for much of its existence. We can see, then, that the film will emphasise the imbrication of subjective and cultural traumas. I will also discuss, although briefly, the performativity of identity,[3] particularly in relation to the elusive character of Ángel/Juan/Ignacio/Zahara. But the chapter's main focus is not on the representation of bodies or the logic of identity.

To some degree, my interpretation of Almodóvar's film may suggest an 'allegorical reading', in which individual traumatic experiences and memories – here related mainly to death, loss or sexual abuse at the hands of representatives of the Catholic Church – can be displaced onto the collective history of the nation, which was so scarred by the Franco regime's political repression.[4] D'Lugo points out that *La mala educación* can be interpreted as a 'self-conscious acknowledgement of where [Almodóvar] was in 1980 and how, through the evolution of a style and a conception of filmmaking, he has moved to a critique of his own past and the culture out of which his cinema has taken shape' (2009: 383). I agree that the film is highly autobiographical, although it also problematises the concept of autobiography. I also agree with D'Lugo that its allusions to historical context are very important, particularly in relation to the Franco regime of the 1960s and to 1977 and 1980, both important years for the Spanish transition from dictatorship to democracy. Nonetheless, in this chapter I aim to discuss primarily cinema's mimetic properties, as well as how the film articulates a self-reflexive discourse about cinema's mediation of the traces of past traumatic experiences, which allows for a witnessing and re-enacting of those fragments of memory that may escape linguistic symbolisation. D'Lugo explains that: 'for a film that represents Almodóvar's first "historical narrative", in which all action is set in the clearly labelled "historical" past, historical representation itself seems under continual siege by the film's [emphasis on the] enunciative apparatus' (2006: 120). D'Lugo's emphasis on the enunciative apparatus's significance does not undermine the film's historiographical function. Following his line of thought, I argue that *La mala educación* unfolds the traces of the characters' traumatic experiences, in particular Ignacio's, as well as the traces of these particular dramatic moments in Spanish history. It does this not by accurately reconstructing the past, but by transmitting, in a complex way, these traumatic experiences, so that they impinge on our mind and body. *La mala educación* thus problematises the understanding of the archive as the exclusionary transmitter of the historical past.[5]

I interpret the film, then, from a visceral, bodily encounter involving a physical response to the work as well as an interpretive engagement with its textuality and materiality.[6] I focus particularly on three sequences in the film: the opening credits; Zahara's performance; and the scene in which Enrique and Ignacio watch Mario Camus's film *Esa mujer* (*That Woman*,

1969). These sequences epitomise Almodóvar's concern with the inscription and transmission of the fragments of memory and traces of past traumatic experiences in this film. The sequences reverberate, permutate and proliferate in echoes throughout the film, allegorically encapsulating the spectator's own affective and interpretive engagement with the film's aesthetics, ethics and politics. My interpretation emphasises how the spectator's contingent aesthetic experience of *La mala educación* becomes a requirement for the completion of the film's meaning.

'Torn Screens'/Shattered Subjectivities

A black screen, appearing as a monochromatic black surface, contains the letters of Almodóvar's production company: *El Deseo*. This is followed by a series of frames showing black screens, each one containing the name of an institution that contributed to the financing of the film. These frames bring to our notice the intermittent, opaque blackness, those intervals that are the condition of possibility for the production and perception of cinematic images, the continuum of film.[7] Then, a different black frame fills the screen. This surface has been scratched, as though children had engraved on it an infinite number of graffiti faces, sexual organs and texts; they may remind us of the images drawn on the walls and doors of public bathrooms, or on blackboards in school classrooms, as if such anonymous, subversive or illegal acts of vandalism, such violent destructions of the surface, had become the only way of revealing or exorcising our political views, sexual fantasies or anxieties. The film's soundtrack takes a dark and sombre tone. It evokes, aesthetically and subjectively, the enthralling riddle, the mystery underpinning the film, which, Vernon suggests, is associated with 'moral and psychic ambiguity' (2009: 54). The soundtrack's articulation of suspense may imply that the film's meaning resides in the interstices of language and vision, a suggestion that is further enhanced by the film's complex layering of different diegetic levels (Kuhn 2009: 273).

A vertical white strip on the scratched surface disrupts and obstructs our vision of the images scratched onto the screen, further emphasising the dispersions and obliterations of the field of representation. We see the director's name. His signature is visible between the cracks and fissures of the torn surface. We can understand the presence of the filmmaker's signature here in the light of Nicholas Roy's engagement with Derrida's reflection on the signature in general, 'in the direction of the impossibility of the signature – in other words, towards a recognition of the *negative* force of this "almost", the necessarily *residual* undecidability of every signature-event' (1995: 96, emphasis in original). Derrida argues that the relationship between the signature and the text undermines the dichotomy between the inside and the outside. He explains that: 'In the form of the whole name, the inscription of the signature plays strangely with the frame, with the border of the text, sometimes inside, sometimes outside' (1984: 120). Almodóvar's cinematic signature, although a small part of it, takes hold of the cinematic text. As I will discuss shortly, this reflects a productive tension between the cinematic text and the author's signature.

The next frame shows fragmented photographs formed into a collage crucifix. Almodóvar was nurtured in a culture profoundly influenced by Catholicism; Daniel Boyarin argues that the irreconcilability of sexuality and spiritual practices in Christianity (with its emphasis on the dichotomy between the body and spirit) contributed to the stigmatisation of rabbinical hermeneutic practices. Rabbinical Jews emphasised the importance of sexuality and reproduction as part of our corporeal existence: '[R]abinnic Judaism invested significance in the body which in the other formations was invested in the soul. That is, for rabbinic Jews, the human being was defined as a body – animated, to be sure, by a soul – while for Hellenistic Jews [. . .] and [. . .] Christians [. . .], the essence of a human being is a soul housed in a body' (1993: 5).[8] Hence, for Boyarin, Judaism's emphasis on the body allows us to recognise the existence of the human subject as being fundamentally grounded in corporeality (1993: 29). Similarly, Elizabeth Grosz draws on Spinoza's anti-Cartesian monism to suggest that '[t]he mind is the idea of the body to the exact degree that the body is an extension of the mind' (1994: 12). Despite these arguments, however, the juxtaposition of religion and sexuality that Boyarin sees in rabbinical Judaism is made manifest in the film's opening credits. This will become a central theme in *La mala educación*. It is inherent in the film's *mise-en-scène*.

The graphic design pattern that I have just described is repeated differently throughout the opening credits. Each frame consists of red, black or white graphics, and looks like a poster made of disjointed, fragmented parts, which cannot be sutured. The text peels away the different layers of the visual *leitmotif*, reminding us of the painful process of peeling away or excavating the subjective and shared traces of traumatic experiences and fragments of memories. The peeling away reveals a mosaic of images and texts that evoke different objects of desire: male bodies; narcissistic egos; female divas or retro-style images of femininity; religious symbols such as crucifixes; images evoking the use of drugs, such as syringes; and allegorical images of death itself, such as skulls, which – according to the Benjaminian notion of allegory – can represent catastrophic history (I will come back to this point shortly).[9] As Adam Lowenstein explains, 'the death's head, that elusive sign of the allegorical representation of history, may be found where we least expect it – as the past erupts in the present, in the flicker of a cinematic image, in a disorienting turn of phrase' (2003: 76). Smith has noted that the film's 'seedy hotel rooms are transformed by rich red drapes', and its 'squalid apartments [are] enlivened by eccentric mosaics' (2004b: 17). The opening credits are thus a visual and tactile 'mosaic' made of divergent, fragmentary registers. On this mosaic, testimonies and premonitions resurface – whether intelligible or unintelligible, visible or invisible, tangible or intangible, they indicate the pleasure and pain of those spectral and material memories and past traumatic experiences that will be re-enacted or im-possibly worked through in the film. The non-diegetic space into which the opening credits are inserted can be associated with the present time. It inscribes shards of individual or collective traumatic experiences and memories, which intrude in the present through the repeated mosaics, whether thick or thin. They emphasise Almodóvar's concern with the cinematic technology's ethical and political function to mediate the spectral and material past, the present and undetermined future.

The credit sequence ends with Almodóvar's name once again appearing on the screen. Through the destruction of the field of representation, that is, the condition of possibility for cinematic 'writing', Almodóvar imprints or inscribes his cinematic signature, and so reclaims his text. But, rather than making the director fully present in the film, Almodóvar's efforts to relate this scattered text back to his signature could have the effect of making his absent presence a kind of present absence. It would thus problematise the dialectical relationship between presence and absence, and allow for the possibility of the cinematic text escaping the signature, which would otherwise imprison and entomb the text itself.[10]

Marsh identifies the signature less as the presence of the author than as a trace that points to the author's elusive absence (2013). His theory foregrounds Derrida's association of the signature with 'spacing', which implies temporal deferrals, spatial displacements, disseminations and differentiations between temporalities and spatialities, or disruptions of the structures of identity construction. Derrida explains:

By definition, a written signature implies the actual or empirical nonpresence of the signer. But, it will be said, it also marks and retains his having-been present in a past now, which will remain a future now, and therefore in a now in general, in the transcendental form of nowness (*maintenance*). This general *maintenance* is somehow inscribed, stapled to present punctuality, always evident and always singular, in the form of the signature. This is the enigmatic originality of every paraph. For the attachment to the source to occur, the absolute singularity of an event of the signature and of a form of the signature must be retained: the pure reproducibility of a pure event. (1982: 328, emphasis in original)

I suggest that, if the signature is a reality that exists outside the text, the latter does become emancipated, albeit ambiguously, from the signature that attempts to entomb and cover it. And if the signature only exists within the text – if it is a fragment or part of the text – the signature cannot link the text to a centre, an ultimate signified, the author's intention or the author as the origin of the text (Todd 1986). More interestingly, the tension established here between the presence and absence of the subjectivity of the filmmaker is consistent with the textual process of elusive presences and present absences, the impression and inscription of the traces of writing and the erasure of such traces that underpin the *mise-en-scène* and thematics of *La mala educación*. Derrida associates Freud's conception of the psychical apparatus with the inscription of a system of writing, and argues that the inscription of traces is predicated on their erasure. The impression of those traces is already based on the iteration and erasure of such traces, and on their being readable and unreadable (1972: 112–13). Following Derrida, I suggest that Almodóvar's film points to such an ambivalent relation or double logic at the core of the production of cinematic 'writing'. The film's thematic, then, is 'the im-possibility of not-writing otherwise'.

The opening credits dissolve into a poster of a film 'written and directed by Enrique Goded', which hangs on Goded's production office – a repetition that insists on and undermines the signature's relating of the cinematic text back to an origin and the way it takes the place of the absent author in an undetermined future. In effect, the non-diegetic space of the credits collapses into the diegetic space of the film, suspending the distance between the characters' fictional time (the diegetic space of the film) and the spectator's 'real' time as they view the film (the non-diegetic space of the credits). This juxtaposition of temporalities could also be interpreted as an example of the heterogeneity and discontinuity of time in the film. We listen to a voice-over narrative and, as the camera pulls back and pans to screen left, we realise that the voice is that of the filmmaker, Enrique Goded, in his production office. He is reading aloud a series of chilling stories published in a 1980 newspaper – presumably based on real events. Goded is trying to find inspiration for his next fiction film (see Figure 3.1). This is just one case of the film's blurring the distinction between fiction and reality or between writing and reading. The realm of reality and that of fiction, or the process of reading and that of writing, constantly overlap in *La mala educación*. This foregrounds the dialectical tension between repetition of the Same and the interruption of singular difference – which articulates that which has not yet been articulated, or that which may be articulated in an undetermined future, and underpins the act of creative expression.

Figure 3.1 Enrique Goded reads aloud a series of chilling stories published
in a newspaper

The 'torn frames' of the credits both resonate and find disjunctions
throughout the film. For instance, Goded's future film is based on Ignacio's
'auto-fictional' story *La visita* (*The Visit*); Ignacio was Goded's lover when
they were at a religious boarding school together in the 1960s.[11] D'Lugo
rightly notes that Goded's visualisation of the film is also a 'flashback to a
fictionalized past that, ironically, is also the projection into the future of
Enrique's next film' (2009: 359). A shot of Enrique reading the manuscript
dissolves into an objective shot of Cine Olympo, an abandoned cinema
in the province of Valencia, as if the fragments of memories are already
being juxtaposed with the repertoire of cinematic images that Goded
has precariously stored in his mental archive. Such juxtapositions self-
reflexively articulate the way that, in this film, 'memories of earlier movies
are frequently more important than historical events' (Kinder 2009: 270).
Another objective shot shows the letters of the cinema's name as the
camera tilts down. The walls of Cine Olympo are covered with torn posters
from past electoral campaigns; the different layers of 'torn surfaces' reveal
how national history and our personal and shared memories are violently
joined or precariously imbricated. We can recognise, for instance, Felipe
González, who led the Socialist Party (PSOE) and became president in
1982. This is significant – the 'film-within-the-film' is set in 1977, when

Spain's Socialist Party was legalised after decades of political repression at the hands of Franco's totalitarian regime. After legalisation, the Socialist Party became the most important party in the Opposition to the UCD, the party of Adolfo Suárez, the first democratically elected president of Spain after the Franco dictatorship.

González is juxtaposed with a fragmented image of Zahara's face – a transvestite, who will be introduced in the ensuing sequences. In his cultural history of homosexuality in twentieth-century Spain, Alberto Mira notes that the image of the transvestite came to prominence in Spain during the late 1970s: 'The images of transvestites proliferated on the streets, in magazines, on movie screens, in television scripts, in night clubs and in the pages of the daily press' (2004: 434–5, my translation). Mira argues that the transvestite functioned as a kind of exotic spectacle for the hegemonic, heteronormative society. Similarly, Kinder suggests that, unlike Almodóvar's previous films, in which sexual mobility was often associated with progressive politics, *La mala educación* turns transvestism 'into a venal form of opportunism, stripping away its political edge and glamour' (2009: 286). The juxtaposition of González and Zahara could, then, be an attempt to connect a progressive politics of gender identity, associated with transvestism, with the left-wing national politics of the Socialist Party. Nonetheless, in line with Kinder's more complex reading of sexual mobility in the film, I suggest that transvestism could be read here as part of the allegorical conception of the *mise-en-scène*. In other words, the fragmented image of the transvestite here is ambiguously and unexpectedly associated with the moment in which history is replaced by an image, as in Walter Benjamin's thinking. Rolf Tiedemann writes about the image of the *Angelus Novus* in Benjamin's concept of history:

> The basis for Benjamin's image of the pile of debris growing up into the skies and the basis for the catastrophic concept of history in the Theses goes beyond its linguistic conceptualization. It is in essence an image, one that the observer can only stare at, condemned to silence, unable to differentiate or to identify details. (Cited in Lane 2005: 53)

As a material fragment that points to the replacement of (catastrophic) history by an image, transvestism in *La mala educación* can be identified with an allegorical moment, undercutting what Benjamin calls historicism's homogeneous, empty time. This empty time is that of the narrative of historical progress on which the previously mentioned progressive politics of identity is predicated. The narrative of historical progress neutralises the shock of the allegorical moment, which is the condition of possibility for the revolutionary moment, in which the history of the oppressed is recognised and remembered, but in which facile feelings of empathy towards the oppressed are avoided. From this Benjaminian perspective, in which the relationship between the past, the present and the future is reorganised in order to 'blast open the continuum of history' (Benjamin 1968: 262), we can conceive the image of Zahara as 'an instant in which an image of the past sparks a flash of unexpected recognition in the present. This moment is disruptive, unpredictable, and dangerous' (Lowenstein 2003: 75). Moving away from a conception of history as progress, and from homogeneous, empty time, this allegorical moment in Almodóvar's film 'flashes up at a moment of danger' (Benjamin 1968: 255). It can be conceived as an anti-redemptive recognition and re-formulation of social stigmatisation and, to use Benjamin's term, oppression.

So transvestism in the film cannot be understood in terms of empathy or by focusing on the positive or negative images of queer characters in the film.[12] It can only be understood through the production of queerness within psychic and moral ambiguity (as Vernon would put it (2009)). In other words, in Almodóvar's cinema, and particularly in *La mala educación*, the embrace of moral and psychic ambiguity leads to a celebration of the anxieties and/or pleasures that are socially and psychically stigmatised by patriarchal and heteronormative society. Almodóvar's representation of morally and psychically dubious characters offers an antidote to reality; we can interpret characters like María Cardenal in *Matador*, Ricky in *Átame* (*Tie Me Up! Tie Me Down!*, 1990), or Benigno in *Hable con ella*, as a re-signification of socially and psychically marginal positions.

More importantly, Almodóvar's characters completely withdraw from conventional forms of sexuality and sociality beyond good and evil, which provokes in us a questioning of our feelings of sympathy, empathy, apathy or antipathy with their passions and actions. For instance, in *Hable con ella*, Benigno's rape of Alicia, though unquestionably a crime, may also be identified, on a metaphorical level, as Benigno's bodily expression of his desire to become Alicia's 'amante menguante' (shrinking lover). *Amante menguante* is the silent black and white film that Benigno narrates to Alicia on the night that he rapes her. This film is thus seen as a unit linked, symbolically, to the main action of Almodóvar's film. Benigno's sexual crime is thus associated with an im-possible desire to merge, bodily, with an irreducible other. Benigno's act of aggression, however reprehensible, is unlike the sexual violence in *La mala educación* or *La piel que habito*, because it is as an im-possible attempt on his part to become the other by being contained within the body of the other or emerging from inside it. In the hospital, Benigno embraces, however troublingly, the ethics of embodied care, on which I focused in Chapter 1, for the comatose Alicia. He meets Marco, who is caring for the comatose Lidia, a bullfighter who was gored by a bull. The two men develop an affective friendship based on the lack of verbal communication between them and the two psychically absent yet physically present women. The hospital thus becomes a space where the four characters' lives are spatially and temporarily suspended. In this context, Benigno's rape of Alicia can be seen as an attempt to return to the pre-Oedipal stage of subjectivity, which implies complete fusion with the other, while always already being haunted by its relation to the cut of castration and the phallic signifier. Benigno does not distinguish between 'I' and 'non-I', between mother and self, between external reality and internal fantasy. Yet, although this could be interpreted as a psychotic foreclosure of the symbolic order, one could argue in the context of this film that Benigno's crime does enable a movement and inclination towards the irreducible other, thereby potentially transforming extreme solipsism into an openness to irreducible difference through undoing internal psychic boundaries. Almodóvar poses a difficult moral question in *Hable con ella*, and the spectator is left with a moral void that cannot be filled within the symbolic universe created in the fiction film.

To return to the torn posters on the Cine Olympo's walls: we next see the posters, defaced, in close-up. The camera's overproximity to the posters gives the perception of this image a haptic quality, ambivalently inscribing the dialectic between touch and sight as the fundamental condition of vision, the perception of external phenomena in general, and, in particular, the perception of film. The 'sense of touch [thus] becomes an index of vision - a temporal imprint of looking' (Fer 2004: 20). The perception and cognition of cinematic images requires the functioning of the thinking mind (consciousness) as well as a bodily response (our visceral encounter with the film medium). *La mala educación* encourages an affective response to cinema and foregrounds the body as always already implicated in the process of perceiving and understanding the film. In other words, subjectivity is constituted through and in language, but, in phenomenological terms, we are conscious of our bodily way of 'being-in-the-world', even if language mediates our perceptions of the external world and enables us to symbolically articulate those embodied perceptions. Almodóvar's film enables us to reflect on how we bring sensory knowledge (associated with the body) and logical reasoning (associated with the mind) together in our perception and understanding of phenomena, without reifying a plenitude of being. As Fer suggests in a different context, the dialectical tension between sight and touch here reveals the fragmentary, disorientating conditions of a precarious and frayed subject's perception, when that subject's contemplation and all-perceiving gaze disintegrates in the process of viewing the film (2004: 11).

As the camera zooms in, the layers of history inscribed on the torn poster become more and more unintelligible, more and more blurred, forcing us to ask how close it is possible to get to, how far it is possible to go from, the cinematic image before the symbolic matrix of representation is lost or the architecture of cinematic vision crumbles (Fer 2007: 80). The traces of personal and shared history here are less linguistically articulated than inscribed in the textuality of the unconscious, or imprinted on our body. This disturbance of the field of vision enacts what Fer calls 'the precarious coming into vision of pictorial [cinematic] representation' (2007: 80). The rupturing of the field of representation or the field of vision points, albeit metaphorically, to the tearing of the image screen.[13] Therefore, as the cinematic camera moves closer to the torn posters, we are deprived of the distance needed for cinematic vision, thereby aggravating, imploding or even annihilating our cinematic perception (Shaviro 1993: 55). Once we interpret the cinematic screen as torn by the overproximity of the cinematic camera to the posters, we can see that our cinematic experience does not reconstitute our subjectivity at the imaginary or symbolic level. Instead, cinematic vision reveals the blindness intrinsic to cinematic perception and vision itself.[14]

But let us focus on Almodóvar's concern with the pain of personal and shared history, as it impinges on the body. For instance, this is made manifest when Zahara and her friend Paquita are placed on the steps of Cine Olympo to plan a visit to Zahara's old religious boarding school. The abandoned cinema becomes a precarious experiential site, which triggers cinematic memories and memories of Zahara's first sexual experiences with Enrique Goded. The pain and pleasure of the spectral and material past actualised in Ignacio/Zahara's body and psyche prompts her to insert drugs just as, earlier, she had inserted Enrique's penis into her/his own body, in order to im-possibly fill the constitutive void that precariously structures and traumatically ruptures one's subjectivity.

So I want my allegorical reading of the film to foreground the linking of the body to individual and collective fragments of memory, to ruins of history and traces of trauma. In other words, allegory, as an 'other-discourse', reveals the ruins and remnants in the present of history that has 'physically merged into the setting' (Cowan 1981: 117). Allegory in *La mala educación* resists integration into a totalising structure of signi-fication, through the film's ambiguous emphasis on the fragment and the remnant. This enables us to think of the imbrication of material ruins and human suffering as constitutive of historical experience. Such experience impinges on our mind and body in an affective and phenomenological, as well as a discursive and representational manner, thereby foregrounding a conception of the world as writing – which is, of course, associated with allegory. As Bainard Cowan rightly suggests:

> If experience is always already given in signs, insofar as any experience is significant, then the very concept of experience – designating as it does 'the relationship with a presence' – becomes 'unwieldy' and must be replaced by a term which gives notice that the mind in encountering reality is already writing, even at the zero-point of this encounter. (1981: 112)

The Benjaminian notion of allegory complicates the relationship between representation and what is represented by adding layers of signification to the field of representation. These layers paradoxically point to the impossibility of completing the event. The structure of allegory produces a total disruption of the past, present and future in order to emphasise an understanding of temporality based on repetition. Allegory fragmentarily and ambiguously reveals the fragmented and ephemeral condition of nature and the painful and transitory nature of life, which is allegorically encapsulated in the image of the death's head, to which I referred above. This culminates in a non-transcendental, non-redemptive death.[15] For Samuel Weber, 'Death is at work in allegory however not just as decline and decay, but more intimately, as that which separates each thing from itself: from its essence and from its significance' (1991: 496). The Benjaminian concept of allegory enables us to think about the problematic imbrication of the particular with the general, the material with the immaterial, the internal with the external, or the past with the present and future.

In this context, I want to suggest that the relationship between personal and collective history and their intoxicating, long-lasting effects upon Zahara's bodily memory in *La mala educación* allows us to think about how the totalitarian regime of Franco and its perverse association with the Catholic Church impinges not just upon external, physical reality but also upon internal, immaterial reality – just as Rolnik argues in the context of the Brazilian military dictatorship (2008a: 155). For Rolnik, the intoxication can have lasting effects, and one may need to find strategies of psychic protection from such an affliction by 'anaesthetising the marks of the trauma in the affective circuit' (2008b: 156). Nonetheless, as I explained in the Introduction, Rolnik suggests that one should take into consideration how the macro-political and the micro-political affect each other in order to provide a more mobile cartography. From this perspective, in the late 1970s and early 1980s, Spanish society was still haunted by the legacy of political violence and threatened by the potential re-emergence, as I explained in the previous chapter, of micro- and macro-fascisms. We might ask whether *La mala educación* points towards the intensification of individual and collective creativity and resistance, which is epitomised in the film by the 'counter-cultural' phenomenon of *La Movida*, to which Almodóvar belonged.[16]

Traces of the fragments of personal and collective history seem to float, appearing obliquely rather than directly, thanks to the *mise-en-scène* of the abandoned movie theatre and its mutilated posters. These fragments disappear just as one tries to grab hold of them.[17] The dialectical relationship between writing and its erasure, between visibility and invisibility, makes present the spectral and material traces of the fragments and layers of personal and shared history embodied in the mosaic of torn posters, thereby undercutting the logic of mimetic representation and signification (Deleuze and Guattari 1984). This contributes to what Hannah Feldman calls an 'as-yet-undefined' public discourse (2004: 95). At this point, the shot of the posters blends into that of an undefaced poster. The *mise-en-scène* reveals once again Almodóvar's conception of time's heterogeneous and discontinuous movement between the present, past and future. The intact poster announces a burlesque show by the company *La bomba*. Its main star is Zahara.

Almodóvar's allegorically associates the *mise-en-scène* with traumatic history by emphasising the destruction at the core of cinematic representation. This enables me to draw on wider discourses about the relationship between artistic representation and violence. It is useful to relate this sequence in *La mala educación* to Georges Bataille's discussion of primitive art, for example. In 'L'Art primitif' (1930), Bataille associates primitive art with the production of violence, rather than with the creation of form. He advocates a creative process in which phenomena are destroyed, and introduces the concept of *altération* (1930: 389–98), which can be used to discuss the work of all artists who are preoccupied with the violent process of physical decomposition and disintegration, which is implied in the process of representation (Krauss 1985). Works of art reintroduce repressed material existence as well as physical and psychical pleasure and pain into the field of representation. This de-sublimation in artworks suggests that works of art are linked to productive destruction rather than repressed creation. So we can understand works of art as being constructed through an instinctual liberation of libidinal impulses, rather than through a formal process of sublimation. From this perspective, artistic representation can be conceived as a violent and obsessive, yet productive process of liberating unconscious desires (Fer 1995: 157).

The physical and sadistic dimension associated with Bataille's concept of *altération* is made manifest in the torn surfaces that appear throughout *La mala educación*. These surfaces allegorise cinema's questioning of the cinematic medium's own destructive–creative process. Almodóvar's film makes us think of how the meaning of a film is also expressed in the process of obliterating the film. For instance, film editing is always already predicated on the violent cutting, annihilation and obliteration of unsuitable shooting material, which is excluded from the final version of the film. The self-reflexive discourse of Almodóvar's film thus implies alteration and destruction. The chain of violent actions found in artistic creation, and particularly in cinematic production, exorcises repressed, irrational, self-destructive impulses,[18] thus re-enacting the return of trauma through compulsive repetition.[19]

So the film's concern with the traces of trauma and fragments of memory is already inherent in its *mise-en-scène*; this can be seen particularly in the film's torn surfaces, which can be associated with an 'im-possibility of not-writing otherwise'. But I most want to emphasise the linking of those torn surfaces with traumatic encryption and inscription. In this context, compulsive repetition is linked to the symptomatic, non-narrative re-enactment of trauma. Hence, repetition, or the 'unconsciousness of representation', as I explained in the previous chapter, reveals the absent presence of trauma. The torn surfaces in Almodóvar's film illustrate the irruption of traces of trauma by playing out on the surface's 'skins' the tension between being unfinished (defaced) and traumatic repetition. These surfaces collapse the boundaries between the inside and the outside. In metaphorical terms, the torn surfaces here can be seen as physical and psychic wounds, as if the different layers and fragments that composed these graphic images created the effect of wounded flesh, resulting in an amorphous image that is stripped of its own identity by having its own 'flesh' be torn away from a formless body, on which one can no longer distinguish 'flesh' from 'skin'. The torn surfaces in *La mala educación* suggest that the film focuses on matter in order to articulate the pleasure or the pain caused by the memory of our individual and collective (traumatic) experiences. This relationship demonstrates Almodóvar's preoccupation with the imbrication of matter with subject matter (Wilson 1995: 172–92). So the torn surfaces in *La mala educación* make the physical and psychic experience of being unfinished or emotionally mutilated precariously visible and tangible; they suggest that communication with and/or relation to the 'self' or the irreducible 'other' is achieved through devastating ruptures, through violent, 'negative narcissistic'[20] or physical injuries or, to use Andrew Asibong's words (2009), through a 'bleeding kinship', which the film associates with the death drive.

Figure 3.2 Ignacio and Father Manolo singing

Figure 3.3 When Ignacio falls to the ground and hits his forehead on a rock

This can be seen, for instance, in the pastoral scene at the swimming hole after the young Ignacio has escaped from Father Manolo's attempt to sexually abuse him (see Figure 3.2). Ignacio falls to the ground and hits his forehead on a rock. Almodóvar freezes the frame, giving us a close-up

of Ignacio's face with blood dripping down his forehead (see Figure 3.3).
Acevedo-Muñoz notes how 'the face is split open down the middle, into
a split-screen that reveals the profound darkness inside, and that marks
explicitly and melodramatically the turning point of Ignacio's life' (2007:
271). The red line of blood tears both Ignacio's face and the cinematic
screen. In a voice-over, Ignacio says that, like his torn face (and like the
torn screen), his own subjectivity will always be shattered due to the abuse
and violence inflicted on his body and psyche by representatives of the
Catholic Church during the Franco regime. In effect, as Ignacio's face
splits into two parts, the face of Father Manolo is revealed, as if he were an
obscure shadow that will always lurk behind, take possession of, and split
Ignacio's wounded existence – which will culminate in a non-transcendental, non-redemptive death. Yet, through the writing of *La visita*, Ignacio
leaves a trace that will survive his own mortality – a mortality which is
associated with the iterability of writing. Later, we see Father Manolo
reading Ignacio's story in his office in the late 1970s (see Figure 3.4). He
is here haunted by the traces of language that return from the irreducible other. The film then cuts to Goded reading the same story, which he
will turn into his film in the 1980s. This later film re-inscribes Ignacio's
signature, as well as Goded's own, in the process of adaptation.[21] This
graphically innovative image of Ignacio moves away from the indexical

Figure 3.4 Father Manolo reads Ignacio's story

condition of the cinematic medium. It is rendered by means of technology not available during the 1960s, when the scene is set. Time here splits the present, as Deleuze notes, 'in two heterogeneous directions, one of which is launched toward the future while the other falls into the past' (cited in Stewart 2006: 190).

Almodóvar's use of digital technology in this sequence shows how the material and spectral traces of trauma and fragments of memory will uncannily return from the past or from the future,[22] thereby shaping and affecting the experience and interpretation of similar, yet different, undetermined, traumatic events.[23] For instance, one of the final scenes in *La mala educación* shows Ignacio dying of a heroin overdose. Although Ignacio's brother and Señor Berenguer are responsible for the administration of the drug, this death due to addiction can best be seen as the ultimate consequence of Ignacio's tendency towards self-destruction and self-shattering. In slow motion, we see Ignacio's forehead hitting his typewriter. It is important to note here that one cannot experience one's own death. Death is an inevitable event that one will never actually live; it is 'incommensurable with the events of one's life', and exposes a 'fracture between everyday language and another kind of speaking' (Armstrong 2012: 9). In his reflection on Maurice Blanchot's 'The Instant of My Death', Derrida associates the moment of one's death with an 'inexperienced experience'. 'Death', he suggests, 'has already taken place [. . .] Yet this past, to which I testify, namely, my death itself, has never been present' (Blanchot/Derrida 2000: 50). This scene of Ignacio falling onto his typewriter reverberates with the earlier scene of Ignacio falling onto a rock. The event of Ignacio's death already places him out of the world. Yet the reverberation of these two scenes foregrounds the way that the remnants of Ignacio's inassimilable past traumatic experiences or undetermined, future traumatic events, including his singular self-annihilating encounter with the non-relational event of death, overwhelmingly affect and intensely penetrate each other. Asibong points out that this traumatic shattering of Ignacio's subjectivity leads 'to nothing but a sensation of radical despair, a despair felt as intensely by the spectator' as by Ignacio (2009: 191). From this perspective, compulsive repetition in *La mala educación* reveals that trauma returns violently into the symbolic beyond linguistic symbolisation and articulation. Trauma uncovers the gap that is covered over by symbolic representation, thereby producing an 'otherwise than writing' or a 'writing in the Real'.

In psychoanalytic understandings of the traumatic event's catastrophic impact on the psyche and body of the victim, as in the work of Caruth, the incomprehensibility and temporal unlocatability of traumatic memories

leads to a sense of fragmentation that might cause psychic disorientation, destruction and disintegration (Caruth 1991). Following Freud,
Caruth explains that the experience of trauma cannot be linguistically
represented, as it has become an un-cognised reality external to the
subject, which is not mediated by her or his consciousness. Trauma
cannot be symbolically articulated, but only compulsively repeated as a
non-remembered, overwhelming experience. This produces a wound in
one's system of meaning, because the return occurs only in a symbolic
manner (Caruth 1991). According to Caruth, the traumatic event thus
produces a rupture in the subject's cognitive mechanism. The subject
cannot articulate or symbolically represent the experience of that trauma.
As I discussed in Chapter 1, this can paralyse the subject, who needs to
resort to narrative in order to potentially integrate the encryption of the
unprocessed traumatic event into her/his cognitive mechanism. Such a
linguistic structuration of traumatic experiences may help the subject stop
her/his compulsive repetition and re-enactment of unprocessed, belated
traumatic experiences, and, instead, to fully integrate and assimilate those
experiences into her/his psyche.

But here I do not want to focus on how the subject might master
remnants of trauma through integrating them and assimilating them
into consciousness. I wish, instead, to emphasise how the torn surfaces
in *La mala educación* are associated with the shattering of the subject of
language, thus subverting the linguistic articulation of traumatic experiences. Here, instead, we see the imaginary's inability to fully capture the
traces of trauma, and the symbolic's inability to fully elaborate these traumatic experiences through and in language. In this context, our cinematic
encounter with trauma's belatedness and incomprehensibility point to an
ethical and potentially political relation to the traces of the other's trauma
in an 'unplaceable place', a 'time out of historical time' (Ettinger 2000: 93).
Foregrounding this potential transformation of the aesthetic encounter
with traces of trauma beyond assimilation and integration, Pollock argues,

> a certain compulsion or activity indexes both a presence of the unknown and
> unknowable and the subject's actions as the symptomatic site of its pressure
> and translation. Thus not content but gesture, what we would now name the per-
> formative process in artwork [or in cinema], that takes, and indexes, its own time
> and creates a new space of encounter, may become the place of a transformative
> registration. (2009b: 42)

Almodóvar's film's attention to 'torn screens' epitomises such a de-
formation of the symbolic representation or linguistic articulation of
traumatic experiences. In doing so, it moves beyond what Pollock calls the

phallic model of trauma. As I explained above, a phallic model of trauma attempts to encapsulate fully or redeem the scattered effects of trauma by using narrative to translate the trauma into communicable memory. It is then relegated to a closed past (Pollock 2009b: 46). As Freud suggests, memory functions therapeutically for traumatised subjects, who are 'obliged to *repeat* the repressed material as a contemporary experience instead of, as the physician would prefer to see, remembering it as something belonging to the past' (Freud 2003 [1920]: 56, emphasis in original).

Instead, *La mala educación* points to our aesthetic encounter with, or our *wit(h)nessing* of, the remnants of trauma. As I have explained throughout this study, the ethical and political potential of this trans-formative registration, to use Pollock's terms, does not reside in the linguistic mastery of trauma. Such mastery is predicated on the separation of the subject from the Real within the symbolic order, which is itself predicated on producing the Real as lack (Ettinger 2016: 152–3). As an aesthetic practice that allows the possibility of encountering or borderlinking with the traces of the trauma of the Other, Almodóvar's film underscores the affective impact or after-effect on the spectator of the non-narrative, spectral re-enactment or inscription of the symptoms and 'traces of oblivion' (Ettinger 2000: 114). Instead of focusing on mastery or calculated transformation through representation, I emphasise the affective process in which the spectator becomes fragilised by com-passionately *wit(h)nessing* the trauma of the Other, a trauma that 'glitters from the other side behind this invisible and untraversable limit' or threshold between the Real and phantasy via aesthetic practice and aesthetic experience (Ettinger 2016: 153).

Embodied Inter-subjectivity and Prosthetic Memory

The torn frames in *La mala educación* connote a tension between matter and subject matter; we can also read Zahara's body as a kind of surface on which is inscribed the materiality of skin; the artifice of clothing; and the expressiveness of the identical as well as singular gesture in the performativity and performance of bodily identity and subjectivity.[24] *La mala educación*'s emphasis on 'embodied inter-subjectivity' and 'prosthetic memory' plays into my ongoing concern with Almodóvar's cinema and the transportability and 'im-possibility of not-sharing' the irreducible other's traces of memories and fragments of (traumatic) experiences of irreducible others beyond the autonomous, discrete subject.

Consider the scene in Enrique Goded's film of Paquita and Zahara's nightclub performance. Paquita introduces her friend, Zahara, to an unsympathetic audience as a mixture of 'desierto, casualidad y cafetería' (the desert, chance and a café). A close-up of Zahara's back emphasises her/his tight, flesh-coloured dress adorned with feathers and sequins. The camera lingers on Zahara's body, thereby accentuating her/his voluptuous, androgynous body. When she/he turns around, we can see that the tight dress is adorned with a female pubis and, as the camera tilts up, we can also see nipples on the dress and nails painted on Zahara's gloves. Almodóvar describes Zahara's dress as 'flesh-colored, tight-fitted to the neck like a second skin that gives the impression of total nudity. The ass, the tits, and the pubis are made with sequins and brown and pink glass beads and tones. The dress in itself represents false, naked femininity' (cited in D'Lugo 2006: 152). In a profile-view close-up of Zahara, we watch Gael García Bernal's lip-synching to a song sung by Sara Montiel. Montiel was both a sex symbol for heterosexual men and an icon for transvestites during the Franco regime and the transition to democracy. She was, for example, the object of Ignacio's desire; Juan/Ángel has now incorporated Montiel into her/his own body and subjectivity.[25]

This sequence crosscuts between shots of Zahara singing within the diegesis, and shots of the very attractive Enrique Serrano. Though the character has a different surname, Enrique Serrano is clearly Enrique Goded's fantasy projection of himself in his film. The alteration of Enrique's surname problematises and undermines the conventions of autobiography. This genre requires that the author, narrator and character share the same proper name. In this way, the autobiographical text – the writing of the self – is entirely circumscribed within the signature of the author. But in *La mala educación* autobiography is re-conceived as the condition of possibility for the incorporation and inscription of the irreducible other into one's subjectivity in the process of writing, or the incorporation or inscription of the self into the subjectivity of the irreducible other in the process of reading. We see here once again the film's *leitmotif* of bodily conflations: the collapse of one body onto another (Montiel's body onto that of Ignacio, Juan/Ángel, or the Montiel impersonator). Here, too, subjectivities collapse into one another (Ignacio's subjectivity into that of Juan/Ángel); one memory onto another (Ignacio's memories onto those of Juan/Ángel); life transformed into art, the sacred into the profane, the position of the victim into that of the victimiser, the present into the past, or the past into the future. Like *Todo sobre mi madre*, *La mala educación* generates a precarious space of coexistence between multiple, interchangeable, transmissible bodies, identities, subjectivities, memories, spaces and times. As Victor Fuentes suggests, 'the duplicity and doubleness of the story and the characters contribute to a non-linear cinematic experience, full of flashbacks and flash-forwards to different times [. . .] and different places [. . .], in which points of view proliferate and real and imagined events collide' (2009: 437).

In the shots of Zahara, meanwhile, we see her mimetically reproduce feminine gestures, which, as we learn later, Juan/Ángel has mechanically incorporated into his body language by mimicking another Montiel impersonator – this, in order to get the part of Zahara in Enrique Goded's film. Juan/Ángel's gestures epitomise the citational nature of gestures, which itself depends on the irreversible irruption of singularity. As Weber puts it,

> [There is a] transformation of repetition from a process aimed at reproducing identity to one that allows for the aporetical resurgence of the singular: aporetical because the singular as such is not identically repeatable, reproducible, unique – but its uniqueness is also not separable from a certain repetition. Such repetition 'produces' the uniqueness of the unrepeatable in the form of those unexpected, often uncontrolled movements. (2006: 73)

In this context, Ángel/Juan's mimetic inscription of feminine gestures simultaneously reproduces and undermines cultural norms and, more interestingly, points to the degree that they could become pure potentiality due to their own fragility and mutability (Dickinson 2011). Juan/Ángel's assimilation, and (re)production of the Montiel impersonator's feminine gestures is driven by a particular intention or purpose (in order to play the role of Zahara). Zahara's gestures, however, can be read as, 'neither the means of addressing an end, nor an end in itself [. . .] but "the process of making a means visible"' (Bennett 2007: 436; Bennett here engages with Agamben's theory of the gesture). Zahara's corporeal movements thus contribute to unmaking and undoing Ángel/Juan's instrumentalisation of those gestures, those decomposed actions, which refuse to be inserted into a constricted form of teleology.

Zahara's extravagant, flesh-like dress can thus be read as a parodic signifier, which connotes Zahara's excessive investment in the performativity of feminine identity through the artifice of clothing and the expressiveness of the identical and singular gesture. As a non-linguistic form of expression, the identical and singular gesture mediates physical and emotional experiences when signifying language seems to slip or even fail. Gesture thereby stands at an ambivalent point between the realm of the communicative and that of the introspective (Bennett 2007). Yet, gesture is not merely a form of communication and mediation. Rather, gestures self-reflexively express their own 'being-in-a-medium', to use Agamben's phrase (2000). They thereby point to the way in which corporeal movements are predicated on their own mediality. Gesture can be associated with a 'non-communicative speechlessness' located on the other side of language, precisely because gestures interrupt language just as the latter manifests itself (ten Bos 2005: 40).

It is also useful to relate the skin-like effect of Zahara's dress to Anzieu's psychoanalytic understanding of the significance of the skin in the constitution of subjectivity; I will return to this theoretical point in my analysis of *La piel que habito*. According to Anzieu, 'the skin, which is a system of several sense organs (perceiving touch, pressure, pain, heat), is itself closely connected with the other organs of external sense (hearing, sight, smell, taste) and with the awareness of body movement and balance' (1989: 14). But the skin is not merely an organ of sense, since it also fulfils several biological functions: breathing, perspiring, secreting, expelling, maintaining the tonus, stimulating respiration, circulation, digestion, excretion, or reproduction (1989: 15). In addition, while the skin protects us from external disruptions, Anzieu argues, it is also the surface on which these disruptions are marked. Because the ego incorporates the other through the skin prior to its absorption by the mouth (Anzieu 1989: 19), the skin is integral to the formation of our subjectivity and to our recognition as embodied beings.

So Zahara's skin-like dress points to the materiality of our body as, to use Anzieu's terms, formative of the (relational) self. Consequently, Zahara's subjectivity, which already embodies the subjectivity and memory of her/his brother Ignacio, points to the way in which 'appearance, which is constantly on the point of passing itself off as reality, must constantly reveal its profound unreality' (Sartre 1954: 10). For Jean-Paul Sartre, as he discusses Jean Genet's *Les Bonnes* (1947), the fluid interchangeability between appearance and being problematises ontology, which, though the study of being, also depends on non-being – so that the latter becomes being (1954: 30). Sartre provides us with a theory of ontological relatedness that depends on the way in which the one in the other, or the other in the one, bears witness to the im-possibility of being either oneself or the other. Sartre's focus on the ontology of the subject problematises the relationship between being's realisation and de-realisation, thus undercutting the Western ontological tradition. Ontology is based on the metaphysics of presence, in which 'being' is understood as 'presence' (Debevec Henning 1982: 231). Zahara resonates with the characters in Genet's *Les Bonnes*: they all emphasise the 'processes of constant folding and unfolding of experience. There are no fixed centers [. . .]; instead, bits and pieces are constantly moving in and out of the folds to become intertwined with other surrounding unfoldings in a "spiraling distributive process'" (Hequembourg 2007: 158). Through the representation of Zahara, Almodóvar proposes a form of being and a mode of ontological relatedness that disrupts and undercuts the metaphysics of presence by emphasising, like the textual process described above, an ambivalent and interminable process of deferrals, substitutions and supplements. There are no originary, stable centres or teloi. Instead, we shift endlessly and belatedly from presence to absence, from closure to interruption, or from identity to difference.[26] Derrida explains:

> Everything begins with reproduction. Always already: repositories of a meaning which was never present, whose signified presence is always reconstituted by deferment, *nachträglich*, belatedly, *supplementarily*: for *nachträglich* also means *supplementary*. The appeal of the supplement is primal here and breaks open what will be reconstituted by deferment as the present. The supplement, which seems to be added as a plenitude to a plenitude, is as well that which compensates for a lack. (1972: 92, emphasis in original)

Similarly, Zahara's embodiment of Ignacio's subjectivity and her/his memories of him are inscribed in her/his subjectivity and on the 'flesh' and 'skin' of her/his body, which functions as 'a reminder of what was not been allowed to be forgotten [. . .] The "unforgettable" is etched on the body itself' (Grosz 1994: 132). In other words, the body receives and transmits fragments of memories and traces of trauma. The body feels and viscerally experiences the indelible physical and psychical traces of individual and shared memories, through affect and sensations beyond re-cognition.

Almodóvar's representation of Ángel/Juan as an 'imposter' who appropriates his brother's subjectivity and memory for his own benefit has to be understood within his cinema's moral universe. Almodóvar's work has, since the very beginning, expanded and exceeded our own moral conventions, which are based on reductive preconceptions and clear-cut distinctions between, and definitions of what is, 'right' and 'wrong', 'true' and 'false' or 'authentic' and 'inauthentic'. In *Prosthetic Memory*, Landsberg explores how the technology of cinema can transport us across different spaces and times, emphasise experience as a mode of acquiring knowledge, or lead us to be affected empathically, bodily and psychically, by experiences and memories which are not organically linked to us. According to Landsberg, cinema undercuts the polarity between subjective and collective memory, while recognising that the memories and experiences of others cannot be reduced to our own self-consciousness. She suggests: 'A practice of empathy is an essential part of taking on prosthetic memories, of finding ways to inhabit other people's memories *as* other people's memories and thereby respecting and recognizing difference' (2004: 24, emphasis in original). Landsberg's emphasis on empathy as the condition of possibility for experiencing the memories of others may run the risk of assimilating the other's experiences and memories into a familiar structure, thus neglecting the other's opacity and irreducibility. But she also stresses that memories must be inhabited as other people's memories. Her insistence on the transmissibility of memory across subjects (2004: 43) opens up new ways to think about shared experiences and memories by dissociating identity from an essentialist logic and undercutting authenticity as the essential component of memory (2004: 46). 'Prosthetic memory' thus becomes 'the grounds for political alliances and the production of new, potentially counter-hegemonic public spheres' (2004: 34). Landsberg puts great emphasis on how the modern mass media mediate memories and experiences that were previously transmitted through more direct 'embodied action', to use Taylor's term (2003), and then, too, on how the media make those memories and experiences available to us. But she still pays attention to the importance of the visceral or affective encounter in experiential practices and embodied spectatorship as the condition of possibility for the production of prosthetic memory (Landsberg 2004: 4).

Almodóvar proposes a form of 'embodied inter-subjectivity' through Zahara's embodiment of the subjectivity and memory of Ignacio. Here, we have a capacity, whether intentional or not, to carry the inscription of and im-possibly of not sharing in our own subjectivity, and on our own body, the traces of another's traumatic experiences and fragments of memories. For instance, Juan/Ángel's and Ignacio's mother suffers from heart disease; her suffering is paradoxically transferred to the body and psyche of their aunt.[27] But we should also consider the transgression of the individual subject's boundaries. In these examples, we seem to have an instance of inter-subjectivity, in which two discrete subjects, each confined within the boundaries of their own bodies, share a trauma. We should also consider trans-subjectivity, which I discussed in my previous chapter. Here, those boundaries are transgressed. In the trans-subjective, sub-symbolic psychic sphere, different-yet-co-emergent and separated-yet-joint partial objects and partial subjects share each other's trauma and *jouissance* in distance-in-proximity and proximity-in-distance through borderlinking (Ettinger 2016: 155). From this perspective, *La mala educación* forces us, as Pollock notes,

to imagine not merely inter-subjective exchange and impacts but the subject as always a trans-subjective meeting point both in time and out of time, in her/his own immediate family history and beyond through what might be passed to and encrypted within her/him that already links others to others and others to worlds, to traumas and events never known or knowable by him or her except as these transposed traces of otherness lodged within. (2009b: 49)

The ethical and political potential of such an 'im-possibility of not-sharing' the traumas and *jouissance* of the other at a trans-subjective level does not lead to redemption or even calculated emancipation. Ettinger explains that 'joining is first of all joining within/by the trauma that weakens and bifurcates me, and creates a danger of regression and dispersal in the process of receiving, passing on, and transmitting' (2016: 159). Following Ettinger, I suggest that an emphasis on the vulnerability and fragilisation of the self in relation to the irreducible other is the condition of possibility for opening up our psyche and body to, affectively encountering or com-passionately *wit(h)nessing* the traces of past traumatic experiences and fragments of memories coming through and transmitted by irreducible others at a trans-subjective level that may or may not lead to transformation in an undetermined future. As Ettinger puts it:

Different aspects of trauma and jouissance are dispersed by and with affects, and their traces circulate between I and non-I. Events that profoundly concern my soul and psyche, and that I can't contain and elaborate entirely, are transformed and they fade away and get dispersed in others that thus become wit(h)nesses of/to my own trauma. We can think of events whose traumatic weight is so heavy that I would not be able to contain its memory traces at all. In the matrixial borderspace 'my' traces will transgress my limits and will be inscribed in another so that the other crossed in/by me will mentally elaborate them for me. (2000: 113)

To reiterate the arguments deployed in Chapter 2, *La mala educación* enables us to think of the film medium as a borderspace, a threshold where it may be possible to com-passionately encounter or *wit(h)ness* the traces of trauma and fragments of memory coming from irreducible others, with whom we are matrixially borderlinked. Such a fragilising encounter may provide the occasion for a trans-formation of the remnants of trauma, without necessarily leading to a complete working through of the traumatic, un-cognised void.

Embodied Witnessing

In the final sequence I will focus on, the two children, Ignacio and Enrique, go to the cinema to watch Mario Camus' *Esa Mujer*. They are escaping, for a few hours, repression and abuse at the hands of their religious boarding school's priests, in Goded's 'film-within-the-film'. As I have argued throughout this chapter, the sexual abuse perpetrated by representatives of the Catholic Church can be associated with the political oppression and repression at the core of the Franco regime.[28] Although the children are in 1964, Almodóvar, whether consciously or unconsciously, has them attend a film made five years later. D'Lugo suggests that 'the premise of the evoked past is not necessarily based on faulty history, but on faulty memory' (2009: 384). Such an anachronistic 'blind-spot' produces a radical rupture, fissure or loss in the system of meaning, so that the fragments of memory – including absences, repressions, excesses and uncertainties – are not bound or sutured into a unitary, single and coherent narrative. *Esa mujer* can be seen as a graft, which is incorporated into the film within *La mala educación* to point to how the traces of trauma and fragments of memory are mediated through a precarious cinematic archive – an archive that opens onto the future. *Esa mujer*, the 'film-within-the-film-within-the-film' was produced late in the Franco regime (a historical period to which Goded's *La visita* refers). It is an irreducible alterity that is already constitutive of, and trans-generationally haunts, Almodóvar's heterogeneous film. We see here, clearly, how the traces of other films are inscribed in the texture of *La mala educación*. These traces are not limited to this moment, either. We see a scene from Camus' film in which a former nun, now turned 'fallen woman', returns to her former convent. This is literally and symbolically, if not secretly, related to the action and theme of both *La visita* and *La mala educación*. The scene from Camus' film is a kind of lost, constitutive object, like a ghost that haunts or is encrypted in the textual unconscious of Almodóvar's film.

We can understand this through Derrida's discussion of Abraham and Torok's concept of cryptonymy; *Esa mujer* functions in *La mala educación* as a 'heterocryptic ghost that *returns* from the Unconscious *of* the other, according to what might be called the law of *another generation*' (1986: xxxi, emphasis in original). Instead of reifying a totalising identity or unitary linearity, the cryptic and explicit incorporation of one film in Almodóvar's film produces a 'complicated interwoven structure', to use Kristeva's terms (2002), which encourages the dialogical reading of texts through other texts that inhabit their topography, or the reading of the embedded texts through the texts in which they are inserted (Lloyd Smith 1992). A tracking shot of the two boys walking along the street cuts to a long shot of Cine Olympo, which advertises the screening of *Esa mujer* (see Figures 3.5–3.6). Almodóvar cuts to the scene from the film mentioned above, which we watch as if it occupied the diegetic space of *La mala educación*. The dissolution or slippage between texts points to the collapse or opening of the cryptic text (*Esa mujer*), which had been secretly entombed in the textual unconscious and body of *La mala educación*. Now, it strangely leaks

Figure 3.5 Ignacio and Enrique go to see a film

Figure 3.6 Cine Olympo advertises the screening of *Esa mujer*

out from Almodóvar's film. A shot from the point of view of the movie theatre's screen shows the two boys, captivated by the cinematic experience. They look at each other and talk about Montiel's beauty, which is affectively registered through close-ups of her face. The film's focus on

Montiel's facial expression foregrounds the disconnection of gesture from action, or gesture's suspension of action, thereby pointing, as I discussed above, to the solitary rather than the communicative, while still expressing 'the experience of "being in" an interaction' (Bennett 2007: 441). Yet, Ignacio and Enrique's conversation is juxtaposed with the conversation of *Esa mujer*'s female characters (the former nun turned into a 'fallen woman' and the Mother Superior of the convent).

In staging the 'film-within-the-film-within-the-film' in this manner, I suggest that the sense of hearing momentarily displaces the primacy of sight and mind to emphasise instead how the corporeal, the bodily, is always already implicated in the process of perceiving and understanding cinema. In other words, as I discussed in Chapter 1, the emphasis on sound in Almodóvar's film could be identified as a meta-cinematic discourse, by which the film calls attention to the aural condition of the cinematic medium. Almodóvar's use of diegetic sound thus acquires a relative autonomy *vis-à-vis* the image and produces a corporeal and haptic resonance or intensity in the spectator. This then de-emphasises the filmmaker's responsibility for visualisation and emphasises instead the spectator's responsibility to engage with the film (Hallas 2007: 39). Melissa Ragona claims that this attention to sound undercuts the hegemony of image that has conditioned the history of both popular narrative and experimental cinema (2004). Michel Chion refers to those unanchored, seemingly disembodied sounds, which he calls the 'acousmêtre', that make us feel the intense vibration of the irreducible other within our own bodies (1999). This can also be read in terms of the history of philosophy. The emphasis on sound in *La mala educación* undercuts the Cartesian philosophical tradition, which has insisted that sight and vision are the privileged locus of knowledge. According to Susan Bordo, 'Cartesian perspectivism', which has been the hegemonic scopic regime of Western modernity, is associated with a conception of seeing that is predicated on the clear-cut dichotomies between interiority and exteriority, or subject and object. For Bordo, this tradition underpins the hegemony of a disembodied, mastering subject who can perceive and understand the outside world from an elevated, distanced and neutral position (1990). If 'Cartesian perspectivism' is associated with a transcendental, rational subject whose gaze is located at the centre of the field of vision, the film's attention to sound here may re-configure our perceptual and cognitive experience by displacing or subverting the conceptions of subjectivity and signification associated with the Cartesian philosophical and epistemological tradition. As an 'a-signifying' element, sound in *La mala educación* becomes an 'asemiotic' excess.[29] It points to our affective, bodily, sensorial, but indeterminable relation to the cinematic medium or event. Such a visceral encounter does not prevent us, as we will see shortly, from remaining conscious of the impossibility of mastery, immediacy and presence at the core of the experience of the present.

As the film cuts to a shot of the backs of the two children, we can still glimpse the close-up of Montiel's face on the screen in the background. When the camera tilts up, the film shows the two boys masturbating each other, as if they were watching a porn movie, which encourages (or imposes) a mimetic, sexual, corporeal response in the spectator to the desired images or actions represented on the screen. It is worth quoting at length Garrett Stewart's reading of this scene and Almodóvar's concern with the relationship between desire and cinema:

> Escaping from the sexual coercions of the pedophile schoolmaster into a movie theater, yet finding in the screen's sensuous version of religious iconography an alternative route to sexual obsession, the two boys masturbate each other for the first time while watching an actress (Sara Mont[ie]l) they both find desperately beautiful in the role of an ex-nun, 'Mother Soledad'. What emerges in the resulting rear-projected shot is nothing less than a twofold distillation of cinema's eroticized apparatus of psychic projection [. . .], even as it becomes in its own right a 'time-image' of sexuality's forking future paths. Beyond the star's feminine perfection on screen, nothing is mentioned – at either pole of the boys' eventual desires – about this enthrallment by the screen image. Yet the boys are outed nonetheless in their creative (or self-creating) impulses. The one's libido is so inflamed by sexuality's link to female performance that he will want to *become* the woman, the other's so cathected around the display itself that he ends up being a director of such enacted screen spectacles. (2006: 169–70, emphasis in original)

But what interests me in Ignacio's and Enrique's sexual arousal, or the visceral effects of the cinematic image, is that we can define cinematic expression as a contagious, embodied experience, which is not contingent upon the signification of the cinematic image. In other words, exceeding its representational function, cinematic expression, which relates to the materiality of the film, becomes disconnected from the semiotic condition of the cinematic medium, thereby reconfiguring the spectators' affective, perceptive and cognitive experience of cinema beyond a rational comprehension of the structures of signification. If the spectator pays attention to the cinema's visual, aural and visceral expression, which Guattari defines as the 'assemblage of cinema' (cited in MacCormack 2005: 341), just as Enrique and Ignacio do, she/he will be bodily affected by her/his connection to and participation with the cinematic image – without reducing such ungovernable affective intensities to identifiable, articulated emotions.

Almodóvar's emphasis on experiencing cinema via what, following Guattari's line of thought, Rolnik defines as 'the resonant body'[30] is also made manifest in the narration of Father Manolo. He is now as physically ravaged as the abandoned Cine Olympo, but emotionally ravaged, too. Now known as Señor Berenguer, he narrates the events of 1977 from the perspective of 1980, which is indicated in the film by shifting from long subjective flashbacks focalised by Señor Berenguer to shots showing Señor Berenguer interpellating Enrique as his interlocutor. Sally Faulkner, in her discussion of Carlos Saura's *La caza* (*The Hunt*, 1966), argues that medium shots and close-ups let us become part of the process of witnessing through an affective transmission, which takes place in the phenomenological encounter between the spectator and the camera's attention to the other's ageing face (2006: 155). Señor Berenguer, who defines himself as 'el malo de la película' (the bad guy in the film), shows the age and fragility of his body (his chronic coughing could be a symptom of a pneumonia caused by AIDS; this was unknown in 1980, and an important theme in *Todo sobre mi madre*, as I discussed in the previous chapter).[31] MacCormack suggests that the face of the irreducible other enables us to im-possibly read her/his subjectivity in a way in which 'flesh becomes sign' (2005: 354); Señor Berenguer's im-possible testimonial presence thus emphasises '*not* the drama of communication, but the immense tiredness of the body, the tiredness there is beneath [. . .], which suggests to thought "something to incommunicate", the "unthought", life' (Deleuze 1989: 189, emphasis in original). In this context, as I explained in Chapter 1, Almodóvar problematises the dialectical relationship between the victim and the oppressor. A reductive polarisation of these positions could perpetuate a dichotomy between passivity and agency. D'Lugo tells us that the 'unexamined past, never fully repudiated within the culture of the transition, seemed presciently embodied in the very ambiguous figure of Berenguer' (2009: 303).

Almodóvar does seem to feel com-passion, which I have distinguished in this book from empathy, for Father Manolo's/Señor Berenguer's paedophile passions. Empathy is predicated on translating the suffering of the other into a familiar structure within one's consciousness. For Ettinger, com-passion takes place beyond empathy and understanding, as one can be com-passionate towards perpetrators of one's oppression, for instance, without feeling empathy towards, or understanding them, because, as Ettinger explains, 'primary compassion is a spontaneous way of trans-subjective knowing of/in the unknown Other before and beyond any possible economy of inter-subjective exchange' (2006b: 124–5). Operating at a trans-subjective level beyond the social and political sphere, com-passion is predicated on the fragilising yet resistant openness of the 'I' to the suffering of the other in an encounter-event. Yet, com-passion can become a psychic resource or ability for thinking about responsibility towards the irreducible other, who always already precedes the ontology of the subject, in the social and political field, thereby becoming the 'primary event of peace' (Ettinger 2006b: 124).

So, although the film is politically unsympathetic towards those who were complicit with the Franco regime, such as the Catholic Church – which is epitomised by Father Manolo – or those who embodied, as D'Lugo suggests, the culture of oblivion and silence that characterised the transition, which is epitomised by Señor Berenguer, Almodóvar does put pressure on our disposition not to listen to testimonies of those whose ideological and political positions may be antithetical to ours, thereby articulating a subjective ethical position that requires the performative act of bearing witness to the irreducible other's experiences, a position located beyond the moral and macro-political level. Labanyi argues that '[s]uch an approach is not only helpful in dealing with the suffering of victims of injustice but also, I suggest, opens up a way to deal with the suffering of those whose politics we cannot condone' (2007: 112). Bearing witness opens up an intersubjective space or, as I have argued is more important, a trans-subjective encounter/event which reconciles, or establishes productive tensions between, our incompatible subjective and shared experiences, without reducing or incorporating, in an empathetic fashion, the irreducible other's experiences into our own consciousness.

One of the experiences narrated by Señor Berenguer emphasises Almodóvar's concern with the cinematic medium as a witnessing practice, which both produces knowledge and transmits memories through an emphasis on embodiment.[32] I am referring to the sequence in which Juan/Ángel has sex with Señor Berenguer (see Figures 3.7–3.8) on the couch in the Valencia apartment where Juan/Ángel and Ignacio live. They themselves film this 'un-pleasurable' experience. The technological reproduction of the sexual act becomes an event itself, which highlights the coexistence of different temporalities and spatialities, as the event is predicated on its infinite reproduction or deferral in a future to come.[33] Such an association of the cinematic image with bodily affect resonates with the sequence showing the two young boys masturbating each other in the cinema, and could be interpreted as a similar yet different, belated re-enactment of sex between Father Manolo and Ignacio, which comes in and out of time to haunt one's and/or the other's body and psyche in the present and in an unpredictable future.

Figure 3.7 Ángel/Juan has sex with Señor Berenguer

Figure 3.8 Señor Berenguer is infatuated by Ángel/Juan

This sequence crosscuts between subjective shots from Juan/Ángel's point of view of Señor Berenguer, subjective shots from Señor Berenguer's point of view, and objective shots of the couple having sex. The alternating subjective shots of the sex act are at some moments mediated through the Super 8 camera that they hold; the trembling of these shots seems to reflect psychological and emotional disturbance as well as physical fragility and disorientation. Spontaneity and pre-cariousness underpins the filming technique, which becomes part of the enunciative process, replicating the way in which filming themselves has become a way of exposing their own vulnerabilities – particularly those of Señor Berenguer, who can be blackmailed by Ángel/Juan. The somewhat incoherent movements of the camera and the inexact framing enhance our own kinaesthetic response to the movements of the camera. But they also point to the impossibility of fully apprehending the trace of the cinematic image, which is always already virtually constituted through its own non-presence. At other moments, rather than the characters' Super 8 camera, Almodóvar's camera mediates our encounter with the scene. Hence, this particular sequence emphasises embodiment, epitomising the film medium as a mediator of subjective and shared experiences, undercutting the medium's implicitly voyeuristic position and the primacy of vision as the 'organizing term, a term or process which hierarchically subordi-nates the other senses (or bodily zones) under its direction and control' (Grosz 1994: 220). From a phenomenological perspective, this could lead us to think of the full participation of the bodily self in the cinematic experience. This conceptualisation of the bodily self's participation in the cinematic experience may allow us to rethink the film medium's ontologi-cal and epistemological nature, thereby problematising the relationship between the re-presentational image on the screen and the physical body of the spectator. However, a phenomenological perspective is predicated on the illusion of an immediate and direct access to experience, without layers of mediation. It thus foregrounds an originary, pure thing outside the infinite play of signifiers, and perpetuates a metaphysics of presence. As Derrida claims:

> [T]he presence of the perceived present can appear as such only inasmuch as it is *continuously compounded* with a nonpresence and nonperception, with primary memory and expectation (retention and protention). These nonperceptions are neither added to, nor do they *occasionally* accompany, the actually perceived now; they are essentially and indispensably involved in its possibility. (1973: 64, emphasis in original)

For Derrida, the metaphysics of presence is associated with a teleological move towards absolute knowledge, which implies complete mastery of heterogeneous difference, the disavowal or reappropriation of loss and the reduction of death to a universalising structure of knowledge (McGowan 2013).

At one point, Goded narrates the story of a woman who embraces an alligator as she is devoured by it. The woman attains the impossible *jouissance*. This stands metaphorically for the self-destruction at the core of Goded's own emotional relationships and, to return to Bataille's concept of *altération*, to his creative practices. Cinema as a witnessing practice contributes to the absolute loss of self-control and the fragmentation of the self, or the rupture within one's being such that one's encounter with death cannot be obscured, rather than contributing to mastery, disavowal or reappropriation of loss and negativity.

Hence, the practice of testimony in general, and Señor Berenguer's narration in particular, is associated in *La mala educación* with bodily affection, pointing to the way that language, as mediated through the cinematic image, is inextricably linked to the body. *La mala educación* makes us think about how cinema becomes a witnessing practice through our embodied encounter with the film medium. From this perspective, body and language point to the subjective and shared psychological and material process of enacting and/or abreacting subjective and shared traces of trauma and fragments of memory. The fragments of memory and history and traces of trauma precariously endure in the present, as we can see in Ignacio's encounter with death, as performed and traumatically enacted by his brother, or imprinted on the last letter he wrote to Enrique.

In *La mala educación* Almodóvar articulates the ethical and potentially political process of acting out or working through the fragments of memories and traces of past traumatic experiences, through the mediation of the cinematic image. Such a juxtaposition of conflicting and incompatible memories and past traumatic experiences cannot be localised within a single point or an original centre. Rather, are located in the folds, in lines of flight, or between different bodies and subjectivities at a trans-subjective level. I would like to conclude this chapter by noting how the film ends. We see a long shot of the black gate to Goded's house. Ángel/Juan and Enrique walk towards the door, on the left side of the frame. Here, Enrique literally closes the door on Juan/Ángel, thus symbolically cutting this 'imposter' out of his life. The dark gate reminds us of a grid. The panels composing the grid are maximised and recede. Like vignette bubbles, texts inside the panels inform us of Juan/Ángel, Enrique Goded and Señor Berenguer's fates. This extra information implies that *La mala educación* extends the actions of the characters beyond the film's diegetic space and time, perhaps all the way to our present time. Given that Almodóvar conceives of time as moving in different directions between the past, the present and the future, the *mise-en-scène* here turns the film into a flashback narrative from the time frame of *La mala educación*'s production. In one panel, we are told that Enrique Goded continues to make films with the same passion he brought to them in the late 1970s and early 1980s.[34] The word 'passion' swells against the black field and recalls the way that the opening credits filled the screen (Smith 2004b: 18) until it loses its intelligibility. Like Ángel/Juan/Ignacio, who has altered his body to become Zahara, these elastic and precarious forms of being encapsulate our precarious subjective constitution in relation to the bodies, memories and traumas of others who are affected by the pains of history and their enduring impact on our own subjectivity and body.

I have suggested that cinema is incorporated into the archive, or functions as an archivisation of the traumatic event. With that understanding, we can see that Almodóvar's focus on cinema as a witnessing practice, through his emphasis on embodiment, alludes to a kind of 'counter-archive', or what Taylor defines as a 'repertoire' of shared affects, in which our fragments of memories and traces of past traumatic experiences cannot be captured by or are symptomatically erased from the archive. The latter, which is instrumental in constructing or preserving the past history of the nation for the future, cannot register, or violently represses our own visceral, bodily encounters with the not-yet known, not-yet experienced, not-yet remembered pains of history, as they are transmitted by and through other bodies and subjectivities at a trans-subjective level in the present and in an unpredictable future.

Yet, *La mala educación* enables us to problematise the archive's logic of preservation. It takes into account the cross-temporal condition on which the traumatic event, or its archivisation/reproduction as production of the event, is based. Almodóvar's film emphasises the paradox at the core of the traumatic event or the reproduction of the traumatic event as producing the event. Traumas stand between the past, the present and the future, between appearing, reappearing, and disappearing. They leave or infinitely defer their scattered marks or traces, which relate to other traces and events, as well as evoking the possibility that the trauma may be re-enacted or re-produced differently in an unpredictable future, without perpetuating the teleological, archival logic of preservation.[35] In addition, the affective intensity produced by individual and shared fragments of memory and traces of traumatic experiences in *La mala educación* affects us before they are rendered intelligible through rational comprehension of the structures of signification – and affects us beyond such rational comprehension, as well. This affective intensity resists the domestication of traumatic events. It refuses to render them available and comprehensible to mainstream culture. It exceeds the emphasis on detached cognition or unreflective emotion in conventional Spanish cinematic recreations of the past.[36] Finally, I want to note how Señor Berenguer literally returns to the film set, the present of the diegetic reality of *La mala educación*. In this case, the present may symbolically succumb to the dark shadows of the elusive, spectral past. My final chapter, devoted to *La piel que habito*, focuses on the 'im-possibility of not-succumbing'.

CHAPTER 4

Im-Possibility of Not-Succumbing:
La piel que habito

[P]hilology is that venerable art which exacts from its followers one thing above all –
to step to one side, to leave themselves spare moments, to grow silent, to become slow
– the leisurely art of the goldsmith applied to language: an art which must carry out
slow, fine work, and attains nothing if not *lento*. For this very reason philology is now
more desirable than ever before; for this very reason it is the highest attraction and
incitement in an age of 'work': that is to say, of haste, of unseemly and immoderate
hurry-skurry, which is intent upon 'getting things done' at once, even every book,
whether old or new. Philology itself, perhaps, will not 'get things done' so hurriedly:
it teaches how to read well: i. e. slowly, profoundly, attentively, prudently, with inner
thoughts, with the mental doors ajar, with delicate fingers and eyes. (Nietzsche cited
in Galt Harpham 2009: 37, emphasis in original)

In this final chapter, I explore how *La piel que habito* reflects and responds
to the vicissitudes and catastrophes of the past and present. Whether they
be individual or collective, national or trans-national, they are all inscribed
on and irrupt through the surface of the body. This reading encourages
spectators to ponder how the fragments of memory and history are actualised and endure from the vantage point of the present, and how the traces
and shards of the traumatic past exceed temporal boundaries. They haunt
or contaminate our experience of the present, so that the traumas of the
violent past are re-staged, condensed and displaced.[1] The traces of memory
and history are externalised, but also erased as they are impressed. Or, they
are imprinted in the subjectivity and body without external articulation,
thereby escaping from linguistic symbolisation. From this perspective, we
can associate the scientific development of biogenetics and biotechnology,
one of the main themes in the film, with a 'synthetic wounding' of the
human body by scientific, technological, political and economic power
– a wounding that is both literal and symbolic. This reading obliges us
to keep questioning and re-conceptualising our theoretical discussions
about embodied human existence. As Gianna Bouchard argues, '[a]s the
body has become increasingly exploited, manipulated, commodified and

commercialised by biotechnologies, so unease has escalated about control over and proprietary interests in all bodies, both human and non-human' (2012: 94). Bouchard does not establish a hierarchical distinction between humans and non-humans (I will come back to this point shortly), but her argument does seem to be predicated on a liberal notion of the 'autonomy of the individual', who has a right to make choices –and is, thus, inextricably linked to a liberal conception of sovereignty, and the associated discourse of mastery. Because Bouchard leaves these concepts unquestioned, she remains caught up in the binary logic and hierarchical thinking that she attempts to undermine.

With regard to the 'autonomy of the individual', I shall reiterate that the ontological subject is always already predicated on one's relation to irreducible others. To put it differently, our relation to the irreducible other precedes and exceeds our ontological condition of subjectivity; as Butler puts it, 'relationality not only [is a] descriptive or historical fact of our formation, but also [. . .] an ongoing normative dimension of our social and political lives, one in which we are compelled to take stock of our interdependence' (2003: 16–17). Butler is concerned with the ethical and political questions raised by the way that subjectivity is constituted by precariousness and vulnerability; and by the distinction between those subjects who are worthy of being grieved and those who are not; and by the infrastructural distribution of precariousness and 'bare life' (a term to which I will come back later on). In this context, Butler draws on Lévinas' ethics of alterity (see Introduction) to propose that the call of the irreducible other, with whom we are bonded, constitutes our ethical relation to the irreducible other. For Butler, individuation is posterior to the irreducible other's solicitation and the response to that solicitation. Because of this, subjectivity cannot be reduced to the calculated choices of an egoistic self or the contractual obligations of autonomous individuals (2012).

Before continuing to discuss the issues at stake in this chapter, I will clarify how Butler's focus on precarious life can be put into a productive tension with Ettinger's psychoanalytic concepts in this study. In a conversation between the two theorists (2011), Butler seemed anxious about Ettinger's emphasis on the ethical and political valence at the core of our matrixial trans-subjective encounters. For Butler, Ettinger's focus on self-fragilisation as a condition of possibility for responding to the irreducible other's ethical call may be antithetical to her emphasis on the ethical relation which we are always already in, and which precedes and exceeds the ontological subject. According to Butler, our acceptance or refusal of the other's solicitation does not supersede that ethical relation. She insists that those affirmations are not predicated on the egoistic calculation of an autonomous subject, and are thereby already conditioned by the undecidability at the core of the concept of responsibility (see Introduction). But I suggest that these two thinkers are not mutually exclusive, even if Ettinger emphasises the resources already engendered within subjectivity for a psychic disposition and ability to respond to the solicitations of the other. Ettinger's psychoanalytic focus on partial subjectivity and trans-subjectivity avoids any reconstituting of the autonomous individual, precisely because matrixial time is outside linear historical time and therefore operates beyond the boundaries of the discrete subject. Ettinger's notion of a 'subjectivity as encounter at shared borderspaces' is not, in fact, antithetical to Butler's emphasis on the way in which we are acted upon by, and act upon the other. In effect, Ettinger's emphasis on borderspaces is an additional resource for thinking ethically and politically about irreducible others – the central concern of Butler's use of Lévinas and Arendt.

To return to Bouchard's argument, let us begin by asking how we can reflect on the persistent threat to our embodied human subjectivity posed by scientific and technological intrusions on the human body, particularly when they are complicit with modern sovereign power and biopolitics. We can do it, I suggest, precisely by questioning these categories of thinking in order to foreground their instability. In this context, the depiction of biogenetics in *La piel que habito* could be seen as a fantasy, which reveals Almodóvar's reliance on some elements of the science fiction genre.[2] But the film can also be interpreted as figuring anxiety about the imbrication of sciences and technology – particularly the genetic sciences – with political and economic power, and their increasing role in our social and political lives. At the same time, the film turns the operations of modern sovereign power against themselves. On the one hand, then, I propose that the film's attention to Vicente/Vera's incarceration and forced mutilation, and Dr Ledgard's scientific manipulation of her/his body, can evoke historical events, including the traumas induced and marks left by totalitarian regimes on the individual and the social body and psyche.[3] On the other hand, I argue that *La piel que habito* evokes a traumatic return from the present to the painful past. It makes us aware of the possible dangers of perpetuating the 'concentrationary' logic at the core of the structures of power that sustain our global society. 'Concentrationary' logic is predicated, in part, on the disposability of bodies and the attempt to eradicate the human, or on the production of a precarious humanity through techniques of terror and the destruction of the political subject or the subject of politics. The structures of totalitarian political regimes and state terrorism, like the Franco regime, have, historically, been sustained by these techniques of power – as Arendt showed in her seminal *The Origins of Totalitarianism* (1951).

Yet, the film renders totalitarianism and its infiltration of contemporary culture only obliquely. It is important to emphasise and clarify, then, that there are important ontological and historical differences between the horrific and exceptional violence perpetrated by totalitarian political systems, and what we understand as our current culture's reliance on bio-technology and biogenetics in particular, and technology and the sciences in general. There are also, however, important similarities in how these technologies and sciences allow for the control, exploitation, commodification and manipulation of the human body, and how these impinge upon our subjectivity, as well.

Dr Ledgard embodies phallic masculinity. We can associate this with modern sovereign power and biopolitics precisely because the concept of liberal sovereignty is predicated on the im-possibility of the liberal sovereign controlling the incalculable elements that exceed the operations of its own machinery. In his analysis of the shift from sovereign power to bio-power, Foucault explains that sovereignty involves the sovereign's right to give life or death to others without responding to a legislative or juridical apparatus; this is mainly visible in – in Derrida's terms, 'erected' by – acts of spectacular violence.[4] Foucault argues that biopower can be seen in the controlling and disciplining of bodies through multidirectional discursive apparatuses and state institutions. This discipline produces docile subjects who have internalised the dictates of the biopolitical regime so that they can function in a capitalist society based on reproduction (see Foucault 1990 [1978]). Vicente/Vera, for instance, embodies both literally and symbolically a gendered subjectivity. As Butler explains, such a subjectivity shows how the constitution of our embodied human subjectivity is always grounded in our vulnerability, our 'nudity', before the other – and the other's before ourselves.[5] Vicente/Vera's 'wounded gender'[6] seems to illustrate how the acquisition of, the becoming of, gender is always already predicated on a process of undoing or dispossessing the subject. As Butler argues,

> when we speak about 'my sexuality' or 'my gender', as we do and as we must, we nevertheless mean something complicated that is partially concealed by our usage. As a mode of relation, neither gender nor sexuality is precisely a possession, but, rather, is a mode of being dispossessed, a way of being *for* another or *by virtue of* another. (2003: 13, emphasis in original)

For Butler, if we are exposed to the vulnerability of the irreducible other, the other's 'nudity', we become aware that vulnerability and precariousness are constitutive elements of our own subjectivity, as well. This exposure to our shared vulnerability is not based on a symmetrical relation – Butler insists that the other is irreducible, and cannot be translated into or contained within an intentional structure in one's consciousness. If the other is constituted through the undoing of her/his subjectivity, and by being dispossessed of it, we too are constituted through undoing and dispossession. For Butler, this is the condition of possibility for an ethical relation between us and the irreducible other. As we will see in the film, it is based on one's ethical responsibility for the irreducible other's 'bodily conditions of life', both material and symbolic (2012).

Agamben ties his reflections on biopolitics to the concept of hyperbolic sovereignty. He connects modern sovereign power to biopower, which can become a '"death machine" supported by a "state of exception" that suspends the rule of law to totalize it in and as its other' (Weber 2006: 68). Whereas Foucault suggests a distinct shift from hyperbolic sovereignty to biopower, Agamben associates the idea of the concentration camp with the current biopolitical way of ordering experience. He sees biopolitics as reliant on an 'anthropological machine'. Here, that which is considered non-human is excluded as a constitutive element of the human. On this understanding, the body is reduced to disposable matter, and is entirely vulnerable to the degrading force of sovereign power (Braidotti 2006: 13). Agamben explains:

> Instead of deducing the definition of the camp from the events that took place there, we will ask: What is a camp, what is its juridicopolitical structure, that such events could take place there? This will lead us to regard the camp not as a historical fact and an anomaly belonging to the past (even if still verifiable) but in some way as the hidden matrix and *nomos* of the political space in which we are still living. (1998: 166, emphasis in original)

Following this line of thought, Weber summarises Agamben's argument that it is through sovereignty 'which a certain Western tradition of "biopolitics" seeks to assimilate the heterogeneity on which it depends and thereby to treat it as the integrating element of its own "death machine"' (2006: 65). From this perspective, I propose that the traces of a 'concentrationary' logic emerge and re-emerge as a kind of spectre to haunt us and de-form our human subjectivity outside and beyond the historical reality of the concentration camp. Concentrationary logic is integral to the late-modern economic and political system, because state violence, failing infrastructures, and the commodification of bodies – this latter being the most important in the film – all allow for the production of disposable bodies.

La piel que habito takes place in Toledo, a city that evokes the ruins of Spain's imperial past, as if the city could be associated with that allegorical moment in which 'history is replaced by its setting' (see Chapter 3). Although Almodóvar's film does not explicitly refer to Francoism or recreate the past, I argue that the film allegorically, and hence obliquely, evokes Spain's recent traumatic past, in particular, as well as trans-national history, and the intoxicating effects of those traumas. In doing so, it establishes a non-dialectical relationship between particular and universal.[7] Allegory implies a crisis of referents, which underpins the structure and economy of trauma. I have explored allegory in Chapter 3; allegorical representation and interpretation here points to the 'historical devastation, the ruining of meaning, but also the work on the ruins of a disfigured totality that transformed its traces into the redemptive promise of a broken historicity that continued to vibrate in the folds of its falling' (Richard 2000: 274). From this perspective, *La piel que habito* is a self-conscious cinematic practice that allegorically represents how some elements of totalitarian political regimes' violence, in particular Francoism, can still seep, whether noticeably or not, into forms of modern sovereign power in the present – and, in doing so, the film performs an act of political criticism. Yet, *La piel que habito* performs what I call 'productive inconsistencies', in which the articulation of one category of thinking relies on the coexistence of an antithetical category. The categories do not, however, invalidate each other. Instead, the coexistence of incompatible discourses opens up alternative ways of thinking about both political sovereignty and the sovereign subject.

My concern with both the material and the discursive conditions of the human body and embodiment[8] is intended to avoid the logic underpinning the 'anthropological machine', which would refuse to bear witness to beings considered below the category of the human (Dickinson 2011). Similarly, I avoid the reduction of the human to an abstraction, in particular that associated with the liberal enlightenment's understanding of universalism, which has been so inadequate at protecting actual human beings from the violence of modern sovereign power (Fraser 2004; Bernstein 2005). This understanding of the human in the abstract is itself predicated on a supposedly clear binary distinction between the human and the animal. Kelly Oliver explains:

> [T]hese oppositions are too simplistic and cover up complicated and fluid differences within the categories. For example, there is not just one type of man (think of women, the history of mankind, cultural differences, racial differences, etc.), and there is not just one type of animal. [. . .] [I]t is obvious that the category *animal* covers over vast, nearly infinite, differences between species and individuals. (2013: 6, emphasis in original)

Oliver foregrounds the undecidable operation at the core of Derrida's concept of *différance*, not in order to dismantle binary oppositions, but in order to explore how undecidability 'works fo[r] and against the binary oppositions' (2013: 7), and to reveal the 'mechanistic operations' at work on both sides of the binary (2013: 7). To simply invert a binary would be to imply complicity with the opposite position, so Oliver foregrounds instead the irresolvability of such binary oppositions. She thus multiplies the 'differences and fractures [of] traditional boundaries. Once we wedge the machine in between the binaries animal–human and nature–culture, however, their oppositional stance grinds down, if it does not come to a complete halt' (2013: 8).

However, I want to propose that *La piel que habito* agitates us and helps us to remain hypervigilant; I think with the film, through the prism of the 'concentrationary', about the recognition of the memories of the Franco regime and totalitarian regimes in general, which attempted to produce a precarious humanity, and the associated threat to our embodied conditions of being. The toxic effects of 'concentrationary' logic can contaminate the memory of the body far into the future, and the concept of hyperbolic sovereignty continues to infiltrate, or repeat differently in, our contemporary neoliberal culture. So, I argue that *La piel que habito* points to the articulation of a perverse fantasy of power and mastery, embodied by Dr Ledgard, over the irreducible other, embodied by Vicente/Vera. This fantasy is predicated on the repression of any awareness of its own nothingness, and this unrecognised lack is projected onto the irreducible other.[9] Hence, *La piel que habito* insists on the complexities and ambivalence of those symbolic structures, in order to point, symptomatically, to their precariousness, inconsistencies and fissures. It encourages us to remain hypervigilant in the face of the dangers of the 'im-possibility of not-succumbing' to the logics of power on which totalitarian regimes are predicated.

Technology/Opacity/Hapticality

A panoramic view of the old city of Toledo is juxtaposed with an expository intertitle. It informs us that the film takes place in 2012. The image of Toledo carries the weight of the past, while the intertitle signals that the film is set more or less in the present (the film was produced in 2011). Hence, this opening scene, in which past and present are conflated into 'the concentrated time of a Deleuzean [*crystal-image*]' (Cisneros 2006: 63, my emphasis), acquires great significance. It illustrates, in cinematic terms, Almodóvar's political concern with a concept of time as convoluted, in which past and present are juxtaposed or coexist within the same space, thus 'vacillating between multiple temporal registers, including the future, that remain irreducibly distinct' (Cisneros 2006: 60). The bifurcated temporality proposed here challenges a linear conception of homogeneous time. This linear conception is associated with a teleological notion of history, in which the present seems to be the result of a logical progression from past events. But in the film, the intertitle allows for the inscription of the shards of individual and collective past traumatic experiences and memories, as figured by the image of Toledo – an image that evokes Spain's past. The superimposition of temporalities points to the intrusion of history into the surface of the image, so we connect, critically, what is visible with that which is located beyond the visible (Silverman 2015).

This image is followed by an establishing shot of the mansion, in which most of the film's action takes place. The estate's name is tiled on one of the walls, and we see a close-up of the name, El Cigarral. According to Jeremy Biles, this name alludes 'to the insect that "dies" beneath the earth to be metaphorically "resurrected"' (2012: unpaginated).[10] A panning shot of the same wall that surrounds this magnificent house emphasises, from the outset, the oppressive, symbolic authority of architecture, the monumental, which is associated with phallic power, as if, as we later learn, the visible fortress-house covers, like a tomb, the underlying, invisible structures of psychic and political perversion and repression that haunt, and are re-enacted in this enclosed architectural space. The civilised mansion thus becomes a document of barbarism.

The camera pans once more from right to left. We notice the metal intercom used to communicate with the residents of the prison-like mansion, which pays a key role in a later scene: Zeca (Marilia's criminal son, brother of Dr Ledgard) has been filmed by security cameras while robbing a jewellery store. To avoid police detection, he dresses up, ridiculously, as a tiger. He uses the intercom camera to talk to his mother, and proves that he is her son by showing her his buttocks – she recognises his mole.[11] The modern intercom contrasts jarringly with the house's otherwise antique appearance, so we notice, as we might not have in other circumstances, that the relationship between mother and son is mediated by technology.

The film further develops its focus on the technological mediation of our everyday experiences and intersubjective encounters in a sequence showing Dr Ledgard watching Vera (an act repeated differently later in the film). A medium shot of Dr Ledgard looking off-screen and trying to reach the remote control of his TV cuts to an objective shot of his back. We now see that he is watching Vera, who, though reclining, turns to him. A close-up of Dr Ledgard is followed by a shot from his point of view. He gazes voyeuristically at his 'victim' and/or 'object of desire'. Almodóvar forces us to share Dr Ledgard's voyeuristic, phallic position, so that we perpetuate and participate in his sadistic gaze (I will come back to this point shortly). Yet, Almodóvar immediately undercuts this objectifying, voyeuristic, sadistic, phallic vision. As the camera lingers on Vera, the surface of her naked body seems to collapse onto the surface of the screen that mediates Dr Ledgard's 'cinematic' experience, and onto the cinematic screen, which mediates our own perception of the film. Depth-of-field is thereby distorted, and the image of Vera's naked body is turned into images of fragmented flesh, as if our encounter with the cinematic image could only be achieved through our perception of irreducible abstract forms instead of a recognisable human figure. Vera's naked body is turned into a fleshy, unyielding and opaque surface, which fills the spectator's field of vision, creates an over-proximity and enhances our feeling of dislocation – just as the red curtain did in *Todo sobre mi madre*. But, despite this over-proximity, the spectator can haptically perceive the texture of Vera's body, and the tonal differences and shadows of the fleshy surface encourage us to think about the film medium – whether celluloid or digital – as an embodied experience. Vivian Sobchack rightly associates such experience with the radical 'material condition of human being that necessarily entails both the body and consciousness, objectivity and subjectivity, in an *irreducible ensemble*' (2004: 4, emphasis in original). I shall return later to the film's reflexive considerations of cinematic representation and perception in order to emphasise the visceral, disruptive relation or experience in the phenomenological encounter between the spectator and the film, based as it is on pure bodily affect. Shortly, I will explore how the spectator's absorption in the film is constantly interrupted (Fer 2004: 17).

In his description of this scene, Smith suggests that 'the slow pan over a nude sleeping Vera, closely observed by the doctor on his wide screen TV, reminds us of the voyeurism of reality television that Almodóvar critiqued so presciently in *Kika* (1993)' (2011: unpaginated). Here, as with the answering machines in *Mujeres al borde de un ataque de nervios*, Almodóvar shows how modern technologies, including cinema, inevitably mediate, but also threaten human communication. I suggest that Almodóvar's attention to the relationship between humans and machines points to the possibly liberating and transforming effects of modern technologies for human perception and thought, as well as the alienating effects. Both of these possibilities can be seen in Benjamin's work. He was deeply concerned with modern capitalism's impact on human experience and with the threat of fascism in modern society; he recognised history as a living practice involving a recognition of trauma and death (Lowenstein 2003: 74). But Benjamin also recognised, in a rather contradictory, yet productive manner, the way in which modern technologies could forge new collectivities, or, on the other hand, could be appropriated for propagandistic purposes; they could be symbols of progress or lead to disaster (Benjamin 1968; Lane 2005). For Benjamin, modern technologies could anaesthetise human sensitivity and mask the brutal conditions of production and domination, to paraphrase Michael Jennings (2014); or, if used differently, modern technologies could lay bare the conditions of oppression, and encourage us to become conscious of those oppressive mechanisms (Benjamin 1968).

To return to the house where the film's action takes place: the camera focuses on the mansion's iron gates, further associating it with a carceral, surveilled, architectural space. As we will later learn, this resonates with Bentham's plan for the panopticon, which Foucault meticulously analysed in his attempt to think more broadly about the modern, mechanistic procedures of discipline and control (1975). In other words, for Foucault, the panopticon, a political technology for the exercise of power, is not only figured in confined spaces, such as the film's mansion; it can also be understood as the institutional and discursive apparatus that is internalised by subjects, thereby effecting, automatically, its power. Silverman explains: 'for Foucault, disciplinary power is not simply confined to penal institutions', rather, it can be seen in 'any space in which human beings are subject to [the] unregulated bio-political power of the state' (2015: 193). The mansion, the architectural space shown in the film, does seem to produce social good behaviour – that is, to institutionalise subjectivity – through surveillance and discursive binary divisions.[12] But, to the contrary, these political technologies can also produce aberrant behaviour due to the de-forming, intoxicating effects of excessive power on human subjectivity. As we see the exterior path to the house, the camera cuts to an objective shot of one of the mansion's windows. We can see, within, the silhouette of someone practising yoga. The windows are secured by iron bars, again suggesting that we see the old mansion as what Smith and Rob White call a vigilant space. Through this attention to gates, bars and enclosure in the *mise-en-scène*, we are led towards a sense of claustrophobia; we feel the de-formation and intoxication caused by excessive power. Later, we will see, this sensation parallels those of the as yet unknown yogi.

The camera cuts to the interior of the room, of which we have just seen the exterior. An objective shot shows a round surveillance camera; it looks like an orifice on the wall. The camera watches over Vera, thus, it seems, exemplifying the modern, panoptical technologies through which the power of the modern state impinges upon people's bodies, and constitutes their subjectivities. But the round surveillance camera could also be a detail or fragment in the scene that operates as what Mulvey calls a *cinematic punctum* (2006).[13] The surveillance device's shape suggests the orifice in which the vacuum cleaner is kept; Vera uses it to clean up the clothing that she has violently cut to pieces, in an effort to externalise her discomfort. The floor looks like a Jackson Pollock painting, on which the painter's corporeal movements are inscribed by drips of paint as he moves around the canvas.[14] The floor becomes a tactile surface full of incident – the scattered pieces of fabric create an opacity, which is the condition of possibility for visual perception (Fer 2002: 93). Opacity is a form of inscription in the *negative*, scratched on the surface and in the field of vision. The scattered fragments of fabric look like the blind spots in the visual field. But this tactile surface allows us to rethink of vision as incorporating touch.

> [This] pure event of perception, as a matter of fold, is the seeing that sight cannot see, a blindness that is the condition of all sight as well as its limit. This enabling interruption, as the potentiality of visuality (to see and to not-see), is a lure that draws out perception by incessantly withdrawing vision and the visual. (Ricco 2002: 67)

The film's emphasis on the haptic is also illustrated in the repeated sequence of Dr Ledgard watching Vera on his TV. Despite the graphic similarities between the two sequences, the second one is slightly different; it shows Vera, larger than life, dressed in a tight bodysuit, facing the camera and reading a book (see Figure 4.1). Smith and White aptly describe this scene:

> Robert zooms in on the ultra-high-definition plasma image of Vera in a pose that resembles the Old Master painting hanging next door. An incarcerated body, then, but not at all a docile one. Almodóvar thus gives an intriguing spin on the surveillance theme by emphasizing both the gaze's reciprocity and the highly aestheticized quality of the images that the house's video screens exhibit. (2011: unpaginated)

Pascale Thibaudeau here stresses Almodóvar's own emphasis on the power of Vera's returned gaze; this scene, she proposes, points out that Dr Ledgard's vigilant gaze does not empower, but imprisons him in the act of looking (2013: 203). Yet, Thibaudeau's argument remains caught up in a binary logic, in which the subject's gaze is associated with power and the object of the gaze is associated with powerlessness.

I propose, then, that this scene points to the way in which, in Lacanian theory, the subject becomes aware of her/his own visibility in the act of looking; the subject gazes at an object and thus becomes aware of herself/himself as an object. So the gaze does not imply control and mastery, but

Figure 4.1 Dr Ledgard watches Vera and she watches him (© joseharo)

the failure to control the field of vision, which is, indeed, a threat for the subject. Lacan explains: 'In our relation to things, in so far as this relation is constituted by the way of vision, and ordered in the figures of representation, something slips, passes, is transmitted, from stage to stage, and is always to some degree eluded in it – that is what we call the gaze' (1978: 73). From this perspective, Almodóvar re-formulates a position of visual non-mastery through the destabilisation or, more precisely, the laying bare of the phallic scopic economy that underpins cinematic spectatorship. *La piel que habito* thus disarticulates, in both the political and the subjective sense, the liberal conception of phallic sovereignty that has conventionally been associated with the mastery and control of vision. Ettinger explains: 'In an era of technical gazes and anonymous global eyes, the choice of witnessing to, rather than ignorance [. . .] of [,] internal and external phallic gaze becomes crucial. Direct witnessing is painful, since one can't ignore and deny one's own participation in the phallic gaze' (2006b: 110). The film thus makes us critically aware of our potential perpetuation of, and participation in the sadistic, phallic gaze and reveals the internal psychic mechanisms and blind spots through which phallic sovereignty is technologically erected and undone. This enhances our consciousness of our responsible, witnessing, spectatorial position vis-à-vis the cinematic image.

To return to the haptic; this mode of engagement with the cinematic image makes us aware of the extent to which the body is always implicated in perception and cognition. I propose that Almodóvar's emphasis on technology's mediation of our perceptions, communications and experiences undermine an empathic model of aesthetic experience, which relies on a transcendental subject of perception. Almodóvar's film, to the contrary, emphasises that technological mediation causes discontinuities and interruptions, which are, in fact, the condition of possibility for vision (Fer 2004: 4). In this context, these self-reflexive scenes make us think about the conditions of visibility by revealing how our phenomenological encounter with the film has to be experienced in a discontinuous and interrupted manner. A close-up of Zeca licking the video screen on which he can see Vera practising yoga, for instance, suggests that the encounter with the film is always already a discontinuous and interrupted process. It is impossible for Zeca to capture Vera fully on the video screen; this suggests the impossibility of fully apprehending the cinematic image, or, in ethical terms, the impossibility of empathising with or translating the experiences of the irreducible other into a familiar structure within our own consciousness (see Chapter 2). The film, then, stresses discontinuous encounters with phenomena, and downplays the possibility that a subject could be reconstituted in perception. It points to the precarious and vulnerable condition of our subjectivity; to the inability of our gaze to contemplate fully or master phenomena; and to the gaze's disintegration in the process of perception. The latter is always already predicated on the subject being captured by the gaze. *La piel que habito*'s emphasis on the haptic could lead us to think about the full participation of our bodily self in the cinematic and aesthetic experience, and to a more immediate and visceral experience associated with embodied vision and pure empathy (Fer 2004). However, the technological mediation of the perceiving subject's bodily and sensory experience does not lead to a wholly reconstituted subject. Rather, it implies a loss and rupture for the subject, which are itself constitutive of subjectivity. So our encounter with the film implies a condition of embodied viewing that does not lead to pure empathy. Instead, the spectator suffers a loss in the process of perception (Fer 2004). A rupture is produced in the non-transcendental subject, as our relation to the cinematic image is de-familiarised. And, at the same time, the encounter undercuts the normative structures of cinematic vision, which are based on distance and objectification.

Surveillance and Mutilation

To return to the surveillance camera: it seems like a cut on the wall of this rather aseptic and claustrophobic interior space. Although it is included in the field of representation as a surveillance camera, as a cut or void in the visual field it is symbolically excluded from the field of representation, which would undercut the camera's function as a surveillance device. So the camera can be read in divergent and mutually exclusive ways. The film's insistence on how the penetration of almost every space in the house by surveillance technologies symbolises the success of the controlling mechanisms. But identifying the surveillance camera as a void enables us to read the camera as allegorising the incalculable failure of the political technologies that sustain the modern regimes of sovereign power, thereby revealing the 'blind spot in this sovereign gaze that again is both necessary and unsettling' (Oliver 2013: 17).[15]

The camera as cut on the wall can be read as an orifice, which becomes an irreconcilable split, and seems to anticipate the cut that Vicente has suffered in his own body.[16] The film shows us, in flashback, that Dr Ledgard has recently performed a vaginoplasty on Vicente, therefore forcibly mutilating his penis. This is also suggested when a long shot of Vicente dressed in a green robe standing on a chair cuts to a medium shot of his body reflected in a round mirror, as if the mirror's shape implied the additional orifice in Vicente's body. Although flashbacks are an established convention of narrative cinema, Smith has noted that in Almodóvar's film, they work to produce a complex narrative that shifts back and forth, as if time were circumscribed to a loop (2011: unpaginated). From this perspective, the overlapping of different and multiple temporalities seems to replicate, at the level of cinematic form, the temporal structure and economy of trauma. Caruth, for instance, associates flashbacks with traumatic memories, arguing that a flashback can be defined as a temporal and spatial interruption that has a disturbing impact on the subject (1991). The flashbacks in *La piel que habito* could then be interpreted as cinematic devices pointing to the possibility of expression from within an unknown and unprocessed rupture in the subject. In Freudian psychoanalysis, the function of consciousness is to protect one's organism by inserting overwhelming stimulation into an ordered and articulated experience of time. The flashback can thus be interpreted as a cinematic signifier that enunciates the traumatic event's return to the film narrative, just as trauma returns to the subject without having been mediated by consciousness (see Burns 1999: 129–50). Caruth defines compulsive repetition as a painful experience and associates the rhetoric of the flashback with involuntary memories. The repetition of flashbacks is, then, understood in light of the absolute impossibility of avoiding a painful event that is not registered in the subject's psyche (1991). Hence, flashbacks in Almodóvar's film can be read as a rejection of progressive or linear modes of narrating experience,

Figure 4.2 We see Vera dressed in a Lycra bodysuit (© luciafaraig)

because they are representations beyond the linear conception of time. As such, I propose that the flashbacks in *La piel que habito* re-emphasise the (missed) encounter with the traumatic Real, particularly the way in which it is not located 'inside' or 'outside' but between these two spaces, and thus they underscore the repetition of the void. The disorientation that the flashbacks can produce thus replicates the experience of trauma – and here, in particular, suggest that the mutilation and surveillance of Vera/ Vicente's body are traumas that will return psychologically, just as the flashback returns in the film. Mutilation and surveillance are two crucial themes in this film, which are already displaced to or played out on the film's narrative structure and, in a rather suggestive manner, the round mirror and the surface of the wall in Vera's room. The camera in the wall can be seen here as a 'black hole', or as 'a floating flash that illuminates an erotic [and traumatic] blind spot' (Kopelson 1992: 179).

As the camera tilts down, we see Vera, dressed in a Lycra bodysuit which covers her entire body except her face (see Figure 4.2). She is practising advanced yoga postures, which seem to connect her physical with her psychic way of 'being-in-the-world'.[17] This scene is repeated differently three times (see Figures 4.3–4.4). On the one hand, Vera's bodily contortions could make us think of the French psychiatrist Jean-Martin Charcot's photographs of the bodies of hysterical women. He took them to explore how these women somatised psychiatric disorder.[18] On the other hand, I

Figure 4.3 Vera practises yoga (© joseharo)

Figure 4.4 Vera practises yoga (© luciafaraig)

suggest, Vera's postures evoke her physical and psychological 'endurance', which is inscribed on her flexible body's materiality – itself an artificial body. Yet, Vera's bodily postures manifest the embodied ontological and epistemological conditions of her human existence, which enhances the power in the combination of her physical and psychological being, thus resisting the external threat to her inner human condition.

As the camera focuses on Vera, her body holds still, as if time and movement had been frozen. To use Deleuze's concept, we see the emergence of the 'time-image', which affects and transforms our perceptual and interpretive experience of the cinematic image, and thus opens onto other connections (Walsh 2004: 200). As Deleuze puts it: 'The time-image does not imply the absence of movement (even though it often includes its increased scarcity) but it implies the reversal of the subordination; it is no longer time which is subordinate to movement; it is movement which subordinates itself to time' (Deleuze 1989: 271). It is important to bear in mind that the 'time-image' is not only associated with the long take; the 'time-image' cannot be limited to a technical question – for instance, the long take. 'The force or pressure of time', Deleuze suggests instead, 'goes outside the limits of the shot, and montage itself works and lives in time' (Deleuze 1989: 42). The focus here is on a broader philosophical distinction between the 'time-image' and the 'movement-image'. At the same time, Deleuze does see certain cinematic examples of 'slow cinema' (i.e., the cinema of Michelangelo Antonioni) as suspending the logic of cause and effect, and connecting images in terms of external causality (Walsh 2004: 196). Moreover, 'the object of cinema is not to reconstitute a presence of bodies, in perception and action, but to carry out a primordial genesis of bodies in terms of a white, or a black or a grey (or even in terms of colours), in terms of a "beginning of visible which is not yet a figure, which is not yet an action"' (Deleuze 1989: 201). So, while Almodóvar's film differs greatly from the kind of 'slow cinema' often associated with the 'time-image', the long duration of the shot of Vera practising advanced yoga could produce in us the emergence of the 'time-image'. As I shall discuss later, the 'time-image', the emancipation from movement that becomes the condition of possibility for transforming our own relation to the cinematic image, allegorises the potential of Vera moving from a subject position of victimhood, however ambiguous her position as a victim may be, to an ethical affirmation of her psychic and bodily self, without perpetuating the self-enclosure of the cogito. In this context, cinematic form allows us to conceive *La piel que habito* as an aesthetic practice that both politically criticises the way in which technologies of power constitute and de-form subjectivity, as I mentioned above, and at the same time interrupts the impingement on our bodies of biopower and modern sovereignty, through which we are constituted and by which we are threatened – though it does so, to be sure, at the micro-political level, by evoking and foregrounding lines of flight from the operations of power.

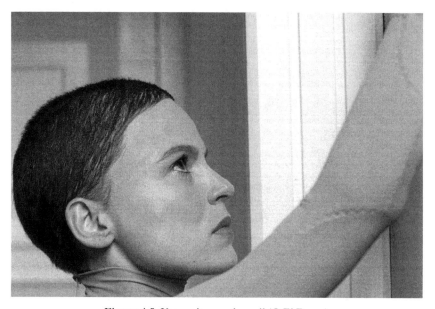

Figure 4.5 Vera writes on the wall (© El Deseo)

Just like Zahara's dress in *La mala educación*, Vera's costume looks like a body made from fragments of skin, an appearance that is further empha-sised by the visible sutures and zippers. Vera also creates sculptures from torn pieces of cloth, inspired by Louise Bourgeois's disjointed, stuffed sculptures; as Nixon explains, Bourgeois' 'use of reclaimed materials and simple construction techniques to fashion these [fabric] figures implies, in contrast to the industrially based fabrication of much late modernist sculpture, a domestic wartime economy of sorting and saving, but also a psychic economy of salvage, separation, and loss' (2005: 9). Vera also writes on the wall repeatedly, filling it with incident in a way that recalls the scratched surfaces described in the previous chapter (see Figure 4.5). These two artistic practices allow Vera to structure and transport the unbound affects induced by her encrypted trauma and, potentially, transform the haunting unprocessed trauma. In addition, Vera's skin-like bodysuit replicates her own body, particularly because her new body is made from pieces of artificial skin made from the blood of killed pigs; Dr Ledgard has been using Vera/Vicente for his experimental trans-genetic transplants. He uses recent scientific and technological developments to transform Vicente into an embodiment of his deceased wife, Gal, thereby destroying Vicente's singular, heterogeneous human subjectivity and replacing it with a commodified, homogeneous object that can serve his dictates and psychic perversions.

Vera also wears a black bodysuit; the camera lingers on her body as she gets dressed, emphasising the suit's colour and texture. It evokes the skin of the doll that Dr Ledgard's traumatised daughter Norma plays with in the garden in Brazil when she witnesses her mother's suicide (we see this scene in a flashback focalised by Marilia, as she tells Vera the story). Norma's inanimate black doll also resonates with Concha Buika's tattooed, black skin. Buika performed at the wedding during which Norma and Vicente meet. A close-up of Buika shows her singing in Spanish the same Brazilian song that Norma sang in Portuguese when her mother died. The film then cuts to a scene of Norma having sex with Vicente in the mansion's garden during the wedding, and we listen to Buika's diegetic, but off-screen singing, which blends seamlessly into the non-diegetic sound of Norma singing the same song. Interestingly, the soundtrack, which is non-diegetic, still functions as a kind of involuntary memory in Norma's mental life. In effect, the Brazilian song triggers in Norma the re-enactment of her unprocessed and untransformed trauma, which leads to an extremely violent physical confrontation with Vicente; later, her father finds Norma lying unconscious on the ground (see Figure 4.6). Dr Ledgard misinterprets this confrontation; he believes that Vicente has raped his daughter, and this becomes the justification for the 'punishment' that follows.

To return to Ettinger's concept of trans-subjectivity, Vera inscribes, condenses and displaces the traces of trauma and fragments of memories and experience coming from and transmitted by irreducible others across times and spaces beyond the boundaries of the discrete subject, just as Huma and Zahara did. *La piel que habito* can be read as an allegory of Ettinger's move from the legal or testimonial implications of the concept of witnessing to her understanding of *wit(h)nessing*, which implies bearing witness with and beside a non-assimilated other. Ettinger explains:

> Here we can conceive of an occasion for [the] realization of an unavoidable encounter with remnants of trauma, in the mental stratum of trans-subjectivity, in a certain jointness that becomes possible only *with-in differentiation*, in a co-emergence with-one-another that is not assimiliation and fusion, in a psychic dimension where a web of connections inside and outside the individual's limits, and self-mutual but nonsymmetrical transgression of these limits, does not favour the total separation of the distinct individual. (2016: 152, emphasis in original)

Following Ettinger, I suggest that Almodóvar's film makes us think of cinema as an aesthetic practice, an encounter/event, through which we can *wit(h)ness* and register the other's trauma at a trans-subjective and trans-historical level. When Vera is raped by Zeca, she explicitly experiences

Figure 4.6 Dr Ledgard finds Norma lying unconscious (© joseharo)

what Dr Ledgard believes his daughter to have experienced in the scene above – but differently. This is an example, then, of Ettinger's concept of being with, without assimilating or fusing with the irreducible other. A *different* re-enactment of the *same* traumatic event makes manifest my main concern with the way in which originary traumatic events are subsequently re-experienced differently, and the way in which subsequent traumatic events affect the experience and interpretation of earlier traumatic events.

Agrado has championed the emancipatory potential of technological and scientific developments vis-à-vis gender and sexual transformation, as is seen in *Todo sobre mi madre,* particularly in the scene I discussed in Chapter 2. As I argued there, Almodóvar's cinematic articulations of trans-sexualism and transgenderism can be celebrated as an intervention in theoretical debates about the performance and performativity of gender identity. But, Smith and White argue, in this film, trans-sexualism and transgenderism are a 'sheer violent mutilation and the cause of torment' (2011: unpaginated). They are conceived in *La piel que habito* as a traumatic imposition on the part of modern sovereign power and bio-power's representative (Dr Ledgard). The explicit, violent imposition of a different gender on Vicente's body points to how medical interventions on the body are predicated on a teleological logic, which demands the move from an 'illegible' subject position to a 'legible' one, and thereby perpetuates patriarchal, heteronormative ideology and binary thinking, as I explained in Chapter 2. However, as I will discuss shortly, while bio-power could be a threat to the human body, even in the worst case it cannot entirely subjugate the self. There is always an inassimilable trace, residue, remainder, or excess, which refuses the process of symbolisation within, and/or subjugation to, the social and symbolic order, and thereby breaks 'away from the absolute predictability of the system' (Richard 2000: 280). Richard associates the heterogeneous remainder with the 'forces of alterity and alteration' (2000: 280). It 'vibrates as an *acting* potentiality', and mobilises the '*zones of uncertainty*' around the *risks* of difference that challenges the model of "imaginary subjectivity"' (2000: 279–80, emphasis in original). The heterogeneous thus prevents the reconstitution of the ontological subject as a supposedly autonomous individual.

Concentrationary: Arendt/Agamben

The camera repeatedly focuses on Dr Ledgard's 'state of the art' scientific laboratory, his medical operating room and the equipment and clinical utensils he uses to carry out his scientific, if not sadistic, experiments on human, non-human or de-humanised bodies. We can read most of the spaces in the film – the laboratory where Vicente/Vera's body is mutilated and fabricated; the claustrophobic, surveilled room where Vera is incarcerated; and the sordid basement where Vicente is first imprisoned and reduced to a dehumanised condition of existence, as if he were an object – in terms of Almodóvar's association of the *mise-en-scène* with concentrationary iconography.[19] This iconography (gates, surveillance cameras, torture chambers, laboratories, prison-houses) links the affluent mansion, carefully decorated with the stylish furniture and artistic masterpieces that signal cultural prestige, to the secret experimental site where Dr Ledgard puts into practice a totalitarian ideology predicated on the dehumanisation, terrorising and destruction of the political subject, Vicente. The latter becomes for Dr Ledgard a subject who is not worthy of being grieved.

A shot showing Vicente screaming, in chains, cuts to a medium close-up of Vicente's mother, whose facial expression reveals her emotional and psychic pain (see Figures 4.7–4.8). It is interesting to note that a sound bridge links the two scenes, as if Vicente's mother could hear her son, as if she knew he was alive; in the ensuing sequence she tells the policeman that Vicente has disappeared, and not died (earlier in the film, she had asked one of her clients whether his wife had left him or disappeared, which we can now see was a premonition of her own confrontation with Vicente's disappearance, even though the earlier scene also provides some comic

Figure 4.7 Vicente is imprisoned in a sordid basement (© joseharo)

Figure 4.8 Vicente's mother feels her son is alive (© joseharo)

relief).Vicente's mother's suffering reminds us that Vicente, like any other being co-inhabiting the world (I will come back to this point), is a subject who is worthy of being grieved – although Dr Ledgard does not see him as such. El Cigarral can thus be read as a 'concentrationary' space, in which

Dr Ledgard exercises violent, total domination and power over Vicente/Vera. We can then recognise how his sadistic practices and his unlimited freedom evoke the violence and horror on which 'concentrationary' logic is grounded.

It is important to emphasise that *La piel que habito* is in no way a realistic representation, nor is it meant to compare El Cigarral with the German genocide of millions of European Jews and Roma people, nor with Nazi concentration camps, in which the inmates were not necessarily killed, but were without question violently dehumanised. Nor does Almodóvar's film directly refer to the atrocities and deaths suffered by Spanish political dissidents in Francoist concentration camps.[20] My reading of the film, rather, suggests that totalitarian political regimes relied on violence and wounding of the individual and social body and psyche, so the concentration camp is just one manifestation of the logic of totalitarianism. And the traces of that violence can still be recognised in contemporary threats to the integrity and dignity of the human body.

From this perspective, I suggest that Almodóvar's film imagines a concentrationary space so that it can focus on embodied subjectivities and human relations afflicted by the intoxicating effects of the totalitarian logic that sustains the concentrationary space – even if those subjectivities and relations are based on abusive intimacy. The iconography, thematic concerns, plot and representations of characters all suggest that *La piel que habito* depicts a concentrationary space. Furthermore, the film's self-reflexive engagement with the spectator's phenomenological, imaginary and interpretive engagement with the cinematic image leads in the same direction, as in the film's emphasis on claustrophobia; our spectatorial identification with and participation in the sadistic gaze; or the film's undercutting of the conventional scopic regime of cinematic spectatorship through de-familiarisation, or its use of what Ettinger calls 'direct witnessing'. Close attention to the aesthetics of Almodóvar's film enables us to think of 'the critical potential in cinema by exposing the viewers, by means of [this] cinematic process, to the insinuation of evil in the everyday and to the familiarization of camp-like logic and structures into the cultural imaginary' (Pollock 2015: 43). In other words, the film demands from us different modes of analysis – psychoanalytic, phenomenological, ethical, aesthetic, political. Together, these allow us to reflect critically on how such potential or real threats to the human body and human life persist in the structures of power that underpin our science- and technology-dominated culture. As the character of Dr Ledgard demonstrates, the complicity of science and technology with our globalised capitalist commodity culture is possible only when the plural, heterogeneous human subject is reduced to a non-differentiated, homogeneous object – an object that can be scientifically and technologically manipulated for private interests, as in the case of Dr Ledgard, or collective economic and political interests.

This interpretation can be filled out if we consider Arendt's argument that one of the main purposes of totalitarianism is to reduce the individuality and spontaneity of human beings to an indistinguishable bundle of reactions; to transform 'the human personality into a mere thing':

> Total domination attempts to achieve this goal both through ideological indoctrination of the elite formations and through absolute terror in the camps; and the atrocities for which the elite formations are ruthlessly used become, as it were, the practical application of the ideological indoctrination – the testing ground in which the latter must prove itself–while the appalling spectacle of the camps themselves is supposed to furnish the 'theoretical' verification of the ideology. (1976 [1951]: 437–8)

For Arendt, totalitarianism is founded on the complete destruction of human dignity, to such an extent that humanity, our social, moral, affective and intellectual being, is rendered superfluous (1976 [1951]: 457–8). Arendt, writing in the aftermath of Nazism, primarily focused on the terrors of Nazi Germany, but she also saw totalitarianism at work in political regimes (i.e. the Gulag system in the Stalinist Soviet Union) that were similarly predicated on horrific violence and dehumanisation. For Arendt, totalitarian regimes, as well as eradicating or exterminating human beings, also deprived them of their right to collective action, which she associates with politics (1958). According to Arendt, humanity is not an essence anterior to the social or the political sphere. Instead, politics, which she understands as collective action, is the condition of possibility for humanity (Pollock 2015: 16). Totalitarianism is antithetical to this understanding of politics, because the latter relies on human spontaneity (the potential for action) and plurality (the production of difference and novelty), while totalitarianism is predicated on the destruction of both. As such, it relies on concentrationary logic (Pollock 2015: 17).

Arendt also warns us that totalitarianism does not end with the defeat of fascism, as its logic can be incorporated into any political ideology based exclusively on utilitarian values: '[t]he danger of the corpse factories and holes of oblivion is that today [. . .] masses of people are continuously rendered superfluous if we continue to think of our world in utilitarian terms' (1976 [1951]: 459). This is relevant today, as Pollock, for instance, has argued by connecting utilitarian values with the logic underpinning neoliberal society: 'In neoliberal capitalism we live under the ideological tyranny of the Market, the blind forces of pure economic necessity against which any notion of what constitutes human life is calculated and found too expensive; even basic life becomes dispensable' (Pollock 2015: 17). This is, of course, the society and culture in which Almodóvar's film is inserted and which it obliquely denounces.

Agamben follows Arendt's analysis of the features of totalitarianism that are not confined to fascism or communism, by thinking about the 'concentrationary' without limiting it to the actual zone of the camp. He explains:

> Insofar as its inhabitants were stripped of every political status and wholly reduced to bare life, the camp was also the most absolute biopolitical space ever to have been realized, in which power confronts nothing but pure life, without any mediation. This is why the camp is the very paradigm of political space at the point at which politics becomes biopolitics and *homo sacer* is virtually confused with the citizen. (1998: 171, emphasis in original)

Agamben proposes that 'concentrationary' logic exceeds the historical actuality of Nazi concentration camps, and can be seen, for instance, in the biopolitical regulation and unregulation of everyday life: 'The political system no longer orders forms of life and juridical rules in a determinate space, but instead contains at its very center a *dislocating localization* that exceeds it and into which every form of life and every rule can be virtually taken' (1998: 175, emphasis in original). The camp is, for Agamben, a hidden logic that haunts and infiltrates the everyday of our current societies (Pollock and Silverman 2011b: 14). The 'concentrationary' system is, of course, associated with the historical reality of the camp, but it is 'a logic which can occur historically in one form but also inform and translate into other instances' (Pollock and Silverman 2011b: 50). Agamben's association of the camp with the new global biopolitical *nomos* (1998: 176) is, then, not oblivious to cultural and historical differences, because the concept cannot be limited to a particular historical moment.

Most relevantly to my work here, Agamben analyses the 'concentrationary' logic at work in contemporary liberal capitalist societies. Totalitariansim can be seen in our societies, for instance, any time sovereign power imposes a distinction between 'valuable' subjects, and those who are reduced to 'bare life' (that is life stripped of form and value), and thereby become a precarious humanity. This can be seen in the use of torture as a technique of domination and repression, the denial of legal rights to stateless people or, most relevant to this film, the state of exception as constitutive of sovereignty. Silverman argues:

> Agamben's argument rests on the idea, first, that what starts out as a state of exception in which the rule of law is temporarily suspended, actually becomes the norm and, second, that what is defined as the exception is not, strictly speaking, outside

the norm anyway but profoundly articulated with it, as the one can only define itself in relation to the other. (Silverman 2015: 193)

Agamben's philosophical and political propositions can help us to reflect on how *La piel que habito* suggests that the horrors of the past and the camp-like structures can be repeated in forms of violence that are integral to modern sovereign power in the present, a form of power itself predicated on its multiple, interminable divisions and on its incalculable failures, impotence and inconsistencies (I will come back to this point shortly).[21] The film allegorically evokes a 'concentrationary universe'[22] where, to use Arendt's famous words, 'everything is possible'. Almodóvar's film makes us hyperaware of how the traumatic past can contaminate the present, or how the present reiterates, albeit in a different form, the underlying structures of totalitarian logic. It thus allows us to reflect critically on how the traces and memories of political terror, violence and total domination affect us both spectrally and materially, and impinge, as I have argued throughout this study, not just on visible reality, but also on intangible spaces (Rolnik 2008b). As I explained in Chapter 3, for Rolnik, these lasting effects force us to find ways to protect ourselves, most obviously by preventing the trauma from resurfacing. I suggest, then, that Almodóvar's film can make us aware of how the horrors of our past 'occur historically in one form but also inform and translate into other instances', for instance, in the hold of 'bio-power' over our embodied humanity thanks to the achievements of technological and scientific control, exploitation and commodification of human and non-human life. Žižek, for instance, shows us that biogenetics is complicit with economic, social and political power; he argues that biogenetics can serve the 'interests of corporate capital and of the state agencies tempted to rely on it in order to increase their control of the population' (2004: 132). It is important to clarify that not all the technological and scientific developments perpetuate 'concentrationary logic'; technology is an exteriorisation or supplement to humanity, and can be used well or used poorly, can add to or subtract from human abilities (Hansen 2010: 65). But *La piel que habito* certainly suggests that we should question whether abuses of scientific and technological power over our bodies and subjectivities might eventually reduce us all to 'bare life' and so destroy the ontological distinctiveness of human subjectivity.[23]

For instance, Ian James draws on the concepts of totality, convergence and synchronisation to show how new technologies converge with the symbolic structures underpinning advanced capitalist systems to produce a synchronised subjective and collective experience that supports capitalist economic interests. James connects totalitarian logic with the ideological structures underpinning our consumer, media and technology-dominated culture, with 'which we are enthralled' (Pollock 2015: 41). The structures of capitalism dehumanise us and threaten our singular, divergent and de-synchronised human subjectivities, which are the condition of possibility for our definition as political subjects. He does not overlook the potential democratising effects of the new technologies through which those symbolic structures are accomplished; nor is his discussion of this convergence trapped in a universalising grand narrative. He is interested in 'describing more or less hidden ideological, technological, cultural and socio-economic, but ultimately contingent, processes, which, in their convergence and shared inner logic, *tend* towards totality, a violent totalization, and a totalitarian logic' (James 2015: 95, emphasis in original). In this context, *La piel que habito* offers an oblique political critique of the totalising logic underpinning our culture's reliance on scientific and technological advances. This logic leads to the production of homogeneous, synchronised, disposable subjects, who can become, albeit contingently, de-politicised and unreflective – subordinated, then, to private or collective economic interests.

The Beast

The film's repeated overhead shots of a headless dummy, and of Dr Ledgard applying fragments of artificial skin to Vera's body, point to the confusion between the animate and human, and the inanimate and non-human, body; this confusion is further emphasised by a dissolve from a shot of the dummy to one of Vera (see Figure 4.9). This association of human beings with inanimate objects is familiar to us from the comparison of Norma's black doll and Buika's black body. The dialectical relationship between animate and inanimate beings engages with the theme of dehumanisation, which is seen, for instance, when Vicente dresses a mannequin in his mother's clothing store's shop window. Vicente's action of dressing the mannequin will be re-staged differently when Dr Ledgard 'dresses' Vicente, in this case the object, and turns him into Vera. The store's mannequin is made of straw, which resonates with the burnt skin of Dr Ledgard's deceased wife, Gal. Almodóvar's ambivalent attention to Vera's skin-like bodysuit and to the pieces of artificial skin applied to Vera's body points to the way in which skin constitutes our subjectivity, and to the impossibility of surviving without it. For Anzieu, the skin is the threshold, the space of contact between the subject and the exterior world. The skin protects and isolates the subject from the outer world; and yet the subject is psychically constituted through her/his contact with the skin of the

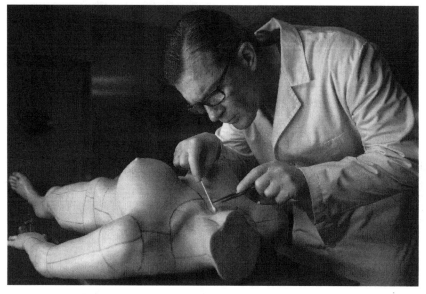

Figure 4.9 Dr Ledgard uses a headless dummy to practise his experiments
(© Lucia Faraig)

(m)other's body. Hence, the skin is one of the most important features of our embodied being. It fulfils complex cultural, anatomical and physiological functions in human subjectivity (see Chapter 3 above).[24] So Gal's emaciated body and burnt skin situate her between life and death, in a state of embodied being, but a state of being in which human subjectivity has been obliterated. Gal can touch and smell her burnt skin, but when she sees her face reflected in her room's window, she decides to commit suicide, as if to exercise the only control she has left over her obliterated humanity.

Vera has extremely pale skin, as if she were the material result of a political ideology based on the supremacy of the white race. We see Dr Ledgard applying a kind of fire machine to that skin or trapping an insect between Vera's body and a glass, scenes which suggest that Vera's extremely pale skin is immune to burns or insect bites. So, we may think that her artificial body is immune to pain. However, Vera does externalise her internal emotions by crying, and her body is still sensitive to physical pain. We can see this most obviously when she is violently raped by Zeca, a scene captured by the video screens in the mansion's kitchen; it might remind us of 'torture porn' movies (see Figure 4.10).[25] Sara Ahmed argues: 'It is through experiences such as pain that we come to have a sense of our skin as bodily surface, as something that keeps us apart from others, but as something that also mediates the relationship between internal or

Figure 4.10 Zeca rapes Vera (© El Deseo)

external, or inside and outside' (2005: 101). Zeca can be seen as a character who provides us, albeit problematically, with some kind of comic relief, since he is dressed up as a tiger. And he could also be seen as the stupid 'beast',[26] which reflects the bestiality of his brother, Dr Ledgard, though in Ledgard's case this bestiality is the basis of his hyperbolic sovereignty. Both brothers, however, operate outside the law and thus do not respond to it (Oliver 2013: 85–114). Zeca's skin-like tiger shirt is left on a kitchen chair behind Marilia, who, bound and gagged, witnesses Vera's rape through the mediation of the security cameras (this scene resonates with the scene in *Kika* in which Juana is tied to a chair by her brother, so that she cannot prevent him from raping her female employer). The detached tiger-skin-like shirt becomes a material signifier indexing the intrinsic relationship and resemblance of the beast to the sovereign (Oliver 2013: 85–114). It thus becomes a haunting trace of the horror of the return of the repressed to this already horrific universe. The detached skin of the beast is itself symptomatic of the spectral horror of the concentrationary logic that underpins modern sovereign power and bio-power in the present. Under this logic, the beast and the sovereign share a similar position; they are connected but also opposed, so that the dichotomy between them is undercut (Oliver 2013: 85–114). But in the film, Dr Ledgard kills Zeca. Here, the film lays bare the mechanistic operations that underpin the concept of sovereignty. We see here, in concrete terms, that Dr Ledgard's indivisible sovereignty is constituted by the unconscious repression of his own bestiality, by his disavowal of his internal instability and multiple, interminable divisions (Oliver 2013: 85–114). Zeca embodies the beast that is the condition of possibility for Dr Ledgard's supposedly self-sufficient sovereignty; in reality, the latter is predicated on the undecidable relationship between the animal and the human (Oliver 2013: 85–114).

Looking at the Perpetrator

La piel que habito's focus on Vera's body and skin problematises a dialectical relationship between the artificial, cosmetic conditions of her bodily self (as a surface that lacks depth, thus undercutting the relationship between inner and outer structure) and the material and discursive conditions (or the relationship between her embodiment and the psychic self, as Anzieu explains). This reveals that one's body is always already prosthetic. In other words, the prosthetic is integrated into the body, which is itself the medium through which we encounter personal and historical experience. For Freud, the body is a 'projection of a surface' that mediates the relationship between the outside world and the inside of the self (1962). Mark Hansen proposes that 'the human evolves by exteriorizing itself in tools, artifacts, language, and technical memory banks. Technology on this account is not something external and contingent, but rather an essential – indeed, *the* essential – dimension of the human' (2010: 65, emphasis in original). Based on Hansen's premise, technology is a supplement to human experience, which problematises, or even disarticulates, the relationship between nature and culture. Technology reveals the prosthetic as the condition of possibility for the constitution of the 'natural'. The film, too, problematises the binary opposition between the 'prosthetic' and the 'natural' (I will return to this point shortly).

Lived experience is materially and symbolically inscribed on the skin, and Almodóvar pays close attention to Antonio Banderas' ageing skin (see Figure 4.11), a feature that is particularly obvious if we compare Banderas in *La piel que habito* to Banderas as he appeared in Almodóvar's *Átame*. There, Banderas played the psychotic Ricky, who kidnaps the woman he loves, and forces her to fall in love with him. Smith notes that 'Banderas' looks, now sadly faded, serve here almost as a comment on that entropy of ageing that surgeons and cineastes alike seek in vain to vanquish' (2011: unpaginated). Dr Ledgard and Ricky could be seen as wrongdoers, but Almodóvar does problematise our sympathy, antipathy, apathy or empathy for Ricky, because he takes a subaltern subject position, is physically beautiful, and is committed to loving and caring of the other, despite his

Figure 4.11 Almodóvar pays attention to Banderas' ageing skin (© El Deseo)

reprehensible violation of another's safety and dignity. *La piel que habito* offers a similar challenge to the ethical and political categories that we use to account for the psychic mechanisms of power and desire: Dr Ledgard ends up falling in love with Vera, and, as Marilia intuitively suspects, this love will be the cause of his demise and ultimate death.

We see, in a dimly lit close-up, Vera's bag, into which she puts the gun that she will use to kill Dr Ledgard and Marilia. This shot shows how the cosmetic façade of Vera's femininity is used strategically to reveal the vulnerability and precariousness of phallic modern sovereignty as embodied by Dr Ledgard. Is Vera's murder of Dr Ledgard simply an instance of the common association of feminine masquerade with calculating dissimulation in patriarchal and heteronormative ideology? Does Vera's murder of Dr Ledgard mimetically reproduce Dr Ledgard's murder of Zeca, so that Vera perpetuates the actions on which his hyperbolic sovereignty is constituted? Vera's subjectivity has been de-formed, at least partially, by the contaminating effects of the totalitarian logic to which she has been subjected; that logic may have induced in her a totalitarian deed. But I suggest that Vera does not point to the threatening female figure hidden behind a cosmetic façade of femininity. Rather, the murder shows how Dr Ledgard's sovereign subjective and social position and, broadly speaking, the technological and scientific structures that sustain modern sovereign power, are predicated on chance elements that contribute to the incalculable failure or impossibility of their completely determining or constituting human subjectivity.

Yet, unlike Ricky, Dr Ledgard occupies and takes advantages of his hegemonic social and economic position, thereby aggravating his misdeeds and preventing any sympathy for him and the ideology of total domination that he puts into practice. In other words, Dr Ledgard fails to fulfil the ethical responsibility that precedes the choices of the autonomous subject; he fails, then, to fulfil the conditions required for coexistence in a world characterised by the freedom of plurality, to use Arendt's term. Instead, he chooses arbitrarily with whom he wants to coexist, thus violating the non-sovereign ethical relation with the irreducible other. He puts into practice an ideology predicated on the destruction of plurality and heterogeneity, stripping subjects of their basic humanity (Butler 2012). Banderas' consciously cold and almost mechanised performance makes it even more impossible to sympathise with Dr Ledgard. It is as if his conditions of existence had already been completely 'contaminated' or 'penetrated' by the inhuman technological and scientific violence of modern sovereignty, even though the bio-power he embodies and perpetrates in a pathological fantasy of total power will result in his own annihilation.

Even here, however, Almodóvar complicates the reductive binary opposition between perpetrator and victim, sympathy and antipathy, or empathy and apathy, because the adoption of one position always implies complicity with the opposite. The film is largely concerned with Vera's skin, but, as I have mentioned, it also pays considerable attention to Banderas' ageing face (see Figure 4.12). The face is, of course, the locus of human subjectivity; we become aware of Dr Ledgard's suffering and loss, of the vulnerability and perishability of his precarious body and subjectivity. *La piel que habito* does not force us to emotionally identify with the perpetrator or to subscribe to his political ideology and actions, but it does encourage us to look at the human face of the other, which is the difficult ethical prerequisite of bearing witness to the other's lived experiences – even though Dr Ledgard himself fails to recognise the humanity of an other. Ettinger explains: 'I don't have to feel empathy for my perpetrators, nor do I have to understand them, but this doesn't mean that I will hand them the mandate to destroy my own compassion which is one of my channels for accessing the non–I' (2006b: 124). It is important to re-emphasise that human subjectivity is predicated on our common vulnerability and precariousness. Because we cannot sympathise with Dr Ledgard, we see more strongly still the asymmetrical relationship at the core of our trans-subjective encounters. We cannot easily fall into an uncritical empathetic relation with the other, by identifying with the other's suffering. By

Figure 4.12 The skin we all live in and through which we encounter the other
(© joseharo)

forcing us to confront the perpetrator's human face, *La piel que habito* makes us aware of the impossibility of understanding or assimilating the other's irreducible experiences and singular acts into our own consciousness. Rather, we must com-passionately bear witness to, *wit(h)ness* or share in distance in proximity and proximity in distance the other's subjective and shared experiences – in this case, as they are inscribed on Banderas' ageing, human face.

To return to Vera's body and skin, one could think that the artificial skin imposed on her through surgical operations imposes new traces on her body and so destroys the traces of Vicente's personal and historical experiences. The artificial skin is made from the blood of pigs; Vera's skin thus inscribes the traces of the violent death of the animal, which is always already the constitutive outside of the human. In addition, as I have argued above, Almodóvar forces us to question the binary logic of 'artificial' and 'natural'. The categories cannot be collapsed, but the film's problematisation of their relationship helps us to see that Vera's body is always already a prosthetic medium. Concerned as I am with an ethical relation based on the bodily conditions of life, whether 'prosthetic' or 'natural', I suggest that Vera's skin carries the scars of totalitarian violence (in Arendt's terms) and modern sovereign power (in Agamben's terms). But the skin is, according to Bernadette Wegenstein, 'the site of encounter and exposure between body and media rather than the site of exclusion and closure' (2010: 33). Vera's body is thus a site on which individual and shared traumatic experiences are materially and symbolically inscribed as traces whose exteriorisation is the condition of possibility for their constitution. The traces' exteriorisation is not anterior to them (Derrida 1980), and yet their impression is predicated on their erasure. Furthermore, such traces are imprinted on subjectivity and body without appearing external; they thereby escape linguistic articulation and symbolic representation.

As is well known, Almodóvar has claimed that, in the context of this film, one's invulnerable identity remains intact despite external morphological mutations (cited in Martín 2014: 110). He thus disconcertingly implies an essentialist conception of identity. We can consider this claim in relation to the suggestive scene at the end of the film. A static camera focuses on Vicente's mother's clothing store. We see Vera reflected in the window as she leaves a taxi and walks towards the shop. The body of a female mannequin on display frames – or imprisons – the reflection of Vera. As I mentioned earlier, when Gal sees herself in the mirror, she is prompted to kill herself. The reflection of Vera (she is a replica of Gal) suggests that she will remain trapped in her femininity. Like a ghostly apparition, the image reflected on the window places her between presence and absence, between visibility and invisibility, thereby pointing symbolically to one's realisation and de-realisation of being (see Chapter 3). Trapped in a female body, Vicente returns '"from the dead", like a modern Lazarus, having died in some dimension without being actually killed' (Pollock and Silverman 2011b: 28). The final scene shows the expression of astonishment on Vicente's mother's face and that of the store worker when they find out that the disappeared Vicente has returned home, as a woman, but identifying himself as Vicente.

I propose that Vicente's final self-affirmation is not associated with essential masculinity, or any other 'authentic' or invulnerable and fixed gender identity. Vicente's assertion is inconsistent with his identification as Vera Cruz in a previous conversation between Dr Ledgard and one of his professional colleagues. The identification as Vera could be interpreted as dissimulation on the part of Vera, who wishes to obtain Dr Ledgard's unconditional trust. But I interpret these inconsistent assertions as the affirmation of the remainder, excess, traces or residue that interrupt the process of symbolisation and/or subjugation on which modern sovereign power and biopower are predicated. Power has materially and symbolically impinged on Vicente by transforming his body into a woman's; this surgery conforms to the teleological logic that enforces the move from one gender to another, as well as the totalising logic that rejects the singularity and heterogeneity at the core of our embodied human condition. The remainder, excess, trace or residue is symbolised here by the photograph of Vicente that Vera sees in a newspaper. The photograph seems to function as the infinite remainder of the void through which we are constituted and ruptured. From this perspective, the inconsistencies at the core of Vera/Vicente's affirmations do not lead us towards binary oppositions or the erasure of limits. Instead, they 'multiply limits, and therefore acknowledge more differences [. . .], thresholds, and Janus-faced concepts to jam the machinery of binary oppositions' (Oliver 2013: 6).

To sum up, *La piel que habito* illustrates my theoretical concern with the psychic effects of the irruption of individual and shared traumatic experiences as they are played out on Vera/Vicente's body and skin and on our own body. Ahmed explains: 'the skin comes to be felt as a border through reading the impression of one surface upon another as a form of violence, where an other's "impression" is felt as negation' (2005: 107). Similarly, Vera's embodiment of Gal's subjectivity and memory, the inscription of them on her flesh and skin, functions as a residue of what cannot be erased or renewed. Vera's body carries the residues or traces of that which cannot be forgotten, which remain inscribed on the surface and the flesh of the body. From this perspective, *La piel que habito* explores how our subjectivities and bodies can actualise the sensory mark or trace of the pervasive presence of the fragments of memory and past traumatic experiences. These are perceptibly or imperceptibly inscribed in the body's memory and in the psyche in the present, but do not perpetuate the self-enclosure associated with 'being as presence' (Rolnik 2008a: 132–7). The traces or fragments of structural (that is, internal to the psychic and bodily self) and historical (external to our subjectivities) traumas are not restricted to social frames, because, in Almodóvar's cinema in general, they are transmitted and com-passionately shared across different subjects, spaces and times, at the trans-subjective and trans-historical level, within and beyond the Spanish nation and the diegetic space of the film. As I explained in the Introduction, such traces and fragments do not lead to a melancholic repetition of the symptom, nor to the closure associated with working through. Instead, they lead to an im-possible process of working through, which creates the conditions of possibility for articulating an affirmation of the ethical and potentially political process of individual and social mourning, which would challenge the instrumentalisation of both amnesia and of commemoration. To reiterate the argument proposed in Chapter 3, Almodóvar's films thus point to the subjective and shared processes of enacting and/or abreacting, both psychologically and physically, our individual and shared traumatic experiences, as mediated by the cinematic image and transmitted through our encounter with the cinematic medium. The second-hand women's dresses in Vicente's mother's store are material signifiers inscribing the traces of absent women's bodies. The cinematic image itself, whether analogical or digital, thus inscribes or imprints the traces of trauma and fragments of memory, precisely because some of those traces can only emerge in a contingent encounter with the cinematic and aesthetic practice. Through my focus on the body and embodiment in *La piel que habito*, I interpret Almodóvar's film as a springboard for an ethical and political reflection on how the fragments of memory and history endure through our own visceral, bodily encounters in the present with the pains of the past – in a present, which is haunted by the silent and yet powerful scream of a mutilated and threatened, if not yet obsolete, humanity.

Lines of Flight

I end this final chapter by returning once more to Vera's yoga practice, which she continues despite Dr Ledgard's threats to her human embodiment. We see, in this 'time-image', Vera's vulnerability and precariousness, but also that she is holding onto her material body. *La piel que habito* insists on the 'mediality of the body' and 'how the body is always our most fundamental medium of knowledge and [human] experience' (Wegenstein 2010: 34). Yoga can, in one way, be seen as a commodity that has been entirely incorporated into the global market of new spiritualities. But Vera uses it to 'endure', bodily and psychically, in time and space, so she might engage actively with different levels of intensity, and so produce an interruption or line of flight from the 'auto-suspension and spectral reproduction of the law' (Weber 2006: 69–70). This engagement with the world 'as a field of forces', as well as with the material and psychical self, which is already another self and with the world, leads to an affirmation of 'the body as an enfleshed field of actualization of passions and forces', without perpetuating her own self-enclosure (Braidotti 2006: 2). Following Braidotti's concept of the 'pathos of our global politics' (Braidotti 2010: 43), I propose that we are unable to resist the present through oppositional nostalgia and melancholia; these would only lead us to disavow the complexities and contradictions of the present. But we, like Vera, may be able to 'endure' the present, and interrupt the process of symbolisation and/or subjugation through which we are constituted and threatened, by seeking lines of flight. As Almodóvar shows us, the present points to the 'im-possibility of not-succumbing' to the dark shadows of the past, which inform and are translated into the atrocities of our times, atrocities that are inscribed on the 'skin that we live in' and through which we encounter the other.

Finally, Almodóvar's cinema demonstrates that we are able to transmit and com-passionately share, respond to or *wit(h)ness* individual and collective traumatic experiences through the film medium. As I have tried to demonstrate throughout this study, our encounter with Almodóvar's cinema foregrounds the potential transformation of our ethical and political relation to personal and historical traumatic experiences. We encounter the cinematic and aesthetic practices affectively and interpretively, and see beyond simple dichotomies between perpetrator and victim, memory and amnesia, representation and its impossibility, empathy and apathy, structural and historical trauma or acting out and working through. As with Nietzsche's reflection on 'slow readings' in my epigraph to this chapter, I hope that this book bears witness to, and transmits to its readers, the need to keep reading cinema critically, slowly and differently, understanding films as theoretical and political resources that might bring to light structures of domination, exclusion and discrimination. I hope to have suggested, too, that psychoanalysis is a valuable tool for such reading, particularly for Almodóvar's films, which reveal so much about the unconscious fears and desires that motivate structures of past and current violence.

To take only one example, Ettinger's matrixial psychoanalysis helps us to foreground the trans-subjective preconditions of the constitution of our subjectivity, without assuming 'a common pre-social, pre-political origin by means of which to transcend the temporariness of current conflict' (Pollock 2013b: 189). Ettinger's emphasis on com-passionate trans-subjective encounters, non-sacrificial hospitality and *response-ability* can be useful resources or supplements to thought about our ethical relations to the irreducible other which always already precede and exceed the ontological constitution of the discrete subject; to see how those relations need not reify the autonomous individual or its rational calculations; to consider again the undecidability of responsibility and hospitality. Ettinger's emphasis on the gift of femininity to human subjectivity and its unconscious contribution to the social and political sphere enables us to envision a complex world co-inhabited by plurality and difference beyond a politics of recognition, providing a valuable underpinning for our attempt to understand humanity in all its infinite differences and in all its vulnerability. Pollock suggests: 'Acts of violence against others violate what is the gift of feminine sexual difference to humanity: a foundational sense that in becoming me, I became human always **with another to whose trauma and jouissance I may be creatively** connected. That is to say that my humanity, which is a product of co-emergence, co-affection, co-poiesis, may be brutally compromised when any other human being's humanity is violated' (2010: 872, emphasis in original). Just as Almodóvar's cinema is predicated on its constant rewriting and revisions, our faithfulness to the events of critical theory and psychoanalysis should remain open to profound and endless questioning of our own critical, theoretical and political positions and our categories of thinking.

Notes

Introduction

1. The term 'post-traumatic' is used in Farrell (1998). 'Post-traumatic' implies a reconsideration of the prevailing effects of traumatic events on the present.
2. Paul Julian Smith was one of the first Almodóvar scholars to contest this claim by foregrounding the significance of the Spanish socio-cultural context in Almodóvar's cinema from the outset.
3. The term 'fragments' does not imply the complete recovery, articulation or suturing of memory into a single narrative, but rather our partial, discontinuous and affective encounter with memory as transmitted via the film medium in the present. The term 'traces' does not imply the destruction of the cognitive mechanism associated with the traumatic event, but our encounter with the belated residues of personal and shared traumatic experiences, as they are processed or accessed via cinema. Such an encounter with traces of trauma may or may not be transformative.
4. See also MacDonald 1991.
5. See Derrida's discussion of the notion of the trace in relation to Sigmund Freud's conceptualisation of memory traces (1972).
6. The bibliography, both in Spain and the Anglo-American academy, is exhaustive. See, for instance, the fascinating study by Estrada of the politics of memory in relation to documentary filmmaking. My focus here is not on exploring how these memory debates contribute to the formation of a democratic subject. Instead, I am more interested in exploring how our intersubjective and trans-subjective encounters with traces of trauma and fragments of memory through the film medium point to the impossibility of reifying a logic of identity. Instead of conceiving democracy as a macro-political, representative political system based on the implementation of a constitutional state in the recent past, I am more interested here in thinking about, to use Derrida's term, a 'democracy to come' within democracy. Deferring democracy opens up the conditions of possibility for the (unfulfilled) promises of democracy. See Derrida 2005. For a Deleuzean discussion of the concept 'becoming-democratic', see Patton 2005.
7. It is important to distinguish affect, which implies an element of ungovernability, from emotion, which is always captured by discourse. My focus on both affect and cognition takes into consideration both the significance

of discourse and sensations that cannot be entirely captured by discourse. Yet, I establish a productive tension between epistemologies that privilege affect and event and those that privilege discourse and structure, such as post-structuralism, in order less to resolve the contradictions and incompatibilities between these different epistemologies than to disallow the possibility of reifying presence. Therefore, my emphasis on affect does not exclude the significance of structure, and yet I claim the necessity to pay attention to affect, which is often excluded from an exclusive focus on structure. It is also important to underscore that the potentiality of affect is not always positive, as affect can also be associated with negative sensations. For instance, in the Spinozist and Deleuzean tradition, affects can be both creative, and cruel and deadening. For an excellent philosophical reflection on affect, see Massumi 2002.

8. I am indebted to Griselda Pollock, whose psychoanalytic feminist contribution to trauma studies and the study of contemporary art shapes my thinking here. I am particularly interested in exploring how the concepts Pollock deploys in relation to visual arts can travel to and therefore be transformed when they encounter Almodóvar's cinema (Pollock 2013a).

9. For a crucial critique of the *Movida* as an apolitical spectacle, see Subirats 2002. Subirats' critique of the *Movida*'s apoliticism is due in part to their exclusive focus on the macro-political level. Txetxu Aguado identifies a transformative potentiality in the *Movida* in general and Almodóvar's cinema in particular by focusing on the micro-political level, thereby foregrounding the production of new forms of subjectivity. I will discuss the relationship between the macro- and micro-political shortly. See Aguado 2009.

10. I would like to thank an anonymous reader of this study at an earlier stage for providing me with this invaluable suggestion and reference.

11. It is important to underscore the danger of reducing the democratic period in Spain to 'post-Francoism'. Cultural historians, for one thing, disagree on when the so-called post-Franco period ends. My intention here is not to define a clear-cut periodisation. Nor am I trying to associate the democratic period in which Almodóvar's films have been produced with post-Francoism. But there is a need to make sense of the traumas caused by war and totalitarianism. In this context, I underscore the belated effects of trauma and memory in the present.

12. Almodóvar has publicly supported demands from family members of the victims of the Civil War and the Franco regime. He has also explicitly supported Manuela Carmena, who represents a group of new left-wing political parties and social movements associated with PODEMOS, as a candidate in Madrid's municipal elections of May 2015.

13. Pérez Melgosa rightly suggests that Almodóvar's critical engagement with the politics of memory in Spain was in part motivated by his concern with the memory of Latin American dictatorships, such as Chile and, as we will see in Chapter 2, Argentina.

14. See Antonio Francisco Pedrós-Gascón's Lacanian analysis of Almodóvar's cinema in relation to the foreclosure of the primordial signifier, which Pedrós-Gascón associates with Francoism. Pedrós-Gascón 2012.

15. See Ibáñez 2013. I am referring to the influential and sophisticated work of Vilarós 1998; Moreiras 2002; Medina 2001; and Keller 2015.

16. See the fascinating issue of the *Journal of Spanish Cultural Studies* dedicated to Spanish film and spectrality edited by Steven Marsh (2014).

17. For a fine Derridean understanding of the figure of the *marrano* in Spanish and Latin American studies, see Graff-Zivin 2014a. Graff-Zivin conceives *marranismo* as a critical practice that is both the 'constitutive outside' on which the totalitarian inquisitional logic is predicated and that moves beyond the logic of identity (the latter is, according to Graff-Zivin, inexorably linked to the inquisitional logic). See also Graff-Zivin 2014b.

18. Throughout this study, I rely on Derrida's distinction between 'future' and 'futurity', which is the translation of the French term 'àvenir'. The latter implies the unpredictability of the future (Derrida 1994).

19. For a psychoanalytic understanding of the difference between presence and meaning, see Scarfone 2011.

20. Moreiras emphasises Almodóvar's critique of psychoanalysis as an epistemological discourse. She argues: 'submitting both psychoanalysis (as a discourse about the formation of subjectivity and identity) and trauma theory to parody through the character of the psychoanalyst and the primal scene of Sexi and Riza (cause of their current sexual positions – nymphomania and homosexuality), deeply questions the dominant discourses and ideologies through which the constitution of the subject is produced, as well as psychoanalysis' value as an epistemological discourse' (2014: 150, my translation).

21. See Protevi 2010.

22. For a fine Deleuzean study of Almodóvar's cinema, one that moves beyond Deleuze's highly influential books on cinema, see Seguin 2009. Seguin's Deleuzean analysis enables him to explore how Almodóvar's films supplement and intersect with other texts, thereby indicating something that is always in excess of the closure of representation. In this context, Almodóvar's cinema becomes a precarious, heterogeneous and unstable representational space that encourages transversal, flexible readings that, instead of reifying a centre, come and go limitlessly through space and time. A different approach can be found in Kercher 2015. Constructing a single point of meaning, one associated with a patrilineal model based on origin and influence, Kercher proves the influence of Hitchcock in Almodóvar's cinema. But Kercher's exclusive focus on identifying the Hitchcockian motifs in Almodóvar prompts me to ask, to what extent does the integration of cinematic texts into other cinematic texts in a different signifying system raise the question of which intertexts might figure in representation, thus replacing or adding layers of signification to the cinematic texts? To what extent may we re-read Hitchcock's cinema itself through Almodóvar's productive

appropriation of his oeuvre? Or, can one engage deeply with Hitchcock's own intertextual reliance on other cinematic practices (i.e., the crucial dialogue between Hitchcock and German Expressionism)? For a discussion of the different forms and functions of intertextuality in Almodóvar's cinema, see Aronica 2005.

23. I am indebted to Francisco José Martínez Martínez's excellent study of Deleuze's book on difference and repetition and, more broadly, on Deleuze's philosophy. See Martínez Martínez 1987.

24. I provide the English translation of the titles of the films when I first mention them. I will use their Spanish titles throughout the book. As I will explain shortly, this book is not a comprehensive study or survey of Almodóvar's entire oeuvre. Instead, I have selected films that, being my case studies, both exemplify and put pressure on my theoretical argument. In other words, for the purpose of foregrounding and exploring in depth the theoretical issues at stake and for the sake of intellectual coherence, this book distinctively has a closer focus on fewer films.

25. See also Rancière 2009.

26. See, for instance, Ettinger 2005. Rolnik has published articles in Portuguese and English, but *Molecular Revolution in Brazil*, which she co-authored with Félix Guattari (see Guattari and Rolnik 2008), remains her only book available in English. An English collection of Rolnik's contribution to aesthetics and psychoanalysis is urgently needed.

27. I am indebted to Tammy Clewell's discussion of Freud's 'Mourning and Melancholia' and 'The Ego and the Id' (1923). See Clewell 2004. Clewell argues that Freud proposes a theory of endless mourning beyond melancholia in 'The Ego and the Id'. Joseba Gabilondo also refers to Freud's own revision of his early distinction between mourning and melancholia to explore the way Almodóvar mourns the loss of the *Movida* and the Spanish Transition (2005).

28. I am applying this term retrospectively. Although the term often refers to the economic policies implemented from the 1970s and 1980s, and traced back to the 1930s, I suggest that the late Franco government implemented a free market economic system that paved the way for the hegemony of consumerist capitalism in the post-Franco period. Instead of thinking of a transition from a 'pre-modern' Francoist period to a (post)modern democratic period, I suggest that the post-Franco period is the logical *consequence* of the economic transformations that took place in the late Franco period.

29. I am indebted to Silverman's discussion of concentrationary memory in which he conceives of memory as a palimpsest.

30. Pollock explains: 'Unlike many current trauma theorists who perceive our response to catastrophic events in terms of obligatory mourning and loss, Ettinger considers art as a potentially creative transformation premised on the intimate relation between aesthetic process/sensibility and com-passion (hyphenated to stress the sharing with a pain or feeling) relations to the other' (2013a: 13). I am inspired by Pollock's departure from testimony and

obligatory witnessing, and the representation or impossibility of representation of trauma in what are now traditional positions in trauma studies, namely those of Cathy Caruth and Shoshana Felman. The latter have been highly influential in the debates on trauma and memory in Spanish film studies and, more broadly, in film studies.

31. In her discussion of Guillermo del Toro's *El laberinto del fauno* (*Pan's Labyrinth*, 2006), Davies warns us of the dangers of exploiting historical memory in Spanish cinema (see Davies 2012).

32. For a critique of Derrida's reading of Jan Patocka in *The Gift of Death*, see Findlay 2002. See also Gasché 2007.

33. For a study of the use of comedy in Almodóvar as a way of going against the grain of fixed boundaries and categories, see Medhurst 2007.

34. *Carne trémula* (*Live Flesh*, 1997) includes a first sequence set in the early 1970s.

35. See Smith 2014; Allinson 2001; D'Lugo 2006; and Acevedo-Muñoz 2007. For edited volumes, see D'Lugo and Vernon 2013; Epps and Kakoudaki 2009; or Morris and Vernon 1995. I have been inspired by other scholarly research on questions of trauma and memory in literary and cinematic practices in contemporary Spain, both in the Anglo-American academy and in Spain, including Moreiras 2002; Resina's edited volume (2000), which deals mostly with literary texts and concentrates more extensively on an early period within Spanish history, namely that of the political transition from dictatorship to democracy (1975–82); or Winter 2006. Ferrán (2007), which offers new theoretical frameworks to existing research on memory in Contemporary Spain by exclusively analysing literary texts, is also a source of inspiration here. For other work beyond Almodóvar and Spanish cultural studies, see Girgus 2010; Walker 2005; Kaplan and Wang 2003; or Wilson 2006. For philosophical and theoretical debates on affect and embodiment in relation to cinema, see, for instance, Beugnet 2007 or del Rio 2008.

36. Pollock defines such an intersubjective encounter through research and writing: 'The model offered here is a creative covenant that utterly rejects the typically Oedipal, destructive relation between old and young, outdated and new, while equally resisting academic adulation. An ethics of intellectual respect – Spivak's critical intimacy is one of Bal's useful concepts – is actively performed in engagement between generations of scholars, all concerned with the challenge of reading the complexities of culture' (2013b: xvi).

Chapter 1

1. For the association of mourning with representation, see Webster Goodwin and Bronfen 1993.

2. For a fine analysis of the association of movement in dance with modernity, see Lepecki 2006.

3. See Gutiérrez-Albilla 2015a.

4. In her article on *Volver*, Kinder explains at length the film's engagement with the culture of death in Almodóvar's native La Mancha (2007).

5. For an analysis of Deleuze's concept of repetition, see Sandro 2003.

6. Flinn provides a discussion of Barthes's association of music with the term *signifiance* and Kristeva's association of music and poetic language with the *semiotic* and the *chora*.

7. This point is also made by Kinder (2007: 8).

8. For a fine reading of the film in relation to Derrida's notion of spectrality, see Marsh 2009.

9. Drawing on Bakhtin's concept of the *chronotope*, which emphasises the indissociability of time and space, I associate here the rural space with the past and the urban space with the present. See Konstantarakos for an application of Bakhtin's concept to the analysis of space in film (2000).

10. See Burdeau's perceptive analysis of the film (2006).

11. See Gutiérrez-Albilla for an analysis of how Pina Bausch's *Café Müller* functions in Almodóvar's *Hable con ella* (2005).

12. I am thinking here of Kristeva's analysis of different types of strangeness. Kristeva focuses on those strangers who are outside society, those who are inside society and on one's strangeness to oneself associated with the *semiotic*, which remains inaccessible to the self, yet felt and experienced (1991).

13. For an excellent study of migratory aesthetics, see Bal 2011.

14. For a study of the theme of exile in Jaime Camino's documentary about the forced exile of Republican children to the Soviet Union during the Spanish Civil War, see Gutiérrez-Albilla 2011a.

15. See Janet Walker's analysis of this kind of cinematic genre (2001).

16. It is important to bear in mind an important point made by Loureiro. He warns us of the dangers of fixing the victim in opposition to the oppressor, thereby failing to explore our complicity (2008). Almodóvar moves beyond such a logic, but the film does foreground the personal and shared experiences of those who were once considered faceless, nameless or voiceless subjects.

17. D'Lugo (2013) rightly explains that this element of the plot is taken from one of the stories that Leo, the protagonist of *La flor de mi secreto*, is writing. According to D'Lugo, this story is based on an event that took place in Puerto Rico. By incorporating cultural referents, characters, or, in this case, stories from Latin America into his films, Almodóvar embraces a 'Hispanic' transnational aesthetic. I am focusing here less on the 'accurate' origin of this element of the plot than on foregrounding the effects of this action upon us, as we encounter Almodóvar's cinema.

18. I am indebted to Marcantonio, who has drawn this analogy between the physical and the symbolic weight carried by generations of women (2006).

19. The term (post)modernism, which is often associated with the post-Franco period, may be seen as another phase within modernism. Therefore, the

notion of late modernity used in this chapter is located within a tele-ological narrative of historical progress that is associated with the legacy of the Enlightenment. See Hal Foster's description of (post)modernism as a deferred action of modernism (1996).

20. Although I am emphasising here the film's denunciation of the social and economic marginalisation suffered by migrants, it is important to clarify that the film also allows us to think of the alternative personal, social, affective and economic relations that these working class Spanish and migrant women are able to forge, thereby radically resisting, suspending and redefining the social and symbolic order in which they are constituted through their exclusion, discrimination and marginalisation. I am foregrounding here the film's denunciative aspect in order not to deny the presence of social divisions and differences.

21. See Nathan Richardson for a discussion of this film in relation to the question of the rural exodus (2002).

22. In her analysis of *Volver*, Mercedes Camino does refer to some of the consequences of the structural changes that took place in the late Franco period, including the Spanish migration to Germany. See Camino 2010.

23. It is important to mention that, while the Francoist regime could be thought of as an archaic interruption of the teleological narrative of historical progress, it can also be seen as a product of modernity itself. See Labanyi for an association of Francoism with what she describes as 'conservative modernity'. Labanyi also identifies (post)modernity as an intensification of rather than a break with modernity (2002).

24. See also Moreiras' fascinating reading of *Laberinto de pasiones* (2014).

25. I am here inspired by Aby Warburg's concept of the 'pathos formula'. For a fine analysis of this concept in relation to psychoanalysis and Benjamin's concept of allegory, see Efal 2000.

26. See Mari Paz Balibrea for a discussion of María Zambrano's critique of modernity's repression of the irrational (2005).

27. Marsh also acknowledges the significant media coverage, especially in what in Spain are defined as 'programas del corazón' (TV shows based on gossips about famous people), of Jurado's pancreatic cancer in the same period as Almodóvar was making *Volver*. In fact, Jurado's death, which became a prominent media event, took place in 2006, the year of the release of this film (Marsh 2009: 355).

28. Allinson 2001 and Smith 2006a.

29. I am indebted to Thomas Elsaesser, who articulates this argument (2001: 196).

30. I thank Smith for our discussions of the alternative argument that TV can be seen as a memory machine that works through vital social issues. Nonetheless, I maintain the opposite position here.

31. *Zarzuela* music was instrumentalised by both the Republican government and the Franco regime.

32. For an analysis of the concept of 'heterosociality', see Stephen Maddison 2000.
33. See Bersani and Dutoit's discussion of the resignification of the penis in Almodóvar's *All About My Mother* (Bersani and Dutoit 2004). For an analysis of the way in which bodily fragments function in Almodóvar's cinema beyond fetishism, see Urios-Aparisi 2010.
34. I am indebted to Maurice Hamington, who defines this notion of 'embodied care' (2004).

Chapter 2

1. For a discussion of *Todo sobre mi madre*'s female identification in the context of gay or queer dissidence, see Maddison's fine discussion of the film (2000).
2. While I connect queer theory to Butler's early work (1990), this chapter does not provide an exhaustive history of queer theory. Instead, I focus on and problematise some of queer theory's concepts – such as the performativity of sexuality and gender – and relate them to those of other epistemological frameworks, such as psychoanalytic feminism or phenomenology.
3. Although our bodily experiences are always mediated by language and the body is never a given, I suggest here that the articulation of those bodily experiences cannot be disentangled from the material specificity of our bodies. See Pollock et al. 1995.
4. For an excellent theorisation of sound in Almodóvar's cinema, see Vernon 2009.
5. I am indebted here to Abraham and Torok's study of melancholia (1984). I will shortly engage with Ettinger's redefinition of Abraham and Torok's notion of the 'crypt' through her concept of 'transcryptum'.
6. The concept of the Real is understood here as both a lack in and an excess of representation. However, my concern with traumatic encryption foregrounds the dissolution of the representational structure. For a fine analysis of the different conceptions of the Real in Lacan, see Shepherdson 1997.
7. See Elsaesser 2001.
8. For a fine definition of these registers, see Pollock 2010.
9. For a fascinating analysis of the relationship between the unconscious and representation in Lacan in relation to contemporary art, see Foster 1996.
10. See Kinder's fine analysis of the film in terms of a fluid intertextual trans-subjectivity. I have been inspired by Kinder's emphasis on a trans-subjective intertextuality, which she sees as energising the narrative and extending 'the life, meaning and mobility of all discreet parts' (2005: 15).
11. For a discussion of the *gracioso* figure, see Greer-Johnson 2001.
12. Establishing an analogy between this particular cinematic technique and the cinema of Ozu, Smith explains that these panning shots, which are not connected to the plot, 'suggest his characters are caught up in the web of

accidents that make up everyday life and cannot be extricated from the highly coloured locations they inhabit' (2014:166).

13. 'Hapticality' is a very pertinent term for those interested in phenomenological film theory, affect and embodiment. See the pioneering work of Laura Marks (2000). In the context of Spanish film studies, see Martin-Márquez 2013 or Evans 2013. As we will see throughout this book, although I draw on phenomenological film theory, I am aware of the risk of perpetuating a metaphysics of presence at the core of phenomenology. The spectral trace resists such a complete phenomenologisation by moving beyond a logic of presence and absence.

14. For a fascinating reading of this scene, see Epps 2009.

15. This scene resonates with the scene in *Matador* that shows Diego, a former bullfighter who is not blind but who does have a physical incapacity, watching a video of the day when he was injured by a bull. Diego realises that his former lover, María Cardenal, witnessed this tragic accident. Brad Epps notes: 'Rising from his chair, and approaching the camera, the camera then shifts to show him coming as close as humanly possible to the television screen, pressing his face against it and forming a kiss in response to María's mouthing of his name' (2009: 311).

16. For a reading of camp in the film beyond the common association of camp with 'insincerity' and 'inauthenticity', see Garlinger 2007.

17. See Pollock et al. for a discussion of Butler's engagement with the materiality and discursivity of the body in *Bodies that Matter: On the Discursive Limits of 'Sex'* (Pollock et al. 1995).

18. Bersani and Dutoit also argue that Agrado and Lola are 'gender transitions without normative end points' (2009: 245).

19. See Isolina Ballesteros' discussion of the film in terms of the subversive, as well as normative, implications of the representation of transgendered subjects (Ballesteros 2009). While I agree with her that some of the transgendered characters in the film, such as Lola, can be rather disturbing, and even sexist, my theoretical analysis goes beyond a focus on positive and negative images of queer characters in film.

20. For a development of these ideas in relation to Jaime de Armiñán's *Mi querida señorita* (*My Dearest Senorita*, 1971), the first Spanish film to deal thematically with the porous boundaries between transvestism, transgenderism, trans-sexualism, hermaphroditism and intersexuality, see Gutiérrez-Albilla 2015b.

21. Ibáñez convincingly connects Esteban's need to spatialise and temporalise his personal experiences to the shared traumatic history of Argentina, which has been transmitted to him by Manuela (2013). I shall focus on the imbrication of personal with collective experience through the character Manuela shortly.

22. I am inspired here by Fer's analysis of Mira Schendel's works of art, where letters seem to transform into insects, thereby dissociating words for their semantic function (Fer 2012).

23. Victoria Rivera-Cordero criticises the film for optimistically, if not unrealistically, ending with Esteban's neutralisation of the HIV virus (2012). I am proposing here to read the film beyond its referential achievements or failures.

24. Samuel Amago's reading of *Todo sobre mi madre* pays great attention to the way African music and African subjects figure in the film as a testament to Barcelona's condition as a multicultural city, making us redefine Catalan and Spanish identity in relation to a global, trans-national context (Amago 2007). Baltasar Fra-Molinero also acknowledges the film's focus on Africa through the use of music and African *figurants* (2009).

25. For an excellent critique of the *Movida*'s institutionalisation, through which the *Movida* is nostalgically idealised as epitomising Spain's embrace of (post) modernity, see Nichols 2009.

26. This took place in Spain in the late 1970s, culminating in the abortive military coup d'état led by General Tejero in February 1981.

27. As mentioned in the Introduction, Almodóvar's concern with the politics of memory in Spain and, by and large, the debates on historical memory in the late 1990s, were influenced by how Chile and Argentina had dealt with transitional justice in their periods of redemocratisation. As is well known, Baltasar Garzón ordered the extradition of General Pinochet to be judged in Spain. This contributed to a rethinking in Spain about the country's lack of transitional justice during the period of the transition from dictatorship to democracy.

28. In *Laberinto de pasiones*, Almodóvar embraces such a liberating, micropolitical attitude by associating Madrid with the most exhilarating city in the world. Since the *Movida* took place prior to the public knowledge of the AIDS phenomenon, *Todo sobre mi madre* acknowledges that AIDS is one of the dramatic consequences to which the use of hard drugs and practice of unsafe sex associated with the *Movida* led. As is well known, an entire generation in Spain has suffered from these dramatic consequences.

29. For a fine reading of the film in relation to its allusion to 1970s Spain and Argentina, see Ibáñez 2013. D'Lugo (2013) and Smith (2014) also refer to how Argentina's 'Dirty War' figures in the film.

30. I would like to thank Akira Lippit for bringing Kracauer's concept of the 'umbilical cord' to my attention.

31. Ernesto Acevedo-Muñoz provides an allegorical reading of the film that associates the human body with the fragmented body of the nation (2004). With regard to the train tunnel's association with a birth canal, Acevedo-Muñoz convincingly argues that it connects the different parts of Spain and, in a more allegorical manner, it can also be read as visualising the rebirth of a nation from within the feminine.

32. For an excellent discussion of the phallic and the matrixial model of trauma, see Pollock 2010.

33. For a sophisticated theoretical analysis of the theme of transplantation in the film in relation to Nancy's personal and philosophical reflection on his own

heart transplant, see Chambers-Letson 2014. For Nancy, having a transplant entails having to share one's body with another body, being in an intimate touching relationship with a stranger, which contributes to the undoing of the sovereign 'I'. One's existence is predicated on plurality and the impossibility of not sharing experiences with others (Nancy 2008).

34. Kinder's focus on a trans-subjective intertextuality also acknowledges the trans-subjective implications underpinning the transmission of the HIV virus across bodies.

35. Pollock remains, to my knowledge, one of the most important interpreters of Ettinger's artistic work, aesthetic theory and psychoanalytic focus on the 'matrixial borderspace'. Although Pollock has written extensively on the work of Ettinger, a fine introduction to Ettinger's complex theories is Pollock's article on feminine aesthetic practices and Ettinger's concepts of 'matrix' and 'metramorphosis' (2004) or her introductory chapter included in Ettinger's first English monograph (Pollock 2006), which is a crucial source for understanding Ettinger's complex psychoanalytical theories.

36. In her discussion of Derrida's conception of sexual difference beyond any possible binary opposition, which became instrumental in the development of queer theory's propositions, Anne-Emmanuelle Berger notes that the cut of castration, which is a bleeding wound, is the condition of possibility for dividing the whole into multiple different parts (Berger 2005). For Ettinger, the several is associated with 'more-than-one' or 'less-than-one' (2006a: 69). The relationship between the several and the singular already operates in the matrixial, thus preceding the cut of castration. For Ettinger, multiplicity is not conditioned by the cut of castration nor does the several perpetuate the binary opposition between the single and the infinite within the phallic logic. Yet, for Ettinger, the subject still needs to go through the Oedipal symbolisation.

37. Although Camino recognises the multiple ways of reading the film's focus on maternity, she warns us of the instrumentalisation of maternity by conservative gender politics (2010). Yet, it is important to rescue maternity from its ideological instrumentalisation within conservative gender politics in order to reflect on the association of maternity, which is articulated beyond patriarchy and heteronormativity, with one's ethical and potentially political capacity to hold the irreducible other.

38. For another critique of the film's emphasis on maternity, see Zecchi 2005. For Ana Corbalán, *Todo sobre mi madre* stands at an ambivalent point between redefining a concept of the family beyond phallocentric culture and perpetuating a notion of maternity which is articulated within that same phallocentric culture that the film intends to subvert (2008). Moving beyond a definition of maternity within patriarchal and heteronormative ideological structures, D'Lugo rightly suggests that maternity in this film should be understood in relation to the performance of motherhood and femininity (2006).

39. The film focuses on both sacrificial and non-sacrificial hospitality. I discuss Ettinger's critique of Lévinas' emphasis on sacrificial hospitality below.

40. I am inspired here by Pollock's call to pay attention to feminist theory in order to underscore the need to embrace the future and life in the face of the culture of death that is the result of the phallocentrism underpinning our current social and political system (2010: 873).

41. For an explanation of the concept of the 'filmmaker in the feminine', see Gutiérrez-Albilla 2013d.

42. I am indebted to recent theoretical work on gallery films, such as that of Catherine Fowler (2004). For Fowler, although gallery films still borrow from the specific *dispositif* of cinema, one has to take into consideration how the out-of-frame affects our viewing experience. I suggest that, since we are now exposed to a variety of screen media, we bring to the viewing of a film our experience of being exposed to different *dispositifs*, even though the film studied here relies on the specific *dispositif* of cinema. Likewise, cinema itself has expanded into other media, such as digital media. In this respect, Spanish cinema studies need new theoretical tools that can account for these new ways of understanding and expanding our cinematic viewing experience.

Chapter 3

1. In this context, memory and history are entangled instead of in opposition to each other.

2. The concept of 'embodiment' underscores our bodily sense of 'being-in-the-world'.

3. As I explained in Chapter 2, the concept of 'performativity' implies that identity is articulated through iterative and imitative practices.

4. It is important to underscore that such an allegorical reading runs the risk of reading the field of references internal to the film as a substitution for, or a 'proper equivalent' of, the historical context in which the film is set or produced. As is well known, this tendency to read films as allegorical representations is in part informed by Jameson's influential essay on 'Third World' literature, which he described as texts that allegorically represent the nation (1986). Betty Joseph has argued that Jameson's reading of texts allegorically could unconsciously assume that allegory is culturally inescapable or a historical given, thereby reducing it to a monolithic referent (Joseph 2012). In order to provide a more nuanced allegorical reading of Almodóvar's film, I will engage with the Benjaminian notion of allegory. This will help me think about the imbrication of the ruins of history with trauma through the film's emphasis on the fragmentary in representation. For a fine study of Benjamin's theory of allegory in Latin American studies, see Avelar 1999 and Graff-Zivin 2014a. Graff-Zivin problematises the way in which scholars in the field of Spanish and Latin American studies have reductively resorted to allegory to think about the representation of political resistance in the face of totalitar-

ian political regimes. For Graff–Zivin, such interpretations are predicated on an understanding of language as transparent and on a facile relationship between signifier and signified. By contrast, Graff–Zivin's engagement with the imbrication of Benjamin's theory of allegory with Derrida's emphasis on hauntology enables her to see allegory 'as a *mode of signification* that exhibits a constitutive aporetic quality, in which the representation of "history" sets the stage for the arrival (from the past as absolute future) of an unexpected event that, through productive anachronism, exposes time as "out of joint"' (Graff–Zivin 2014a: 59, emphasis in original).

5. See Aleida Assmann's discussion of the relationship between the canon and the archive (2008).

6. In line with the methodological approach adopted in this book, this chapter reiterates that the aesthetic experience in general, and the cinematic experience in particular, derive from perception and cognition, as well as from affect and sensation. In his conversations with Fréderic Strauss (2001), Almodóvar himself defined his cinema as a 'visceral cinema'. Hence, Almodóvar implicitly thinks of the cinematic experience in particular, and the aesthetic experience in general, as immanent, as well as of the significance of the senses in this experience.

7. I would like to express my deepest thanks to Teresa Vilarós for bringing this crucial point to my attention.

8. Boyarin does not argue that dualists abhorred the body. He suggests that Christians identified the soul as the essence of the human being, whereas rabbis emphasised the body (1993: 5).

9. For a study of cinema and Benjamin's notion of allegorical representation, see Lowenstein 2003.

10. For an excellent explanation of Derrida's reflection on the function of the signature, see Todd 1986. Moreover, in his discussion of Ana Mariscal, Marsh engages with Derrida's problematisation of the relationship between the signature and the text. Marsh documents the work of this neglected woman Spanish filmmaker, without perpetuating an auteurist approach, which would be predicated on a metaphysics of presence (see Marsh 2013).

11. Almodóvar used the term 'auto–fictional' in an interview included in the extra features of the American DVD of the film. Almodóvar explains that *La mala educación* is itself an 'auto–fiction' of himself. See Víctor Fuentes for a definition of the film as a 'fictional autobiography' and as 'metacinema' (Fuentes 2009).

12. As is well known, the main purpose of gay politics has traditionally been to achieve social visibility, recognition and assimilation into already constituted communities. By contrast, some strands of queer theory, including Bersani's (1995), propose notions of identity and modes of relation that resist incorporation into the hegemonic social and symbolic order. Almodóvar's cinema arguably falls into the latter category.

13. Andrew Asibong puts a similar argument forward in his discussion of *La mala educación* (2009: 190).

14. I am indebted to Foster, who articulates a similar point in his discussion of minimalist art (2004: 288).
15. For a fine explanation of Benjamin's theory of allegory, see Oliván Santaliestra 2004.
16. For a fine historical and theoretical analysis of this 'counter-cultural' movement, see Vilarós 1998.
17. For an excellent discussion of the connection between the Real and the uncanny, see Dolar 1991.
18. For an association of writing (the creative act) with self-mutilation, see Dean 1986.
19. Kinder associates the compulsive repetition enacted in the film with what she terms 'retroseriality', a concept I discussed in the Introduction (2009).
20. I am borrowing this concept from French psychoanalyst André Green, who associates narcissism less with the preservation of the unity of the ego than with the 'devastating effects of the death drive' (2001: xi).
21. I am inspired here by Bernadette Guthrie's fascinating reflection on her own encounter or lack of encounter with Derrida (Guthrie 2011).
22. For a fine discussion of what he defines as the 'digital uncanny' in the film, see Stewart 2006.
23. I would like to express my sincere thanks to Eva Woods for making me aware of Almodóvar's problematisation of the indexical trace through his use of digital technology in this film. Doane rightly points out that digital technology does not undermine the persistence of the logic of indexicality, which is associated with photochemical technologies and mechanically produced images, in visual media, including digital media (2007).
24. The crucial difference between 'performativity' and 'performance' is that the former cannot be defined as an intentional act, whereas the latter is defined as intentional. However, the two practices are not mutually exclusive. With regard to the iterability of gesture, gesture itself is in part predicated on its reproducibility, which implies the emergence of the singular, which is conditioned by repetition (see Butler 2014 and Weber 2006).
25. Montiel came from the same region in Spain – La Mancha – as Almodóvar. She was one of the few Spanish actresses to pursue a career in Hollywood, and Almodóvar is one of the few Spanish filmmakers to have had success in the almost impenetrable American film market. Hence, the image of Montiel functions as a mirror in which the image of Almodóvar is reflected, just as, in the film, the image of Ignacio seems like a reflection of Montiel.
26. I am indebted to Sylvie Debevec Henning's brilliant Derridean reading of Genet's play (1982).
27. I extrapolate this point from the conversation their mother has with Enrique Goded when he goes to Galicia searching for the 'true' identity and origins of Ángel/Ignacio. She says: 'La que sufre de corazón soy yo, pero la que se asusta es ella.' (It is I who suffers from heart disease, but it is she who gets scared.)

28. The horror suffered during so much of Franco's nearly forty years of dictatorship was blocked in the national psyche as a way of exonerating those responsible for the atrocities and the nation itself from the collective shame and guilt that these deeds were produced in Spain.

29. I borrow these terms from Patricia MacCormack, who engages with Guattari's definition of sound, colour, celerity or framing as cinema's 'a-signifying' elements (MacCormack 2005: 341).

30. Rolnik explains: 'This concept designates the capacity of all sense organs to allow themselves to be affected by otherness. It indicates that the whole body has this power to resonate to the forces of the world.' (2007: unpaginated).

31. In her recent book on religion and Spanish cinema, Elizabeth Scarlett makes this observation (2014).

32. I am influenced here by Taylor, who defines performance as an embodied practice in her discussion of the archive and the repertoire (2003). Although it is important to distinguish cinema from performance, the cinematic medium also encourages an embodied spectatorship.

33. For a fine discussion of the concepts of the 'archive' and the 'event', see Steinberg 2016.

34. This is one of the crucial moments which confirms that Goded could represent Almodóvar's alter ego in this 'auto-fictional' film. But, as I have tried to demonstrate in this chapter, autobiography is grounded in the strict coincidence of the proper name of the author with that of the narrator and that of the character. In this film, Almodóvar's authorial signature is both connected to and escapes from the cinematic text. The word 'passion', which is here associated with Almodóvar's creative method, expands until it becomes unreadable, and its expansion can be read as a visual articulation of Almodóvar's authorial bio-degradation, which is the condition of possibility for the process of creating the cinematic text.

35. I am returning here to my evocation of Derrida's deconstructive psychoanalytic interpretation of the archive's 'double logic', which I discussed in the introductory chapter (Derrida 1995b).

36. For a critique of Cvetkovich's notion of a queer archive of feelings, see Edenheim 2014. For Edenheim, Cvetkovich's insistence on making queer traumatic events comprehensible in mainstream history cannot escape the logic of preservation on which the archive is predicated. In addition, such an emphasis on preservation or monumentalisation is antithetical to a queer ethical and political embrace of the not-yet known, not-yet experienced or not-yet remembered.

Chapter 4

1. In Freudian psychoanalysis, 'condensation' refers to the convergences of images into one while 'displacement' refers to the transfer of affects and emotions from one image onto another. These psychoanalytic terms enable us to

think of the workings of memory as a palimpsest that inscribes experiences across times, spaces and subjectivities. For a fine theorisation of palimpsestic memory, see Silverman 2013.

2. Based on Thierry Jonquet's 1995 pulp novel, *Mygale*, *La piel que habito* eclectically draws on different cinematic genres, including science fiction, thriller, horror, melodrama, even comedy. Another important intertext is Georges Franju's film, *Les yeux sans visage* (*Eyes Without a Face*, 1965) (see Marcantonio 2015). It is well known that Almodóvar often negotiates with the conventions of cinematic genres without sacrificing his own authorial style, and he is also often considered through *auteur* theory. But here I am interested in how Almodóvar's film agitates the spectator to make us hypervigilant in the face of the horrors and vicissitudes of the past and the present, while insisting on possible lines of flight, and thereby defies clear-cut characterisations. For a fine discussion of cinematic genres and *auteurism* in relation to Spanish cinema, see Labanyi and Pavlovic 2013

3. See Gutiérrez-Albilla 2013c. The revision of this chapter has enabled me to profoundly question the concepts I deployed in my earlier version. I am using Vicente/Vera and both possessive pronouns. Throughout this chapter, since Vicente is played by a male actor and Vera by a female actress, I will use Vicente and the pronoun 'his' when I refer to a scene with him and Vera and the pronoun 'her' when I refer to her. I will use Vicente/Vera when referring to a theoretical concern pertinent to this singular yet split film character.

4. For Derrida's reflections on sovereign power, see Derrida 2009.

5. For an excellent approach to gender politics in the film, see Martín 2014.

6. The term 'vulnerability' comes from the Latin term 'vulnus', which implies the rupture of the skin. As I will discuss later, such a wound is both literal and symbolic, visible and invisible in the film.

7. As we will see, *La piel que habito* points to how traumatic experiences that took place in a particular time and space can be transported by other subjects in a different time and space.

8. Following on from Chapter 3, I draw here on Spinoza's monism to consider the mind and the body as a unitary whole. Instead of following the Cartesian distinction between the body and the mind, in Spinozan philosophy, mind and body are 'two different expressions, or manifestations, of the one substance' (Gatens 2009: 11).

9. The term 'nothingness' is taken from Lacan's phenomenological account of consciousness (Lacan 1988).

10. The mansion that figures in the film is known as the Quinta de Mirabel, which was built in the fifteenth century and functioned as a country house for the aristocracy and subsequently for the upper classes. The house is now a boutique hotel. By using this house as the set of the film, Almodóvar seems to be concerned with the house's decorative qualities and its carrying of a historical tradition based on class distinctions and unequal material and symbolic conditions of existence.

11. It is interesting to note that we can see members of the domestic service in the background of this scene. These domestic workers have been fired by Dr Ledgard, which is an example, as I will discuss later, of how Dr Ledgard embodies an ideology based on the arbitrary disposal of human people to sustain its own calculated exigencies.

12. Smith and White associate the claustrophobic and vigilant spaces emphasised in the film with Foucault's motif of the panopticon (2011).

13. I associate the surveillance camera with the cinematic punctum's undoing of linear readings of the representational field, emphasising how this cinematic punctum allegorises the way power and control always already depend on incalculable destabilising elements. I will shortly pay attention to the surveillance device's evocation of an orifice to point out that Vicente's 'cut' (orifice) is suggested in the film's *mise-en-scène*.

14. For an association of this scene with Pollock's paintings, see Navarrete-Galiano 2012.

15. I will later explain that Dr Ledgard's absolute power is also predicated on its incalculable failure.

16. For a fine discussion of Vicente's castration in relation to the film's editing, see Price 2015.

17. As I explained in Chapter 3, I am thinking of subjectivity as always already constituted by and in language and within a phenomenological experience of being in the world without reifying a metaphysics of presence.

18. See Didi-Huberman for a fine study of the relationship between hysteria and the photographic medium (2004).

19. For a fascinating reading of Liliana Cavani's *The Night Porter* (1974) in terms of the film's evocation of concentrationary imaginary to offer a political resistance to its intoxicating effects and persistence in the present, see Pollock 2015.

20. Although it is outside the scope of this chapter, I should mention that there were around 180 concentration camps across Spain between 1936 and 1947; although this topic requires further research, some Spanish intellectuals and historians, such as Isaías La Fuente, Javier Rodrigo and David Serrano, have already done important work on the subject. It is believed that at least 250,000 prisoners died in these Francoist concentration camps. Some of these concentration camps followed the model of Dachau. In fact, Heinrich Himmler paid a visit in 1940 to one of the most infamous concentration camps, in Miranda del Ebro. It was closed in 1947. It is also well known that Ramón Serrano Suñer, who was the brother-in-law of Franco and 'Ministro del Exterior' (Minister for Foreign Affairs), worked in collaboration with the Nazis. Therefore, the terror that sustained the Francoist regime can be both theoretically and historically connected to Nazi Germany.

21. Rosi Braidotti is highly critical of Agamben's focus on finitude in his association of biopower with the totalitarian elements that can still seep into forms of sovereign power in the present, including in capitalist, neoliberal

democracies. Braidotti also questions Agamben's definition of 'bare life' as the result of a destructive effect of sovereign power on the subject. In her pursuit of an affirmative ethics, which does not exclude the concept of vulnerability, Braidotti attempts to foreground the generative possibilities of bare life (2006: 2010). Yet, Agamben's reflection on bare life enables us to work through the complex question of the other's exposure to violence in the context of this film before making the transition to explore Braidotti's emphasis on the ethics of affirmation, as articulated in *La piel que habito*.

22. This is the literal translation of the title of David Rousset's book, *L'univers concentrationnaire* (1946). Rousset was a Shoah survivor who, upon return from Buchenwald, claimed that the concentration camp was not a space apart from social life, but fully included in political life (Pollock and Silverman 2011b: 18–19).

23. Although this book problematises the autonomy of the individual and emphasises how our ethical relations precede the ontology of the subject, we still need to pay attention to human subjectivity's ontological distinctiveness in the face of the threats to the human condition I underscore here.

24. For a fine discussion of Anzieu's notion of the 'skin-ego', see Wegenstein 2002.

25. I borrow this term from Xavier Aldana Reyes's fine analysis of the film (2013).

26. 'Bête' means both 'beast' and 'stupid' in French (Derrida 2009).

References

Abraham, Nicholas and Maria Torok (1984), 'A Poetics of Psychoanalysis: "The Lost Object: Me"', *SubStance*, 43.13–2: 3–18.

Abraham, Nicholas and Maria Torok (1994), *The Shell and the Kernel*, Chicago: University of Chicago Press.

Acevedo-Muñoz, Ernesto R. (2004), 'The Body and Spain: Pedro Almodóvar's *All about My Mother*', *Quarterly Review of Film and Video*, 21.1: 25–38.

Acevedo-Muñoz, Ernesto R. (2007), *Pedro Almodóvar*, London: BFI.

Adams, Parveen (1991), 'The Art of Analysis: Mary Kelly's *Interim* and the Discourse of the Analyst', *October*, 58: 81–96.

Agamben, Giorgio (1998), *Homo Sacer: Sovereign Power and Bare Life*, Stanford: Stanford University Press.

Agamben, Giorgio (2000), *Means Without Ends*, trans. Vincenzo Binetti and Cesare Casarino, Minneapolis: University of Minnesota Press.

Aguado, Txetxu (2009), 'Pedro Almodóvar, La Movida y la Transición: memoria, espectáculo y anti-franquismo', *Letras Peninsulares*, 22.1: 23–44.

Ahmed, Sara (2005), 'The Skin of the Community: Affect and Boundary Formation', in Tina Chanter and Ewa Plonowska Ziarek (eds), *Revolt, Affect, Collectivity: The Unstable Boundaries of Kristeva's Polis*, New York: State University of New York Press, pp. 95–112.

Aldana Reyes, Xavier (2013), 'Skin Deep? Surgical Horror and the Impossibility of Becoming Woman in Almodóvar's *The Skin I Live In*', *Bulletin of Hispanic Studies*, 90.7: 819–32.

Allbritton, Dean (2013), 'Paternity and Pathogens: Mourning Men and the Crises of Masculinity in *Todo sobre mi madre* and *Hable con ella*', in D'Lugo et al. (eds), *A Companion to Pedro Almodóvar*, pp. 225–43.

Allinson, Mark (2001), *A Spanish Labyrinth: The Films of Pedro Almodóvar*, London: I. B. Tauris.

Alted, Alicia (2005), *La voz de los vencidos. El exilio republicano de 1939*, Madrid: Aguilar.

Amago, Samuel (2007), 'Todo sobre Barcelona: Refiguring Spanish Identities in Recent European Cinema', *Hispanic Research Journal*, 8.1: 11–25.

Anzieu, Didier (1989), *The Skin Ego: A Psychoanalytical Approach to the Self*, New Haven: Yale University Press.

Arendt, Hannah (1976 [1951]), *The Origins of Totalitarianism*, Orlando: Harcourt.

Arendt, Hannah (1958), *The Human Condition*, Chicago: University of Chicago Press.

Armstrong, Richard (2012), *Mourning Films: A Critical Study of Loss and Grieving in Cinema*, Jefferson, NC: McFarland & Co.

Aronica, Daniela (2005), 'Intertextualidad y autorreferencialidad: Almodóvar y el cine español', in Zurian et al. (eds), *Almodóvar: el cine como pasión*, pp. 57–80.

Asibong, Andrew (2009), 'Unrecognizable Bonds: Bleeding Kinship in Pedro Almodóvar and Gregg Araki', *New Cinemas*, 7.3: 185–95.

Assmann, Aleida (2008), 'Canon and the Archive', in Astrid Grill and Ansgar Nünning (ed.), *Cultural Memory Studies: An International and Interdisciplinary Handbook*, Berlin: de Gruyter, pp. 97–107.

Avelar, Idelber (1999), *The Untimely Present: Postdictatorial Latin American Fiction and the Task of Mourning*, Durham, NC: Duke University Press.

Bal, Mieke (1999), 'Narrative Inside Out: Louise Bourgeois' Spider as Theoretical Object', *Oxford Art Journal*, 22.2: 101–26.

Bal, Mieke (2011), 'Heterochrony in the Act: The Migratory Politics of Time', in Mieke Bal and Miguel Á. Hernández-Navarro (eds), *Art and Visibility in Migratory Culture: Conflict, Resistance, and Agency*, Amsterdam: Rodopi, pp. 211–37.

Balibrea, Mari Paz (2005), 'Rethinking Spanish Republican Exile. An Introduction', *Journal of Spanish Cultural Studies*, 6.1: 3–24.

Ballesteros, Isolina (2009), 'Performing Identities in the Cinema of Almodóvar', in Epps et al. (eds), *All About Almodóvar*, pp. 71–100.

Barthes, Roland (1984), *Camera Lucida: Reflections on Photography*, trans. Richard Howard, New York: Hill and Wang.

Bataille, Georges (1930), 'L'Art primitif', *Documents*, 7: 389–98.

Benjamin, Walter (1968), *Illuminations: Essays and Reflections*, ed. Hannah Arendt, New York: Schocken Books.

Bennett, Jill (2005), *Empathic Vision: Affect, Trauma, and Contemporary Art*, Stanford: Stanford University Press.

Bennett, Jill (2007), 'Aesthetics of Intermediality', *Art History*, 303: 432–50.

Bennett, Jill (2012), *Practical Aesthetics: Events, Affects and Art after 9/11*, London: I. B. Tauris.

Berger, Anne-Emmanuelle (2005), 'Sexing Differances', *differences: A Journal of Feminist Cultural Studies*, 16.3: 52–67.

Bernstein, Richard (2005), 'Hannah Arendt on the Stateless', *Parallax* 11.1: 46–60.

Bersani, Leo (1987), 'Is the Rectum a Grave?', *October*, 43: 197–222.

Bersani, Leo (1995), *Homos*, Cambridge, MA: Harvard University Press.

Bersani, Leo and Ulysse Dutoit (1999), *Caravaggio*, London: BFI Modern Classics.

Bersani, Leo and Ulysse Dutoit (2004), *Forms of Being: Cinema, Aesthetics, Subjectivity*, London: BFI.

Bersani, Leo and Ulysse Dutoit (2009), 'Almodóvar's Girls', in Epps et al. (eds), *All About Almodóvar*, pp. 241–66.

Bersani, Leo and Adam Phillips (2008), *Intimacies*, Chicago: University of Chicago Press.

Beugnet, Martine (2007), *Cinema and Sensation: French Film and the Art of Transgression*, Edinburgh: Edinburgh University Press.

Biles, Jeremy (2012), 'The Skin I Live In', *Journal of Religion and Film*, 16.1 <http://digitalcommons.unomaha.edu/jrf/vol16/iss1/21> (accessed 11 May 2013).

Blanchot, Maurice (2000), *The Instant of My Death*/Derrida, Jacques, *Demeure: Fiction and Testimony*, trans. Elizabeth Rottenberg, Stanford: Stanford University Press.

Bordo, Susan (1990), 'Feminism, Postmodernism, and Gender Scepticism', in Linda Nicholson (ed.), *Feminism/Postmodernism*, New York: Routledge, pp. 133–56.

Bouchard, Gianna (2012), 'Skin Deep: Female Flesh in UK Live Art Since 1999', *Contemporary Theatre Review*, 22.1: 94–105.

Boyarin, Daniel (1993), *Carnal Israel: Reading Sex in Talmudic Culture*, Berkeley: University of California Press.

Boym, Svetlana (2001), *The Future of Nostalgia*, New York: Basic Books.

Braidotti, Rosi (2006), 'The Ethics of Becoming Imperceptible', in Constantin V. Boundas (ed.), *Deleuze and Philosophy*, Edinburgh: Edinburgh University Press, pp. 133–59.

Braidotti, Rosi (2010), 'On Putting the Active Back into Activism', *New Formations* 68: 42–57.

Bronfen, Elisabeth (1998), *The Knotted Subject: Hysteria and its Discontents*, Princeton: Princeton University Press.

Burdeau, Emmanuel (2006), 'Pedro Almodóvar. Rencontre avec un narrateur', *Cahiers du Cinéma*, 612: 18–22.

Burns, Bonnie (1999), 'Cassandra's Eyes', in Ellis Hanson (ed.), *Out Takes: Essays on Queer Theory and Film*, Durham, NC: Duke University Press, pp. 129–50.

Butler, Judith (1990), *Gender Trouble: Feminism and the Subversion of Identity*, London: Routledge.

Butler, Judith (1997), *Excitable Speech: A Politics of the Performative*, New York and London: Routledge.

Butler, Judith (1999), 'Gender is Burning: Questions of Appropriation and Subversion', in Sue Thornham (ed.) *Feminist Film Theory: A Reader*, Edinburgh: Edinburgh University Press, pp. 336–49.

Butler, Judith (2002), 'Is Kinship always already Heterosexual?' *differences: A Journal of Feminist Cultural Studies*, 13.1: 14–44.

Butler, Judith (2003), 'Violence, Mourning, Politics', *Studies in Gender and Sexuality*, 4.1: 9–37.

Butler, Judith (2004), *Undoing Gender*, London: Routledge.

Butler, Judith (2006), 'Bracha's Eurydice', in Bracha Ettinger, *The Matrixial Borderspace*, pp. vii–xii.

Butler, Judith (2012), 'Precarious Life, Vulnerability, and the Ethics of Cohabitation', *The Journal of Speculative Philosophy*, 26.2: 134–51.

Butler, Judith (2014), 'When Gesture Becomes Event', unpublished paper given at 'Theater, Performance, Philosophy', Paris: University of Paris, Sorbonne (June).

Butler, Judith and Bracha Ettinger (2011), 'Judith Butler with Bracha Ettinger. Ethics on a Global Scale', unpublished paper given at Saas-Fee: European Graduate School (July).

Camino, Mercedes (2010), '"Vivir sin ti": Motherhood, Melodrama and *española* in Pedro Almodóvar's *Todo sobre mi madre* (1999) and *Volver* (2006)', *Bulletin of Spanish Studies*, 87.5: 625–42.

Caruth, Cathy (1991), 'Unclaimed Experience: Trauma and the Possibility of History', *Yale French Studies*, 79: 181–92.

Chambers-Letson, Joshua (2014), 'Compensatory Hyperthrophy, or All about My Mother' *Social Text*, 32.1: 13–24.

Chion, Michel (1999), *The Voice in Cinema*, trans. Claudia Gorbman, New York: Columbia University Press.

Cisneros, James (2006), 'The Figure of Memory in Chilean Cinema: Patrico Guzmán and Raúl Ruiz', *Journal of Latin American Cultural Studies*, 15.1: 59–75.

Clewell, Tammy (2004), 'Mourning Beyond Melancholia: Freud's Psycho-analysis of Loss', *Journal of the American Psychoanalytical Association*, 52.1: 43–67.

Cooper, Sarah (2006), *Selfless Cinema? Ethics and French Documentary*, Oxford: Legenda.

Corbalán, Ana (2008), 'Dificultad ante una alternative familiar en *Todo sobre mi madre* de Pedro Almodóvar: ¿Subversión o regression?', *Colorado Review of Hispanic Studies*, 6: 149–66.

Cowan, Bainard (1981), 'Walter Benjamin's Theory of Allegory', *New German Critique*, 22: 109–22.

Critchley, Simon (1995), 'On Derrida's *Specters of Marx*', *Philosophy and Social Criticism*, 21.3: 1–30.

Cvetkovich, Ann (2003), *An Archive of Feelings: Trauma, Sexuality, and Lesbian Public Cultures*, Durham, NC: Duke University Press.

Dasgupta, Sudeep (2009a), 'Resonances and Disjunctions: Matrixial Subjectivity and Queer Theory', *Studies in the Maternal*, 1.2: 1–5.

Dasgupta, Sudeep (2009b), 'Words, Bodies, Times: Queer Theory Before and After Itself', *Borderlands*, 8.2: 1–16.

Davies, Ann (ed.) (2011), *Spain on Screen: Developments in Contemporary Spanish Cinema*, Basingstoke: Palgrave Macmillan.

Davies, Ann (2012), *Spanish Spaces: Landscape, Space and Place in Contemporary Spanish Culture*, Liverpool: Liverpool University Press.

Dean, Carolyn (1986), 'Law and Sacrifice: Bataille, Lacan, and the Critique of the Subject', *Representations*, 13: 42–62.

Dean, Tim (2009), *Unlimited Intimacy: Reflections on the Subculture of Barebacking*, Chicago: University of Chicago Press.

Debevec Henning, Sylvie (1982), 'The Ritual Im-plications of Genet's *Les Bonnes*', *boundary 2*, 10.2: 219–43.

Deleuze, Gilles (1989), *Cinema 2: The Time-Image*, trans. Hugh Tomlinson and Robert Galeta, Minneapolis: University of Minnesota Press.

Deleuze, Gilles (1994 [1968]), *Difference and Repetition*, trans. Paul Patton, New York: Columbia University Press.

Deleuze, Gilles and Félix Guattari (1984), *Anti-Oedipus: Capitalism and Schizophrenia*, trans. Robert Hurley, Mark Seem and Helen R. Lane, London: Athlone.

del Rio, Elena (2008), *Deleuze and the Cinemas of Performances: Powers of Affection*, Edinburgh: Edinburgh University Press.

Derrida, Jacques (1972), 'Freud and the Scene of Writing', *Yale French Studies*, 48: 74–117.

Derrida, Jacques (1973), *Speech and Phenomena, and Other Essays on Husserl's Theory of Signs*, trans. David B. Allison, Evanston: Northwestern University Press.

Derrida, Jacques (1980), *Writing and Difference*, trans. Alan Bass, Chicago: University of Chicago Press.

Derrida, Jacques (1982), *Margins of Philosophy*, trans. Alan Bass, Chicago: University of Chicago Press.

Derrida, Jacques (1984), *Signéponge / Signsponge*, trans. Richard Rand, New York: Columbia University Press.

Derrida, Jacques (1986), '*Fors*: The Anglish Words of Nicholas Abraham and Maria Torok', trans. Barbara Johnson, in Nicholas Abraham and Maria Torok, *The Wolf-Man's Magic Word: A Cryptonymy*, trans. Nicholas T. Rand, Minneapolis: University of Minnesota Press, pp. xi–xiviii.

Derrida, Jacques (1994), *Specters of Marx: The State of Debt, the Work of Mourning, and the New International*, trans. Peggy Kamuf, London: Routledge.

Derrida, Jacques (1995a), *The Gift of Death*, trans. David Wills, Chicago: University of Chicago Press.

Derrida, Jacques (1995b), 'Archive Fever: A Freudian Impression', *Diacritics*, 25.2: 9–63.

Derrida, Jacques (1998 [1967]), *Of Grammatology*, trans. Gayatri Spivak, Baltimore: Johns Hopkins University Press.

Derrida, Jacques (2005), *Rogues: Two Essays on Reason*, Stanford: Stanford University Press.

Derrida, Jacques (2009), *The Beast and the Sovereign*, ed. Michel Lisse, Marie Louise Mallet and Ginette Michaud, trans. Geoffrey Bennington, Chicago: University of Chicago Press.

De Zeguer, Catherine (1996), 'Introduction', in Catherine de Zeguer (ed.), *Inside the Visible: An Elliptical Traverse of 20th Century Art in, of, and from the Feminine*, Cambridge, MA: MIT Press, pp. 19–41.

Dickinson, Colby (2011), 'Beyond Violence, Beyond the Text: The Role of Gesture in Walter Benjamin and Giorgio Agamben, and its Affinity with the Work of René Girard', *Heythrop Journal*, L11: 952–61.

Didi-Huberman, Georges (1984), 'The Index of the Absent Wound, Monograph on a Stain)', *October*, 29: 63–81.

Didi-Huberman, Georges (2004), *Invention of Hysteria: Charcot and the Photographic Iconography of the Salpêtrière*, trans. Alisa Hartz, Cambridge, MA: MIT Press.

Didi-Huberman, Georges (2009), 'Peuples exposés, peuples figurants', *De(s) générations*, 9: 7–17.

D'Lugo, Marvin (2006), *Pedro Almodóvar*, Urbana and Chicago: University of Illinois Press.

D'Lugo, Marvin (2009), 'Postnostalgia in *Bad Education: Written on the Body of Sara Montiel*', in Epps et al. (eds), *All About Almodóvar*, pp. 357–85.

D'Lugo, Marvin (2013), 'Almodóvar and Latin America: The Making of a Transnational Aesthetic in *Volver*', in D'Lugo et al. (eds), *A Companion to Pedro Almodóvar*, pp. 412–31.

D'Lugo, Marvin and Kathleen Vernon (eds) (2013), *A Companion to Pedro Almodóvar*, Malden, MA: Wiley-Blackwell.

Doane, Mary Ann (2007), 'Indexicality: Trace and Sign: Introduction', *differences: A Journal of Feminist Cultural Studies*, 18.1: 1–6.

Dolar, Mladen (1991), 'I Shall Be With You On Your Wedding Night: Lacan and the Uncanny', *October*, 58: 5–23.

Dollimore, Jonathan (1991), *Sexual Dissidence: Augustine to Wilde, Freud to Foucault*, Oxford: Clarendon Press.

Edenheim, Sara (2014), 'Lost and Never Found: The Queer Archive of Feelings and Its Historical Propriety', *differences: A Journal of Feminist Cultural Studies*, 24.3: 36–62.

Efal, Adi (2000), 'Warburg's "Pathos Formula" in Psychoanalytic and Benjaminian Contexts', *Assaph*, 5: 221–37.

Elsaesser, Thomas (1994), 'Historicising the Subject: A Body of Work', *New German Critique*, 63: 10–33.

Elsaesser, Thomas (2001), 'Postmodernism as Mourning Work', *Screen*, 42.2: 193–201.

Epps, Brad (2009), 'Blind Shots and Backward Glances: Reviewing *Matador* and *Labyrinth of Passion*', in Epps et al. (eds), *All About Almodóvar*, pp. 295–338.

Epps, Brad and Despina Kakoudaki (eds) (2009), *All About Almodóvar: A Passion for Cinema*, Minneapolis: University of Minnesota Press.

Estrada, Isabel M. (2013), *El documental cinematográfico y televisivo contemporáneo. Memoria, sujeto y formación de la identidad democrática española*, Woodbridge: Tamesis Books.

Ettinger, Bracha (1992), 'Matrix and Metramorphosis', *Differences*, 4.3: 176–208.

Ettinger, Bracha (1996), 'Metramorphic Borderlinks and Matrixial Borderspace in Subjectivity as Encounter', in John Welchman (ed.), *Rethinking Borders*, New York: Macmillan, pp. 125–59.

Ettinger, Bracha (2000), 'Art as the Transport-Station of Trauma', in *Bracha Lichtenberg Ettinger: Artworking 1985–1999*, Ghent: Ludion, pp. 91–115.

Ettinger, Bracha (2005), 'Co-poiesis', *Framework X Ephemera*, 5.10: 703–13.

Ettinger, Bracha (2006a), *The Matrixial Borderspace*, Minneapolis: University of Minnesota Press.

Ettinger, Bracha (2006b), 'From Proto-Ethical Compassion to Responsibility: Besideness and the Three Primal Mother-Phantasies of Not-Enoughness, Devouring and Abandonment', *Athena*, 2: 100–36.

Ettinger, Bracha (2016), 'Art as the Transport Station of Trauma', in Yochai Ataria et al. (eds), *Interdisciplinary Handbook of Trauma and Culture*, Cham: Springer International Publishing, pp. 151–60.

Ettinger, Bracha and Emmanuel Lévinas (2006), 'What Would Eurydice Say?', *Athena*, 2: 137–45.

Evans, Jo (2013), 'Icíar Bollaín's "Carte de Tendre": Mapping Female Subjectivity for the Turn of the Millenium', in Nair et al. (eds), *Hispanic and Lusophone Women Filmmakers: Theory, Practice and Difference*, pp. 252–63.

Farrell, Kim (1998), *Post-Traumatic Cultures: Injury and Interpretation in the Nineties*, Baltimore: Johns Hopkins University Press.

Faulkner, Sally (2006), *A Cinema of Contradiction: Spanish Film in the 1960s*, Edinburgh: Edinburgh University Press.

Feldman, Hannah (2004), 'Of the Public Born: Raymond Hains and la France déchirée', *October*, 108: 73–96.

Fer, Briony (1995), 'Poussière/peinture: Bataille on Painting', in Carolyn Gill (ed.), *Bataille: Writing the Sacred*, pp. 154–71.

Fer, Briony (1997), *On Abstract Art*, New Haven: Yale University Press.

Fer, Briony (2002), 'The Work of Salvage: Eva Hesse's Latex Works', in Elisabeth Sussman (ed.), *Eva Hesse*, San Francisco: SFMOMA, pp. 78–95.

Fer, Briony (2004), *The Infinite Line: Remaking Art after Modernism*, New Haven: Yale University Press.

Fer, Briony (2007), 'Night', *Oxford Art Journal*, 30.1: 69–80.

Fer, Briony (2012), untitled and unpublished paper given at the 'Mira Schendel Conference', Tate Modern, London (November).

Fernández Agis, Domingo (2009), 'Tiempo, política y hospitalidad. Una reflexión desde Derrida y Lévinas', *ISEGORÍA. Revista de Filosofía Moral y Política*, 40: 191–202.

Ferrán, Ofelia (2007), *Working through Memory: Writing and Remembrance in Contemporary Spanish Narrative*, Lewisburg, PA: Bucknell University Press.

Findlay, Edward F. (2002), 'Secrets of European Responsibility: Jacques Derrida on Responsibility in the Philosophy of Jan Patocka', *Philosophy Today*, 46.1: 16–30.

Flinn, Caryl (1992), *Strains of Utopia: Gender, Nostalgia, and Hollywood Film Music*, Princeton: Princeton University Press.

Foster, Hal (1996), *The Return of the Real: The Avant-garde at the End of the Century*, Cambridge, MA: MIT Press.

Foster, Hal (2004), *Prosthetic Gods*, Cambridge, MA: MIT Press.

Foucault, Michel (1975), *Surveiller et punir. Naissance de la prison*, Paris: Éditions Gallimard.

Foucault, Michel (1984), 'Of Other Spaces: Utopias and Heterotopias', in *Architecture/Mouvement/Continuité*: 1–9.

Foucault, Michel (1990 [1978]), *The History of Sexuality Vol. 1*, trans. Robert Hurley, New York: Vintage Books.

Fowler, Catherine (2004), 'Room for Experiment: Gallery Films and the Vertical Time from Maya Deren to Eija Liisa Ahtila', *Screen*, 45: 324–41.

Fra-Molinero, Baltasar (2009), 'The Suspect Whiteness of Spain', in La Vinia Delois Jennings (ed.), *At Home and Abroad: Historicizing Twentieth-Century Whiteness in Literature and Performance*, Knoxville: University of Tennessee Press, pp. 147–69.

Fraser, Nancy (2004), 'Hannah Arendt in the 21st Century', *Contemporary Political Theory*, 3.3: 253–61.

Freud, Sigmund (1918), *Reflections on War and Death*, New York: Moffat, Yard and Company.

Freud, Sigmund (1962 [1923]), *The Ego and the Id*, trans. James Strachey, New York: Norton.

Freud, Sigmund (1964 [1937–9]), *Moses and Monotheism, An Outline of Psycho-Analysis and Other Works (1937–1939)*, London: The Hogarth Press.

Freud, Sigmund (2003 [1920]), 'Beyond the Pleasure Principle', in *Beyond the Pleasure Principle and Other Writings*, London: Penguin Books, pp. 45–102.

Freud, Sigmund (2009 [1917]), 'Mourning and Melancholia', in Leticia Glocer Fiorini, Sergio Lewkowicz and Thierry Bokanowski (eds), *On Freud's 'Mourning and Melancholia'*, London: Karnac Books, pp. 44–59.

Fuentes, Víctor (2009), '*Bad Education*: Fictional Autobiography and Meta-Film Noir', in Epps et al. (eds), *All About Almodóvar*, pp. 429–45.

Gabilondo, Joseba (2005), 'Melodrama atlántico y migrancia maternal. Apuntes sobre *Todo sobre mi madre*', in Zurian et al. (eds), *Almodóvar: el cine como pasión*, pp. 287–306.

Galt Harpham, Geoffrey (2009), 'Roots, Races, and the Return to Philology', *Representations*, 106.1: 34–62.

García Canclini, Néstor (1995), 'Modernity after Postmodernity', in Gerardo Mosquera (ed.), *Beyond the Fantastic: Contemporary Art Criticism from Latin America*, London: Institute of International Visual Arts, pp. 20–51.

Garlinger, Patrick Paul (2007), 'All about Agrado, or the Sincerity of Camp in Almodóvar's *Todo sobre mi madre*', *Journal of Spanish Cultural Studies*, 5.1: 117–34.

Gasché, Rodolphe (2007), 'European Memories: Jan Patocka and Jacques Derrida on Responsibility', *Critical Inquiry*, 33: 291–311.

Gatens, Moira (2009), 'Introduction: Through Spinoza's "Looking Glass"', in Moira Gatens (ed.), *Feminist Interpretations of Benedict Spinoza*, University Park: Penn State University Press, pp. 1–28.

Gill, Carolyn (ed.) (1995), *Bataille, Writing the Sacred*, London: Routledge.

Girgus, Sam B. (2010), *Lévinas and the Cinema of Redemption: Time, Ethics, and the Feminine*, New York: Columbia University Press.

Glazer, Peter (2005), *Radical Nostalgia: Spanish Civil War Commemoration in America*, Rochester: Rochester University Press.

Golob, Stephanie (2008), 'Volver: The Return of/to Transitional Justice Politics in Spain', *Journal of Spanish Cultural Studies*, 9.2: 127–41.

Gómez, Antonio (2006), 'La política del documental: observadores, observados, unidad y dispersión en *La espalda del mundo*', *Arizona Journal of Hispanic Cultural Studies*, 10, 98–113.

Graff-Zivin, Erin (2014a), *Figurative Inquisitions: Conversion, Torture, and Truth in the Luso-Hispanic Atlantic*, Evanston: Northwestern University Press.

Graff-Zivin, Erin (2014b), 'Beyond Inquisitional Logic, or, Toward an An-archaeological Latin Americanism', *CR: The New Centennial Review*, 14.1: 195–211.

Green, André (2001), *Life Narcissism Death Narcissism*, trans. Andrew Weller, London: Free Association Books.

Greer-Johnson, Julie (2001), 'Sor Juana Castaño: From *gracioso* to Comic Hero', *South Atlantic Review*, 66.4: 94–108.

Grosz, Elizabeth (1994), *Volatile Bodies: Toward a Corporeal Feminism*, Bloomington: Indiana University Press.

Guattari, Félix and Suely Rolnik (2008), *Molecular Revolution in Brazil*, trans. Karel Clapshow and Brian Holmes, Los Angeles: Semiotext(e).

Guerin, Frances and Roger Hallas (2007), 'Introduction', in Hallas et al. (eds), *The Image and the Witness*, pp. 1–20.

Guthrie, Bernadette (2011), 'Invoking Derrida: Authorship. Readership, and the Specter of Presence in Film and Print', *New Literary History*, 42.3: 519–36.

Gutiérrez-Albilla, Julián Daniel (2005), 'Body, Silence and Movement: Pina Bausch's Dance in Almodóvar's *Hable con ella*', *Studies in Hispanic Cinemas*, 2.1: 47–58.

Gutiérrez-Albilla, Julián Daniel (2011a), 'Children of Exile: Trauma, Memory, and Testimony in Jaime Camino's Documentary *Los niños de Rusia* (2001)', in Ann Davies (ed.), *Spain on Screen*, pp. 129–50.

Gutiérrez-Albilla, Julián Daniel (2011b), 'Returning to and from the Maternal Rural Space: Trauma, Late Modernity, and Nostalgic Utopia in Almodóvar's *Volver* (2006)', *Bulletin of Hispanic Studies*, 88.3: 321–38.

Gutiérrez-Albilla, Julián Daniel (2013a), 'Becoming a Queer Mother In and Through Film: Trans-sexuality, Trans-subjectivity, and Maternal Relationality in Almodóvar's *All About my Mother*', in Labanyi et al. (eds), *A Companion to Spanish Cinema*, pp. 563–80.

Gutiérrez-Albilla, Julián Daniel (2013b), 'Inscribing/Scratching the Past on the "Surface" of the "Skin:" Embodied Inter-subjectivity, "Prosthetic Memory" and Witnessing in Almodóvar's *La mala educación*', in D'Lugo et al. (eds), *A Companion to Almodóvar*, pp. 322–44.

Gutiérrez-Albilla, Julián Daniel (2013c), 'La piel del horror, el horror en la piel. Poder, violencia y trauma en el cuerpo (post)humano en *La piel que habito*', *The Journal of Spanish Cultural Studies*, 14.1: 70–85.

Gutiérrez-Albilla, Julián Daniel (2013d), 'Filming in the Feminine: Subjective Realism, Disintegration and Bodily Affection in Lucrecia Martel's *La ciénaga*', in Nair et al. (eds), *Hispanic and Lusophone Women Filmmakers*, pp. 215–28.

Gutiérrez-Albilla, Julián Daniel (2015a), 'Rethinking Spanish Visual Cultural Studies through an "Untimely" Encounter with La Ribot's Dance/Performance Art', *Bulletin of Spanish Studies*, 92. 3, 361–90.

Gutiérrez-Albilla, Julián Daniel (2015b), 'Reframing *My Dearest Senorita* (1971): Queer Embodiment and Subjectivity through the Poetics of Cinema', *Studies in Spanish and Latin American Cinemas*, 12.1: 27–42.

Hallas, Roger (2007), 'Sound, Image and the Corporeal Implication of Witnessing in Derek Jarman's *Blue*', in Hallas et al. (eds), *The Image and the Witness*, pp. 37–51.

Hallas, Roger and Frances Guerin (eds) (2007), *The Image and the Witness: Trauma, Memory and Visual Culture*, London: Wallflower.

Hamington, Maurice (2004), *Embodied Care: Jane Addams, Maurice Merleau-Ponty, and Feminist Ethics*, Urbana and Chicago: University of Illinois Press.

Hand, Séan (1996), *Facing the Other: The Ethics of Emmanuel Levinas*, Richmond: Curzon Press.

Hansen, Mark B. N. (2010), 'Memory, by Bernard Stiegler, with an Introduction by Mark B. N. Hansen', in W. J. T. Mitchell and Mark B. N. Hansen (eds), *Critical Terms for Media Studies*, Chicago: University of Chicago Press, pp. 64–6.

Harris, Geraldine (1999), *Staging Femininities: Performance and Performativity*, Manchester: Manchester University Press.

Harvey, David (1990), *The Condition of Postmodernity: An Enquiry into the Origins of Cultural Change*, Malden, MA: Wiley-Blackwell.

Hatley, James (2000), *Suffering Witness: The Quandary of Responsibility after the Irreparable*, Albany, NY: SUNY Press.

Hequembourg, Amy (2007), 'Becoming Lesbian Mothers', *Journal of Homosexuality*, 53.3: 153–80.

Hirsch, Joshua (2001), *Afterimage: Film, Trauma, and the Holocaust*, Philadelphia: Temple University Press.

Hirsch, Marianne (1997), *Family Frames: Photography, Narrative and Postmemory*, Cambridge, MA: Harvard University Press.

Hirsch, Marianne (2001), 'Surviving Images: Holocaust Photographs and the Work of Postmemory', in Barbie Zelizer (ed.), *Visual Culture and the Holocaust*, New Brunswick, NJ: Rutgers University Press, pp. 215–46.

Huffer, Lynne (1998), *Maternal Pasts, Feminist Futures: Nostalgia, Ethics, and the Question of Difference*, Stanford: Stanford University Press.

Huyssen, Andreas (2001), 'The Mnemonic Art of Marcelo Brodsky', in Javier Panera (ed.) *Marcelo Brodsky: Memory Works*, Salamanca: Universidad Salamanca, pp. 7–11.

Ibáñez, Juan Carlos (2013), 'Memory, Politics, and the Post-Transition in Almodóvar's Cinema', in D'Lugo et al. (eds), *A Companion to Pedro Almodóvar*, pp. 153–75.

James, Ian (2015), 'Totality, Convergence, Synchronization', in Pollock et al., *Concentrationary Imaginaries*, pp. 81–96.

Jameson, Fredric (1986), 'Third-World Literature in the Era of Multinational Capitalism', *Social Text*, 15: 65–88.

Jameson, Fredric (1991), *Postmodernism, or, the Cultural Logic of Late Capitalism*, London: Verso.

Jennings, Michael (2014), 'Toward the Apokatastic Will: Media, Theology, and Politics in Walter Benjamin's Late Work', unpublished paper given at the School of Criticism and Theory, Cornell University, Ithaca (July).

Johnson, Peter (2006), 'Unravelling Foucault's "Different Spaces"', *History of the Human Sciences*, 19.4: 75–90.

Joseph, Betty (2012), 'Neoliberalism and Allegory', *Cultural Critique*, 82.1: 68–94.

Kaplan, E. Ann and Ban Wang (2003), 'From Traumatic Paralysis to the Force Field of Modernity', in E. Ann Kaplan and Ban Wang (eds), *Trauma and Cinema: Cross-cultural Explorations*, Hong Kong: Hong Kong University Press, pp. 1–22.

Keller, Patricia (2015), *Ghostly Landscapes: Film, Photography, and the Aesthetics of Haunting in Contemporary Spanish Culture*, Toronto: University of Toronto Press.

Kercher, Dona M (2015), *Latin Hitchcock: How Almodóvar, Amenábar, De la Iglesia, Del Toro and Campanella Became Notorious*, London: Wallflower.

Kinder, Marsha (2005), 'Reinventing the Motherland: Almodóvar's Brain-Dead Trilogy', *Film Quarterly*, 5.2: 9–25.

Kinder, Marsha (2007), 'Volver', *Film Quarterly*, 60.3: 4–9.

Kinder, Marsha (2009), 'All about the Brothers: Retroseriality in Almodóvar's Cinema', in Epps et al. (eds), *All About Almodóvar*, pp. 267–94.

Konstantarakos, Mirto (2000), *Spaces in European Cinema*, Bristol: Intellect.

Kopelson, Kevin (1992), 'Seeing Sodomy: Fanny Hill's Blinding Vision', *Journal of Homosexuality* 23: 173–83.

Kosofsky Sedgwick, Eve (1993), *Tendencies*, Durham, NC: Duke University Press.

Kosofsky Sedgwick, Eve (2003), *Touching Feeling: Affect, Pedagogy and Performativity*, Durham, NC: Duke University Press.

Krauss, Rosalind (1985), *The Originality of the Avant-garde and Other Modernist Myths*, Cambridge, MA: MIT Press.

Kristeva, Julia (1991), *Strangers to Ourselves*, New York: Columbia University Press.

Kristeva, Julia (2002), '"Nous Deux" or a (Hi)story of Intertextuality', *Romanic Review*, 93.1–2: 7–13.

Kuhn, Annette (2009), 'Screen and Screen Theorizing Today', *Screen*, 50.1: 1–12.

Kuhn, Markus (2009), 'Film Narratology: Who Tells? Who Shows? Who Focalizes? Narrative Mediation in Self-Reflexive Fiction Films', in Peter Hühn, Wolf Schmid and Jörg Schönert (eds), *Point of View, Perspective, and Focalization: Modeling Mediation in Narrative*, Berlin: de Gruyter, pp. 259–78.

Kunst, Bojana (2010), 'How Time Can Dispossess: On Duration and Movement in Contemporary Performance', *Maska* <http://kunstbody.wordpress.com/author/kunstbody/> (accessed 23 July 2015).

Labanyi, Jo (2002), 'Engaging with Ghosts; or, Theorising Culture in Modern Spain', in Jo Labanyi (ed.), *Constructing Identity in Contemporary Spain: Theoretical Debates and Cultural Practice*, Oxford: Oxford University Press, pp. 1–14.

Labanyi, Jo (2007), 'Memory and Modernity in Democratic Spain: The Difficulty of Coming to Terms with the Spanish Civil War', *Poetics Today*, 28.1: 89–116.

Labanyi, Jo and Tatjana Pavlovic (eds) (2013), *A Companion to Spanish Cinema*, Malden and Oxford: Blackwell.

Lacan, Jacques (1978), *The Four Fundamental Concepts of Psychoanalysis*, trans. Alan Sheridan, New York: Norton.

Lacan, Jacques (1988), 'A Materialist Definition of the Phenomenon of Consciousness', in Jacques-Alain Miller (ed.), *The Seminar of Jacques Lacan, Book II: The Ego in Freud's Theory*, trans. Sylvana Tomaselli, New York: Norton, pp. 40–52.

Landsberg, Allison (2004), *A Prosthetic Memory: The Transformation of American Remembrance in the Age of Mass Culture*, New York: Columbia University Press.

Lane, Richard J. (2005), *Reading Walter Benjamin: Writing Through the Catastrophe*, Manchester: Manchester University Press.

Laplanche, Jean (1999), 'Notes on Afterwardness', in John Fletcher (ed.), *Essays on Otherness*, London: Routledge, pp. 260–65.

Leader, Darian (2008), *The New Black: Mourning, Melancholia and Depression*, Minneapolis: Graywolf Press.

Lepecki, André (2006), *Exhausting Dance: Performance and the Politics of Movement*, London: Routledge.

Leighton, Tanya (2008), 'Introduction', in Tanya Leighton (ed.), *Art and the Moving Image: A Critical Reader*, London: Tate and Afterall, pp. 7–40.

Lévinas, Emmanuel (2002), 'Beyond Intentionality', in Tim Mooney and Dermot Moran (eds), *The Phenomenology Reader*, London: Routledge, pp. 529–39.

Lippit, Akira (1999), 'Three Phantasies of Cinema-Reproduction, Mimesis, Annihilation', *Paragraph*, 22.3: 213–27.

Lloyd Smith, Adam (1992), 'The Phantoms of *Drood* and *Rebecca*: The Uncanny Reencountered through Abraham and Torok's "Cryptonymy"', *Poetics Today*, 13.2: 285–308.

Loureiro, Ángel (2008), 'Pathetic Arguments', *Journal of Spanish Cultural Studies*, 9.2: 225–37.

Lowenstein, Adam (2003), 'Cinema, Benjamin, and the allegorical representation of September 11', *Critical Quarterly*, 45.1–2: 73–84.

Luckhurst, Roger (2008), *The Trauma Question*, London: Routledge.

MacCormack, Patricia (2005), 'A Cinema of Desire: Cinesexuality and Guattari's A-signifying Cinema', *Women: A Cultural Review*, 16.3: 340–55.

McDaniel, Diane (1994), 'Children of Almodóvar: An Imagined Past and the Collective Present', *Spectator*, 14.2: 39–51.

MacDonald, Michael J. (1991), 'Jewgreek and Greekjew: The Concept of the Trace in Derrida and Lévinas', *Philosophy Today*, 35: 215–27.

Markuš, Saša (2001), *La poética de Pedro Almodóvar*, Barcelona: Littera.

Maddison, Stephen (2000), 'All About Women: Pedro Almodóvar and the Heterosocial Dynamic', *Textual Practice*, 14.2: 265–84.

Marrati, Paola (2006), 'Time and Affects', *Australian Feminist Studies*, 21.51: 313–25.

Marcantonio, Carla (2006), 'Volver', *Cinéaste*, 31.4: 77–9.

Marcantonio, Carla (2015), 'Cinema, Transgenesis, and History', *Social Text*, 33.1: 49–70.

Marks, Laura (2000), *The Skin of the Film: Intercultural Cinema, Embodiment, and the Senses*, Durham, NC: Duke University Press.

Marsh, Steven (2009), 'Missing a Beat: Syncopated Rhythms and Subterranean Subjects in the Spectral Economy of *Volver*', in Epps et al. (eds), *All about Almodóvar*, pp. 339–56.

Marsh, Steven (2013), 'Ana Mariscal: Signature, Event, Context', in Nair et al. (eds) *Hispanic and Lusophone Women Filmmakers*, pp. 72–82.

Marsh, Steven (2014), 'Untimely Materialities: Spanish Film and Spectrality', *Journal of Spanish Cultural Studies*, 15.3: 293–8.

Martín, Annabel (2014), 'Gendered Logics of Violence: Skin and Cloth, Sutures and Memory. Pedro Almodóvar's *The Skin I Live In* (2011)', *Miríada Hispánica*, 8: 109–33.

Martínez Martínez, José (1987), *Ontología y diferencia: la filosofía de Gilles Deleuze*, Madrid: Orígenes.

Martin-Márquez, Susan (2004), 'Pedro Almodóvar's Maternal Transplants: From *Matador* to *All about My Mother*', *Bulletin of Hispanic Studies*, 81.4: 497–509.

Martin-Márquez, Susan (2013), 'Isabel Coixet's Engagement with Feminist Film Theory: From G (the Gaze) to H (the Haptic)', in Labanyi et al. (eds), *A Companion to Spanish Cinema*, pp. 545–62.

Massey, Doreen (1994), *Space, Place and Gender*, Cambridge: Polity.

Massumi, Brian (2002), *Parables of the Virtual: Movement, Affect, Sensation*, Durham, NC: Duke University Press.

McGowan, Todd (2013), 'The Presence of Phenomenology: Hegel and the Return to Metaphysics', *Mosaic: A Journal for the Interdisciplinary Study of Literature*, 46.1: 95–111.

Medhurst, Andy (2007), 'Heart of Farce: Almodóvar's Comic Complexities', *New Cinemas: Journal of Contemporary Film*, 5.2: 127–37.

Medina, Alberto (2001), *Exorcismos de la memoria. Políticas y poéticas de la melancolía en la España de la transición*, Madrid: Libertarias.

Menard, André (2015), 'La etnohistoria, el suplemento y la superstición', *Diálogo Andino*, 46: 71–7.

Mira, Alberto (2004), *De Sodoma a Chueca. Una historia cultural de la homosexualidad en España en el siglo XX*, Barcelona: Editorial Egales.

Monegal, Antonio (2008), 'Exhibiting Objects of Memory', *Journal of Spanish Cultural Studies*, 9.2: 239–51.

Moreiras, Cristina (2002), *Cultura herida. Literatura y cine en la España democrática*, Madrid: Libertarias.

Moreiras, Cristina (2014), '*Laberinto de pasiones:* lógicas de mercado global y simulacro identitario', *Miríada Hispánica*, 5: 135–52.

Morris, Barbara and Kathleen Vernon (eds) (1995), *Post-Franco, Postmodern: The Films of Pedro Almodóvar*, Westport: Greenwood Press.

Mulvey, Laura (2006), *Death 24 X a Second: Stillness and the Moving Image*, London: Reaktion Books.

Naficy, Hamid (2006), 'Situating Accented Cinema', in Elizabeth Ezra and Terry Rowden (eds), *Transnational Cinema: The Film Reader*, London: Routledge, pp. 111–29.

Nagib, Lúcia (2007), *Brazil on Screen: Cinema Novo, New Cinema and Utopia*, London: I. B. Tauris.

Nair, Parvati and Julián Daniel Gutiérrez-Albilla (eds) (2013), *Hispanic and Lusophone Women Filmmakers: Theory, Practice and Difference*, Manchester: Manchester University Press.

Nancy, Jean-Luc (1991), *The Inoperative Community*, Minneapolis: University of Minnesota Press.

Nancy, Jean-Luc (2008), 'The Intruder' in *Corpus*, trans. Richard A. Rand, New York: Fordham University Press, pp. 161–70.

Navarrete-Galiano, Ramón (2012), '*La piel que habito*: Nueva creación literaria, pictórica y escultórica de Almodóvar', in José Luis Crespo Fajardo (ed.), *Arte y cultura digital: Planteamientos para una nueva era*, Málaga: Universidad de Málaga, pp. 74–86.

Nichols, William (2009), 'From Counter-Culture to National Heritage: "La Movida" in the Museum and the Institutionalization of Irreverence', *Arizona Journal of Hispanic Cultural Studies*, 13: 113–26.

Nixon, Mignon (2005), *Fantastic Reality: Louise Bourgeois and a Story of Modern Art*, Cambridge, MA: MIT Press.

Nixon, Mignon (2007), 'Wars I Have Seen: Louise Bourgeois and Gertrude Stein', unpublished paper given at the 'Louise Bourgeois Conference', Tate Modern, London (October).

O'Bryan, C. Jill (2005) *Carnal Art: Orlan's Refacing*, Minneapolis: University of Minnesota Press.

Oliván Santaliestra, Lucía (2004), 'La Alegoría en *El origen del Drama Barroco Alemán* de Walter Benjamin y en *Las Flores del Mal* de Baudelaire', *A Parte Rei: Revista de Filosofía*, 36.10 <http://serbal.pntic.mec.es/~cmunoz11/olivan36.pdf> (accessed 22 July 2016).

Oliver, Kelly (2013), *Technologies of Life and Death: From Cloning to Capital Punishment*, New York: Fordham University Press.

Oosterling, Henk and Ewa Plonowska Ziarek (2011), 'General Introduction', in Henk Oosterling and Ewa Plonowska Ziarek (eds), *Intermedialities: Philosophy, Arts, Politics*, Plymouth: Lexington Books, pp. 1–7.

Patton, Paul (2005), 'Deleuze and Democracy', *Contemporary Political Thought*, 4: 400–13.

Pedrós-Gascón, Antonio Francisco (2012), 'Hacer cine como si Franco no hubiera existido', in María R. Matz and Carole Salmon (eds), *How the Films of Pedro Almodóvar Draw Upon and Influence Spanish Society: Bilingual Essays on His Cinema*, Lewiston: Edwin Mellen Press, pp. 137–56.

Pérez Melgosa, Adrián (2013), 'The Ethics of Oblivion: Personal, National, and Cultural Memories in the Films of Pedro Almodóvar', in D'Lugo et al. (eds), *A Companion to Pedro Almodóvar*, pp. 176–99.

Perriam, Chris (2013), *Spanish Queer Cinema*, Edinburgh: Edinburgh University Press.

Pisters, Patricia (ed.) (2001), *Micropolitics of Media Culture: Reading the Rhizomes of Deleuze and Guattari*, Amsterdam: Amsterdam University Press.

Pollock, Griselda (2004), 'Thinking the Feminine Aesthetic Practice as Introduction to Bracha Ettinger and the Concepts of Matrix and Metramorphosis', *Theory, Culture and Society*, 21.1: 5–65.

Pollock, Griselda (2006), 'Introduction. Femininity: Aporia or Sexual Difference?', in Bracha Ettinger, *The Matrixial Borderspace*, pp. 1–37.

Pollock, Griselda (2007), 'Notes from a Feminist Front', unpublished paper given at 'Feminist Futures: Theory and Practice in the Visual Arts', New York: MoMA (May).

Pollock, Griselda (2008), 'Feminist Shamelessness', unpublished paper given at 'Sex and Shame in the Visual Arts', Tate Modern: London (December).

Pollock, Griselda (2009a), 'Mother Trouble: The Maternal-Feminine in Phallic and Feminist Theory in Relation to Bracha Ettinger's Elaboration of Matrixial/Aesthetics', *Studies in the Maternal*, 1.1: 1–31.

Pollock, Griselda (2009b), 'Art/Trauma/Representation', *Parallax*, 15.1: 40–54.

Pollock, Griselda (2010), 'Aesthetic Wit(h)nessing in the Era of Trauma', *EurAmerica*, 40.4: 829–86.

Pollock, Griselda (2013a), *After-affects/After-images: Trauma and aesthetic transformation in the virtual feminist museum*, Manchester: Manchester University Press.

Pollock, Griselda (2013b), 'Editor's Introduction', in Griselda Pollock (ed.), *Visual Politics of Psychoanalysis: art and the image in post-traumatic cultures*, London: I. B. Tauris, pp. 1–22.

Pollock, Griselda (2015), 'Redemption or Transformation: Blasphemy and the Concentrationary Imaginary in Liliana Cavani's *The Night Porter*', in Pollock et al. (eds), *Concentrationary Imaginaries*, pp. 121–60.

Pollock, Griselda, Adrian Rifkin, Richard Easton, Herta Gabriel and Toni Suriano (1995), 'A Conversation on Judith Butler's *Bodies That Matter: On the Discursive Limits of "Sex"*', *Parallax*, 1.1: 143–64.

Pollock, Griselda and Max Silverman (eds) (2011a), *Concentrationary Cinema: Aesthetics as Political Resistance in Alain Resnais's Night and Fog (1955)*, New York: Berghahn Books.

Pollock, Griselda and Max Silverman (2011b), 'Concentrationary Cinema', in Pollock et al. (eds), *Concentrationary Cinema*, pp. 1–54.

Pollock, Griselda and Max Silverman (eds) (2015), *Concentrationary Imaginaries: Tracing Totalitarian Violence in Popular Culture*, London: I. B. Tauris.

Price, Zachary (2015), 'Skin Gazing: Queer Bodies in Almodóvar's *The Skin I Live In*', *Horror Studies*, 6.2: 305–17.

Protevi, John (2010), 'An Approach to Difference and Repetition', *Journal of Philosophy: A Cross-Disciplinary Inquiry*, 5.11: 35–43.

Raffoul, François (2007), 'Derrida et l'éthique de l'im-possible', *Revue de métaphysique et de morale*, 53.1: 73–88.

Ragona, Melissa (2004), 'Hidden Noise: Strategies of Sound Montage in the Films of Hollis Frampton', *October*, 109, 96–118.

Rancière, Jacques (2007), *The Future of the Image*, London: Verso.

Rancière, Jacques (2008), 'Aesthetic Separation, Aesthetic Community: Scenes from the Aesthetic Regime of Art', *Art & Research: A Journal of Ideas, Contexts and Methods*, 2.1:1–15.

Rancière, Jacques (2009), 'La división de lo sensible. Estética y política', *Centro de Estudios Visuales de Chile* <http://www.centroestudiosvisuales.cl> (accessed 8 March 2014).

Rancière, Jacques (2011), *The Emancipated Spectator*, London: Verso.

Renov, Michael (2004), *The Subject of Documentary*, Minneapolis: University of Minnesota Press.

Resina, Joan Ramón (2000), 'Short of Memory: The Reclamation of the Past Since the Spanish Transition to Democracy', in Joan Ramón Resina (ed.), *Disremembering the Dictatorship: The Politics of Memory in the Spanish Transition to Democracy*, Amsterdam: Rodopi, pp. 83–126.

Ricco, John Paul (2002), *The Logic of the Lure*, Chicago: University of Chicago Press.

Richard, Nelly (2000), 'The Reconfigurations of Post-dictatorship Critical Thought', *Journal of Latin American Cultural Studies* 9.3: 273–82.

Richard, Nelly (2013), *Crítica y política*, Santiago: Palinodia.

Richardson, Nathan (2002), *Postmodern Paletos: Immigration, Democracy, and Globalisation in Spanish Narrative and Film 1950–2000*, Lewisburg: Bucknell University Press.

Rivera-Cordero, Victoria (2012), 'Illness, Authenticity and Tolerance in Pedro Almodóvar's *Todo sobre mi madre*', *Romance Notes*, 52.3: 311–23.

Rodowick, David N. (1997), *Gilles Deleuze's Time Machine*, Durham, NC: Duke University Press.

Rolnik, Suely (2007), 'The Body's Contagious Memory: Lygia Clark's Return to the Museum', *Transversal* < http://eipcp.net/transversal/0507/rolnik/en> (accessed 8 August 2016).

Rolnik, Suely (2008a), 'A Shift Towards the Unnamable', in Guy Brett (ed.), *Cildo Meireles*, London: Tate Publishing, pp. 132–7.

Rolnik, Suely (2008b), 'Deleuze, Schizoanalyst', in Monika Szewczyk, Chus Martínez and Nicolaus Schafhausen (eds), *Manon de Boer: The Time that is Left*, Frankfurt: Frankfurter Kunstverein, pp. 153–9.

Ross, Christopher (2004), *Spain since 1812*, London and New York: Routledge.

Rousset, David (1946), *L'univers concentrationnaire*, Paris: Éditions du Pavois.

Roy, Nicholas (1995), *After Derrida*, Manchester: Manchester University Press.

Ruedin, Isaac (2002), 'Bodies of Responsibility: Merleau-Ponty and Derrida', *Philosophy Today*, 46.3: 243–54.

Sandro, Paul (2003), 'Putting the Squeeze on Thought: Buñuel's Naturalism and the Threshold of the Imagination', in Gastón Lillo (ed.), *Buñuel: The Transcultural Imaginary*, Ottawa: University of Ottawa, pp. 33–46.

Santaolalla, Isabel (2005), *Los "Otros": etnicidad y "raza" en el cine español contemporáneo*, Zaragoza: Prensas Universitarias de Zaragoza.

Sartre, Jean Paul (1954), 'Introduction', in *The Maids and Deathwatch: Two Plays by Jean Genet*, trans. Bernard Frechtman, New York: Grove Press, pp. 7–31.

Scarfone, Dominique (2011), 'Repetition: Between Presence and Meaning', *Canadian Journal of Psychoanalysis*, 19.1: 70–86.

Scarlett, Elizabeth (2014), *Religion and Spanish Film: Luis Buñuel, the Franco Era, and Contemporary Directors*, Ann Arbor: University of Michigan Press.

Seguin, Jean-Claude (2009), *Pedro Almodóvar o la deriva de los cuerpos*, Murcia: Tres Fronteras Ediciones.

Shaviro, Steven (1993), *The Cinematic Body*, Minneapolis: University of Minnesota Press.

Shepherdson, Charles (1997), 'A Pound of Flesh: Lacan's Reading of the Visible and the Invisible', *Diacritics*, 27.4: 70–86.

Silverman, Kaja (1983), *The Subject of Semiotics*, New York: Oxford University Press.

Silverman, Kaja (1988), *The Acoustic Mirror: The Female Voice in Psychoanalysis and Cinema*, Bloomington and Indianapolis: Indiana University Press.

Silverman, Max (2011), 'Fearful imagination: *Night and Fog* and concentrationary memory', in Pollock et al. (eds), *Concentrationary Cinema*, pp. 199–213.

Silverman, Max (2013), *Palimpsestic Memory: The Holocaust and Colonialism in French and Francophone Fiction and Film*, New York: Berghahn.

Silverman, Max (2015), 'Haneke and the Camps', in Pollock et al. (eds), *Concentrationary Imaginaries*, pp. 187–202.

Skoller, Jeffrey (2005), *Shadows, Specters, Shards: Making History in Avant-garde Film*, Minneapolis: University of Minnesota Press.

Smith, Paul Julian (1999), 'Silicone and Sentiment', *Sight and Sound*, 9.9: 28–30.

Smith, Paul Julian (2003), *Contemporary Spanish Culture: TV, Fashion, Art & Film*, Cambridge: Polity.

Smith, Paul Julian (2004a), 'The Emotional Imperative: Almodóvar's *Hable con ella* and Televisión Española's *Cuéntame cómo pasó*', *MLN*, 119.2: 363–75.

Smith, Paul Julian (2004b), 'All I Desire', *Sight and Sound*, 14.6: 14–18.

Smith, Paul Julian (2006a), *Television in Spain: From Franco to Almodóvar*, Suffolk: Tamesis Books.

Smith, Paul Julian (2006b), 'Women, Windmills, and Wedge Heels', *Sight and Sound*, June: 16–18.

Smith, Paul Julian (2011), 'La piel que habito/The Skin I Live In', *Sight and Sound* <https://sites.google.com/site/pauljuliansmithfilmreviews/Home/la-piel-que-habito-the-skin-i-live-in> (accessed 21 May 2013).

Smith, Paul Julian (2014), *Desire Unlimited: The Cinema of Pedro Almodóvar*, London: Verso.

Smith, Paul Julian and Rob White (2011), 'Escape Artistry: Debating "The Skin I Live In"', *Film Quarterly* <http://www.filmquarterly.org/2011/10/escape-artistry-debating-the-skin-i-live-in/> (accessed 21 May 2013).

Sobchack, Vivian (1999), 'Toward a Phenomenology of Non-fictional Film Experience', in Jane Gaines and Michael Renov (eds), *Collecting Visible Evidence*, Minneapolis: University of Minnesota Press, pp. 241–53.

Sobchack, Vivian (2004), *Carnal Thoughts: Embodiment and Moving Image Culture*, Berkeley: University of California Press.

Steinberg, Samuel (2016), *Photopoetics at Tlatlelolco: AfterImages of Mexico, 1968*, Austin: University of Texas Press.

Stewart, Garrett (2006), 'Vitagraphic Time', *Biography*, 29.1: 159–92.

Stone, Rob (2011), 'Al mal tiempo, buena cara: Spanish Slackers, Time-images, New Media and the New Cinema Law', in Ann Davies (ed.), *Spain on Screen*, pp. 41–59.

Strauss, Fréderic (2001), *Conversaciones con Pedro Almodóvar*, trans. Esperanza Martínez, Madrid: Akal.

Subirats, Eduardo (2002), 'Transición y espectáculo', in Eduardo Subirats (ed.), *Intransiciones. Crítica de la cultura española*, Madrid: Biblioteca Nueva, pp. 71–85.

Taylor, Diana (1999), 'Dancing with Diana: A Study in Hauntology', *The Drama Review*, 43: 59–78.

Taylor, Diana (2003), *The Archive and the Repertoire: Performing Cultural Memory in the Americas*, Durham, NC: Duke University Press.

ten Bos, René (2005), 'On the Possibility of Formless Life: Agamben's Politics of the Gesture', *Ephemera*, 5.1: 26–44.

Thibaudeau, Pascale (2013), 'El cuerpo, la piel y la pantalla: los territorios habitados por Pedro Almodóvar', *Fotocinema: Revista Científica de Cine y Fotografía*, 7: 192–208.

Todd, Jane Marie (1986), 'Autobiography and the Case of the Signature: Reading Derrida's *Glas*', *Comparative Literature*, 38.1: 1–19.

Tuhkanen, Mikko (2009), 'Performativity and Becoming', *Cultural Critique*, 72: 1–35.

Urios-Aparisi, Eduardo (2010), 'The Body of Love in Almodóvar's Cinema: Metaphor and Metonymy of the Body and Body Parts', *Metaphor and Symbol*, 25.3: 181–203.

Varderi, Alejandro (1996), *Severo Sarduy y Pedro Almodóvar: Del barroco al kitsch en la narrativa y el cine postmodernos*, Madrid: Pliegos.

Vernon, Kathleen (2009), 'Queer Sound: Musical Otherness in Three Films by Pedro Almodóvar', in Epps et al. (eds), *All About Almodóvar*, pp. 51–70.

Vilarós, Teresa (1998), *El mono del desencanto. Una crítica cultural de la transición española, 1973–1993*, Madrid: Siglo XXI.

Walker, Janet (2001), 'Trauma Cinema: False Memories and True Experience', *Screen*, 42.2: 211–16.

Walker, Janet (2005), *Trauma Cinema: Documenting Incest and the Holocaust*, Los Angeles and Berkeley: University of California Press.

Walsh, Maria (2004), 'Intervals of Inner Flight: Chantal Akerman's *News from Home*', *Screen*, 45.3, 190–255.

Watney, Simon (1997), *Policing Desire: Pornography, AIDS and the Media*, Minneapolis: University of Minnesota Press.

Weber, Samuel (1991), 'Genealogy of Modernity: History, Myth and Allegory in Benjamin's Origin of the German Mourning Play', *MLN*, 106.3: 465–500.

Weber, Samuel (2006), 'Going along for the Ride: Violence and Gesture: Agamben Reading Benjamin Reading Kafka Reading Cervantes', *The Germanic Review*, 81.1: 65–83.

Webster Goodwin, Sarah and Elisabeth Bronfen (eds) (1993), *Death and Representation*, Baltimore: Johns Hopkins University Press.

Wegenstein, Bernardette (2002), 'Getting Under the Skin, or, How Faces Have Become Obsolete', *Configurations*, 10.2: 221–55.

Wegenstein, Bernardette (2010), 'Body', in *Critical Terms for Media Studies*, pp. 19–34.

Weidner-Maluf, Sônia (2005), 'Embodiment and Desire: *All About my Mother* and Gender at the Margins', *Gender Institute New Working Paper Series*, 14: 1–17.

White, Anthony (2008), 'Industrial Painting's Utopias: Lucio Fontana's Expectations', *October*, 124: 98–124.

Whittaker, Tom (2014), 'Ghostly Resonance: Sound, Memory and Matter in *Las olas* and *Dies d'agost*', *Journal of Spanish Cultural Studies*, 15.3, 323–36.

Williams, Linda (1998), 'Melodrama Revised', in Nick Browne (ed.), *Refiguring American Film Genres: History and Theory*, Berkeley: University of California Press, pp. 42–88.

Wilson, Emma (2003), *Cinema's Missing Children*, London: Wallflower.

Wilson, Emma (2006), *Alain Resnais*, Manchester: Manchester University Press.

Wilson, Sarah (1995), 'Fêting the Wound: Georges Bataille and Jean Fautrier in the 1940s', in Carolyn Gill (ed.), *Bataille: Writing the Sacred*, pp. 172–92.

Winter, Ulrich (ed.) (2006), *Lugares de memoria de la Guerra Civil y el franquismo: representaciones literarias y visuales*, Madrid: Iberoamericana.

Wong, Edlie L. (2007), 'Haunting Absences: Witnessing Loss in Doris Salcedo's *Atrabilarios* and Beyond', in Hallas et al. (eds), *The Image and the Witness: Trauma, Memory and Visual Culture*, pp. 173–88.

Yarza, Alejandro (1999), *Un canibal en Madrid. La sensibilidad 'camp' y el reciclaje de la historia en el cine de Pedro Almodóvar*, Madrid: Ediciones Libertarias.

Zecchi, Barbara (2005), 'All about Mothers: Pronatalist Discourses in Contemporary Spanish Cinema', *College Literature*, 32.1: 146–64.

Žižek, Slavoj (1991), 'Grimaces of the Real, or when the Phallus Appears', *October*, 58: 44–68.

Žižek, Slavoj (2004), *Organs without Bodies: Deleuze and Consequences*, London: Routledge.

Zurian, Fran and Vázquez Varela, Carmen (eds) (2005), *Almodóvar: el cine como pasión*, Cuenca: Ediciones de la Universidad de Castilla-La Mancha.

Index

Note: 'n' indicates an endnote; film titles are shown in *italics*